Fundamentals of Indian Political System

Fundamentals of Indian Political System

Consultant Editor
RAJESH K. JHA

The Pearson–ICFAI University Series is an outcome of a collaboration between Pearson Education India and ICFAI University Press.

PEARSON

Delhi • Chennai • Chandigarh

Associate Editor–Acquisitions: Kaushal Jajware
Assistant Editor–Production: Saima Ghaffar

ISBN: 978-81-317-7040-5

First Impression

Published by Dorling Kindersley (India) Pvt. Ltd, licensees of Pearson Education in South Asia.

Head Office: 7th Floor, Knowledge Boulevard, A-8(A), Sector 62, Noida, UP 201 309, India.
Registered Office: 11 Community Centre, Panchsheel Park, New Delhi 110 017, India.

Compositor: WordsWorth, India
Printer: HT Media Ltd., Noida

Contents

Preface

For any student of political science, politics in India forms the major components of the syllabus. Even the national and provincial level competitive examinations ask substantive number of questions on it. Generally it is thought that it is easy to deal with the issues of Indian politics, but gradually students realise difficulty in dissecting the multifaceted, multi-layered and ever dynamic character of Indian politics. It is a laudable effort by Pearson Education, which has taken the initiativeto bring out this edited volume with its student-friendly format and structuring. This book has been prepared to cover the syllabus of graduate and postgraduate courses of various state and central universities as well as of competitive examinations for civil services. As a consultant editor, I tried to smoothen the rough edges from the students' point of view and tighten the loose ends. This job was quite challenging which I tried to ride over with my decade long teaching experience, and as a chef prepared the pudding with the given ingredients. And the taste of pudding lies in tasting it and wishes everyone enjoys it.

Every chapter starts with 'After reading this chapter, you will be conversant with', which deals with major themes and subthemes of the topic/issue discussed in that chapter. I will advise the students to ponder for a while over these highlighted points here before going ahead. They must try to think here what they know about these themes on the basis of their previous studies and what they would like to know further. Each chapter has been divided into several sections and subsection for the better comprehension. Summary of each chapter would be helpful to the students as a food for thought and in revisions before the examinations. Some questions have been given in the end of each chapter for the practice and clarifying the concepts further. Glossary tries to explain the technical words used in this volume. Bibliography has been prepared in such a way that it should work as a resource for further studies for such readers who develop more interest on the issue(s) raised here.

I was initiated in this endeavour by Mr. Kaushal Jajware, and his colleague Mr. Prashun Chatterjee, of Pearson Education who prodded me to remove my hesitations in undertaking this project. With their patience and perseverance they steered this project to logical conclusion, which deserves more than usual thanks! I am also thankful to Saima Ghaffar for toning up this volume comprehensively. I am failing in my duty without expressing my deep gratitude for my sister – Ms. Mamta and my brother-in-law Mr. Vinaytos Mishra, IPS for their constant encouragement and my wife – Nidhi and daughter – Melu for providing cosy and conducive environment at home. Usual disclaimer applies with deep gratitude to my teachers, colleagues and students for intellectual enrichment of this project, while owning the responsibility for any shortcoming.

Rajesh K. Jha

About the Editor

Rajesh K. Jha is senior lecturer at Rajdhani College, University of Delhi, and a member of the Academic Council of the University of Delhi. After obtaining doctorate degree from the University of Delhi, Jha pursued his career at the University of Fribourgh, Switzerland, and CODESRIA (Council for the Development of Social Science Research in Africa) Dakar, Senegal. He has published several articles in various academic journals and newspapers, and also presented papers in many national and international seminars, and conferences. His areas of interest include federalism, the institutions of democracy, especially the parliament and panchayats. He is consultant to various committees and professional bodies like the Indian Institute of Public Administration (IIPA) and also associated with several voluntary organizations.

1

Indian National Movement

After reading this chapter, you will be conversant with:

- Indian Nationalism
- Moderates Phase
- Extremist Phase
- Gandhian Era

Nationalism is a distinct phenomenon, but it is very difficult to define or give specific meaning to it. It entails close identification of the individual with the State, a sense of love, respect and honour for the nation, and sacrificing oneself to defend and protect its dignity. According to Aurobindo Ghosh, "Nationalism is a religion that has come from God. Nationalism is a creed in which you shall have to live it. It is an "attitude" of heart, of the soul. What the intellect could not do, this mighty force of passionate conviction born out of the very faiths of national consciousness will be able to accomplish. Thus, it will be safe to say that, on the whole, nationalism is a political sentiment, whereas for the people of India during their freedom struggle, it was both a religion and a creed." He identified nationalism with religious spirit.

However, nationalism for a country under subjugation can be said as the rising of its people against imperial powers to drive them away. It also means to relieve the people from miseries and poverty. Indian nationalism has experienced both the conditions. The entire nationalist movement in India revolved around ousting the British imperial power from the country and creating a self-sufficient nation. Nationalism can thus be attributed as the antithesis of colonialism.

INDIAN NATIONALISM

Indian nationalism passed through several phases of development. As it advanced from one phase to another, its characteristics and dimensions underwent transformation. Its social base broadened and its objectives became more pronounced. Increasing strata of the Indian people evolved a national consciousness and perspective and were drawn into the orbit of the nationalist movement. Further, this nationalist feeling found expression in varied spheres of national life—social, political and cultural. The growth of national consciousness in the country was a slow and long-drawn-out process. Initially, it was confined to the progressive sections of the landlords, the emerging middle classes and intelligentsia. However, with the formation of Indian National Congress in 1885, the national movement became the platform for all other sections over a period of time.

A large number of factors were responsible for the National Movement in India. British imperialism was one amongst them. Before the advent of British in India, the South was separated from the rest of the country. British imperialism brought the entire nation under its sovereignty. However the attitude of British was also one of the most important factors for resentment among Indians. The British tried to establish their supremacy and stressed that they had come to rule India. They harboured misconceptions that Indians were culturally, economically and socially backward and were afraid of them.

The year 1885 significantly marked the beginning of a new epoch in the Indian history. For the first time, political organizations were united under the 'Indian National Congress'. The Indian minds became increasingly conscious about its political predicament. United and sincere efforts were made to achieve self-rule. A retrospective examination of the National Movement reveals three phases:

- I Phase - The Period of the Moderates (1885-1905)
- II Phase - The Period of the Extremists (1905-1920)
- III Phase - The Period of Gandhi (1920-1947)

MODERATES PHASE (1885-1905)

The first phase of the National Movement is that of the Moderates. It started in the year 1885 and continued up to 1905. It was confined to the educated middle classes and intelligentsia who drew inspiration from the Western liberal thought. Dadabhai Naoroji, Raja Ram Mohan Roy, Gopala Krishna Gokhale, Feroz Shah Mehta, Mahadev Govinda Ranade, Surendra Nath Banerjee, and other nationalists dominated the Congress policies and were labelled as the moderates. They believed in the British crown and had faith in the British sense of justice. They believed that India's connection with the West through England was a boon. The moderates considered masses as backward and politically passive. They hoped to educate them and gradually bring them into active politics.

Philosophy of the Moderates

The moderates were great scholars and had a clear approach towards the political problems. They opposed violence and used offeree to solve their problems. They believed in non-violence and representations. The Congress as a party was another forum to express the grievances of the people and made them known to the Government. But the Government accepted only those demands that were convenient. The moderates had faith in the solemn pledges made by the people to the British government of India and honoured the 1858 proclamation of the British Queen. Surendra Nath Banerjee called it as 'the Magna Carta of our rights and liberties.'

The moderates believed in the methodical progress and constitutional agitation within the limits of the law. They started educating the people and developing political consciousness in them. They conducted meetings all over the country and criticised the Government through the press. They made several representations to the British government about the prevailing conditions of India. The moderates insisted upon providing employment opportunities to Indian citizens in all higher public offices and membership of the Parliament, so that power could be vested in Indians to make legislation, control finance and administer better. This was possible through goodwill and co-operation with the British.

The moderates constantly worked upon to develop a sense of nationhood. They hoped to make a humble beginning in this direction by promoting close contacts and friendly relations among the people. The economic and political policies of the moderates were also formulated with a view to develop integrity in the people. They organized many agitations at the national level against the tariff duties on imports and also on the imposition of excise taxes on cotton. The moderates urged the British government to provide better facilities to the peasantry by establishing agriculture banks. They also requested the Government to improve the working conditions of the plantation labourers. The moderates demanded the government to change the existing system of taxation which had become a heavy burden to the poor. The moderates brought to the notice of the British government India's growing poverty and economic backwardness. They also blamed the British government polices that were detrimental to the Indian industries and demanded for their immediate development. The moderates campaigned for the use of Indian goods and advocated boycott of the British goods. Their campaign aimed to promote the Indian economy. They complained that the high salary paid to the European officers was a burden on the Indian economy. The retired Europeans who left India were also paid pensions from Indian economy.

Approach of the British Government

The behaviour of Moderates and the establishment of Congress Party changed the attitude of the British government. Lord Dufferin in 1887 attacked the policies of the Congress and criticized the party as a 'microscopic minority of the people'. Hamilton, the Secretary of State blamed Dadabhai Naoroji and stated that, "Dadabhai Naoroji's resistance and association with radical and socialist leaders had deteriorated whatever brains or presence of mind he may originally have possessed". The British officials publicly criticized the anti-governmental policies of the Indian Congress leaders whom they called as 'disloyal babus, seditious Brahmins, violent villains'.In order to weaken the Congress party, the British government adopted the 'Divide and Rule' policy.

CONTRIBUTION OF THE MODERATES

The Moderates played a significant role in the National Movement. They were instrumental in bringing together people of different religions, provinces and communities.

- They created a spirit of public service in minds of the people. They started educational institutions to impart western education, so that young Indians could secure good posts in the public service,
- They made people aware of how the British policies were detrimental to the Indian economy because of deliberate attempts like negligence of industrialization in the country.

Critical Appraisal

The Moderates did not achieve much success and were able to introduce only few reforms. Lala Lajpat Rai criticized them by saying, "After more than twenty years of more or less futile agitation for concessions and redressal of grievances, they had received stones in place of bread".

- Tilak labelled their policy of 'Pray, Petition and Protest' as 'political mendicancy'.
- The Moderates failed to establish roots and disillusioned the members.
- Finally, they failed to understand the growing impatience of the people who were suffering under the foreign rule. In spite of many failures, they laid strong foundations for the national movement to grow.

EXTREMIST PHASE (1905-1920)

The second phase of India's freedom struggle started with the entry of the extremists. This phase extended the aim and scope of the National Movement. The extremists aimed at all-round development and upliftment of the people. They believed that freedom could not be achieved only by making representations. They contradicted the philosophy of moderates, that the Britishers were superior to the Indians. They believed that British were exploiting the Indians and subjecting them to poverty. So, they vehemently opposed the moderates and criticized them as 'arm chair intellectuals'. They inculcated the need for freedom struggle in the people. In order to popularize the movement, extremists started propagating and spreading their views all over the country. Lokmanya Tilak felt conducting festive occasions in public could help induce a sense of brotherhood and propagate nationalism. Four prominent Congress leaders Lala Lajpat Rai, Lokmanya Bal Gangadhar Tilak, Bipin Chandra Pal and Aurobindo Ghosh articulated the aspirations and guided the extremist movement. Tilak coined the popular slogan "Swaraj is my birth right and I shall have it." He believed that without swaraj or self-government there could be no social reform, no industrial progress, no useful education, and no fulfillment of his life.

REASONS FOR THE GROWTH

The factors responsible for the growth of extremist phase are as follows:

- The Indian Council Act, 1892 and its features did not satisfy the extremists as well as the moderates. The extremists felt that the representations of moderates yielded no results.
- The British financial policies created a sense of discontent and unrest in the country. Dinshaw Wacha, R.P. Dutt, Dadabhai Naoroji proved how the British policies were draining the Indian economy.
- The outbreak of famine affected almost twenty million people spread over about seventy square miles. The British government hardly paid any attention to alleviate the sufferings of the people because they were busy celebrating the Diamond Jubilee celebrations of Queen Victoria with the Indian money. This was interpreted as an approach of callousness on the part of government.
- The outbreak of plague evoked similar reaction from the British government. Mr. Rand, the Plague commissioner was reckless in his duties. People were unable to tolerate his negligence. So, he and one of his associates were shot dead on their return from the Diamond Jubilee celebrations at Bombay.
- Lord Curzon's despotic rule was another major factor. He regarded administration as a machine and focused on its efficiency, even if it adversely affected the people.
- The victories of small countries like Abyssinia over Italy, and Japan over Russia inspired and motivated Indians to drive away the British.
- Education infused democratic and nationalistic values in the people.
- Hence, Lala Lajpat Rai, Bal Gangadhar Tilak and Bipin Chandra Pal (Lal, Bal, Pal) called upon the people to agitate against the British policies. They believed that prayers, petitions and protests would not convince British government. Meanwhile, the extremists officially separated from the moderates in 1907 at the Surat Congress session.

Extremists' Programme of Action

The Extremists advocated boycott of foreign goods and use of swadeshi goods. They also advocated the Home Rule Movement, National Education and Passive Resistance.

SWADESHI MOVEMENT

Replacing the British goods with the national goods formed the basic idea behind the Swadeshi movement. The intention behind the boycott movement was to make the Britishers leave the country, so that Indian industries could flourish, thereby offering employment and improve the economic conditions of the suffering masses. The whole movement gained both political and economic orientation. Lala Lajpat Rai, Lokmanya Tilak, Bipin Chandra Pal, Aurobindo Ghosh and many other leaders were associated with this movement.

NATIONAL EDUCATION

Swadeshi was a wide-range term. It included boycotting of foreign clothes, goods, government offices and army recruitment. Scholars like Rash Behari Bose, C.R. Das, Ravindra Nath Tagore started institutions to educate fellow Indians. The National Council of Education was set up in March 1906 and Aurobindo Ghosh was appointed its first principal.

HOME RULE MOVEMENT

Bal Gangadhar Tilak and Annie Besant advocated the 'Home Rule Movement'. Tilak advocated this movement at the Bombay Presidency so as to attain Home Rule or Self-government within the British Empire by all constitutional means in order to educate and organize public opinion in the country. Annie Besant also established a similar Home Rule League at Adayar near Madras. Tilak went on a whirlwind tour of the country in 1916 and appealled the people to unite under the banner of the Home Rule. He declared, "Liberty was the birth right of every man". Annie Besant also toured the country and invoked the spirit of nationalism. Her articles became very popular. Extremists also encouraged co-operative organizations. They promoted voluntary associations to ndertake programmes like rural sanitation, and providing relief duties to famine affected areas. They also formed arbitration committees to decide on civil disputes.

JALLIANWALA BAGH TRAGEDY

Following the Rowlatt Act, many people were arrested in Punjab while they held protest and demonstrations. The people of Punjab took a silent and unarmed procession in protest against the Rowlatt Act. Police fired on the procession. On 12 April 1919 General Dyer declared a ban on meetings and processions. Despite the order, the people of Punjab called for a meeting on 13 April 1919 at Jallianwala Bagh. Several people assembled on that day to demand the release of their arrested leaders. General Dyer ordered his men to fire. This resulted in a massacre of assembled people. This tragic scene shocked Indians throughout the country.

Critical Appraisal

The Extremists explained the need and benefits of democracy and constitutional progress of the country to the people and also the social base of the national movement. They exposed the negative role of the British government in administering India. They demanded for inclusion of a large number of Indians in the administration and to end the economic exploitation. They also realized that pressure tactics and agitations against British government alone would help to achieve these objectives.

THE GANDHIAN ERA (1920-1947)

After the death of Lokmanya Tilak, Gandhi emerged as one of the prominent leaders of the Congress. The liberals and extremists played an important role in the growth of national movement. The moderates challenged the British government and its power when it was more or less an offence to speak anything against both. They made the Britishers apprehend the desire of Indians to run the administration. Contrary to the Moderates, the Extremists made the British realize that Indians were very conscious of the need for independence. Gandhi's presence gave a new turn to the national movement. His policy of Non-Violence and Truth won peoples' hearts. The political career of Gandhi started in South Africa where he launched a Civil Disobedience Movement against the maltreatment meted out to Asian settlers. In 1916, he returned to India and joined the National Freedom Struggle. Gandhi took some time to understand India and the conditions of its people after he came back from South Africa. Gandhi's non-violence and non-cooperation movements proved fairly successful. These movements mobilized the poor and unarmed masses and removed their fear of the British power and violence. It also helped to hasten the transfer of power from the British without heavy loss of life.

Gandhi believed and practised non-violence and non-cooperation in the freedom struggle. His policy reflected his philosophical attitude and was based on 'Truth, Satyagraha and Ahimsa'. Gandhi was a great leader, a saint and a great social reformer. He was pious, truthful and religious. He believed in simple living and high thinking. Everybody who came in contact with him was deeply influenced by his personality. He was a champion of democracy and was opposed to dictatorial rule. Gandhi showed India and the world, the path of truth and non-violence. He believed that truth alone would prevail in the end. According to him, India's real emancipation depended on the Swadeshi movement, i.e. boycott of foreign goods, use of *khadi*, encouragement to village and cottage industries. Gandhi had immense faith in the capacity of the masses to fight the Britisher's. He based his entire policies on their deep involvement and self-sacrificing spirit. Gandhi's involvement in the freedom struggle is regarded as the third phase of the National Movement. His initiatives and involvement are enunciated below:

Non-Cooperation Movement (1920-1922)

Gandhi preached non-cooperation. He advocated seven principles to be adopted for this movement. These were:

- Surrender of titles and honorary offices.
- Refusal to attend government durbars and official functions.
- Boycott of government or government aided schools and colleges.
- Boycott of British courts.
- Refusal to join army as recruits for service in Mesopotamia.
- Boycott of elections to provincial and Central Assembly.
- Boycott of foreign goods.

Chauri-Chaura Incident

Chauri-Chaura was a village in Gorakhpur district of Uttar Pradesh. During the non-cooperation movement, an angry mob of thousands of people attacked a police station and set it ablaze killing twenty two policemen. Gandhi was shocked and abruptly suspended his non-cooperation movement, as it was turning violent. Many prominent national leaders did not agree with Gandhi. Even Jawaharlal Nehru did not appreciate it. M.N. Roy and R.P. Dutt too condemned the action and characterized it as the betrayal of revolutionary forces. Taking advantage of this situation and finding Gandhi's popularity at lowest ebb, the British authorities arrested him and sentenced him to six years of imprisonment. The people immediately reacted against the arrest and intensified the national movement.

Swaraj Party (1923)

C.R. Das and Motilal Nehru founded this party in March 1923. C.R. Das, Motilal Nehru and N.C. Kelkar could not reconcile to Gandhi's decision to withdraw the non-cooperation movement. So, they left the Congress party and formed the Swaraj party. In this connection C.R. Das felt that "the Mahatma opens a campaign in a brilliant fashion, he works it up with skills, he moves from success to success till he reaches the zenith of his campaign but after that he loses his nerve and begins to falter".

The party was formed with an objective 'to wreck from within' and thwart the British policies by becoming members in the Parliament. Leaders like C. Raja Gopalachari decided to remain outside the party. Gandhi was released from jail in 1924. He felt that for the time being there was no alternative other than entering the legislature. The party demanded a new constitution, release of political prisoners, and provincial autonomy. The death of C.R. Das in 1925 resulted in leadership struggle and weakened the party.

Simon Commission (1928)

The British government appointed Simon Commission with an objective to enquire the extent of implementation of the Montague reforms. The Commission consisted of seven members. Sir John Simon was the Chairman. Indians from different sections unanimously decided to boycott this Commission. The Commission landed on Indian soil on 3 January 1929 and found the Indians on hartals voicing slogans 'Simon Go Back'. Lala Lajpat Rai and Govind Vallabh Pant organized demonstrations and received severe lathi blows. The Commission stayed in India for two years to study the prevailing conditions.

Nehru Report (1928)

Lord Birkenhead, the Secretary of State, challenged Indian leaders to prepare a Constitution. An All Party Conference was arranged at Bombay on 19 May 1928. Dr. M.A. Ansari was appointed the President. The Drafting Committee was constituted under the chairmanship of Motilal Nehru to prepare a draft constitution for a responsible government. Mohammad Ali Jinnah also submitted fourteen points to the Drafting Committee in favour of the Muslims. In December 1928, the Congress submitted an ultimatum to the British government that, if their draft was not accepted, it would have no alternative but to start the non-cooperation movement again.

Lahore Session (1930)

Nehru presided over the session that passed a resolution on 'Poorna Swaraj' (Total Independence) on 26 January 1930. Congress observed this day as 'Complete Independence Day'. Pandit Jawaharlal Nehru was the president of the historic Lahore session. A tricolor flag was unfurled on the mid night of 31 December 1929. The Congress proposed a draft resolution in favour of a responsible government which was unanimously accepted.

Civil Disobedience Movement (1930)

After release from jail, Gandhi started the Civil Disobedience Movement on 12 March 1930 at the request of the All India Congress Committee.

The movement focused on the following eleven points:

- Salt manufacture.
- Picketing liquor shops.
- Picketing before foreign clothes dealers' shops.
- Plying *takli* and spinning.
- Burning foreign clothes.

- Eschewing untouchability.
- Making efforts to satisfy the minorities.
- Students to leave governmental educational institutions.
- Public servants to resign and devote themselves to the cause of peoples' welfare.
- Non-payment of all tax arrears claimed by the government.
- Let the majority rest content with what remains after the minorities have been satisfied.

Dandi March

The British government imposed tax on salt. Gandhi felt that levying tax on salt was an injustice to the people. Therefore, he decided to violate this law and manufacture salt from seawater. Gandhi started the Civil Disobedience Movement by breaking the obnoxious Salt Laws. The movement started from Sabarmati Ashram in Ahmedabad to Dandi, which was about two hundred miles from his ashram. Seventy one followers marched behind him and reached Dandi in twenty four days. This movement gained popularity all over India. Large number of women also participated. Nearly sixty thousand people were arrested. Subhash Chandra Bose compared the Salt March to Napoleon's March to Paris on his return from Elba. Following Gandhi's footsteps, salt was prepared by people all over India. The Muslim League did not participate in this movement. But, this movement was organised under the leadership of Khan Abdul Gaffar Khan in the Northwest Province.

Round Table Conferences (1930-1932)

The British government recognized that except the orthodox Muslims, almost the whole of India was behind Gandhi. They requested Gandhi to withdraw the agitation. Gandhi responded that he was prepared to withdraw his agitation only if the government could assure him that in the coming Round Table conference the issue of independence would be conceded. The British government made several efforts to convince Gandhi but in vain. All their efforts failed. They decided to arrange the Round Table Conference at London without inviting any representatives of the Congress party.

FIRST ROUND TABLE CONFERENCE (1930)

On 12 November 1930, the British government convened the First Round Table conference at London. Except Congress, all opposition parties attended the meeting.

The Gandhi Irwin Pact (1931)

The British government realized that in the absence of Gandhi nothing could materialize. So they preferred to invite Gandhi to the Second Round Table conference. It ordered the Governor-General to ensure that Gandhi attended the Second Round Table conference. As a result, Gandhi and his followers were released from jail. On 17 February 1931, Lord Irwin and Gandhi came to an agreement, named as the Gandhi-Irwin Pact. The agreement consisted of the following points:

- To release all the political prisoners.
- To return the properties of the prisoners arrested at the time of Civil Disobedience movement.
- To lift the ban imposed on preparation of salt.
- To withdraw the Civil Disobedience movement.
- To withdraw the proposal to make an enquiry into the police lathi charge on the Indians.

The Gandhi-Irwin pact was accepted by the Karachi Congress session on 25th March 1931.

SECOND ROUND TABLE CONFERENCE (1931)

This conference was held at London on 7 September 1931. Gandhi attended on behalf of the Congress. This conference could not solve the issue of communal representation. It also failed to satisfy the nationalist sections in the country.

THIRD ROUND TABLE CONFERENCE (1932)

This conference was organized on 17 November 1932. Gandhi did not participate. The conference proposed that there should be an All India Federation consisting of British India and the Indian states, but it was not conceded.

Communal Award (1932)

On 16 August 1932, the British Prime Minister Ramsay McDonald announced formation of separate electorates. As a result, separate electorates were formed for depressed classes and seats were also arranged according to communities. This Communal Award was made to weaken the Congress movement. Gandhi opposed this and went on a 'fast unto death' in Yeravada Jail.

Poona Pact (1932)

Gandhi entered into an agreement with Dr. B. R. Ambedkar at Poona regarding the Communal Award. Hence, it is named as the Poona Pact. The British government also amended the Communal Award accordingly. Incidentally, that was the basis on which reservations for SC's and ST's have continued since then.

White Paper (1933)

The British government published theWhite Paper in March 1933. This was based on the division of India and the creation of a separate state of Pakistan. Hence, Indians rejected this paper too.

Government of India Act, 1935

On the basis of the White Paper, a bill was introduced in the House of Commons in 1935, which subsequently came to be known as Government of India Act, 1935.

The Wavell Plan (1942)

Lord Wavell, the Governor-General of India announced a plan consisting of the following objectives:

- Reorganization of the Executive Council of Viceroy by providing opportunity to all political parties.
- Distribution of the membership in the ministry except defense to Indians.
- The establishment of responsible governments in all the provinces.

Cripps Proposals (1942)

In March 1942, the British Cabinet Minister, Sir Stafford Cripps came to India. He promised to provide a Constitution under certain conditions. Congress as well as the Muslim League rejected these proposals, and Gandhi termed this as a 'post dated cheque'.

Quit India Movement (1942)

The breakdown of the Cripps mission forced the All India Congress to think of a further plan. It met at Bombay in August 1942 and adopted the famous 'Quit India movement' piloted by Gandhi. The British government took note of the Quit India movement and arrested the leaders. It banned the Congress organization all over India. Gandhi, vexed by the policies of the British, declared the 'Do or Die' policy.

Mountbatten Plan (1947)

Lord Mountbatten was the last Viceroy of India. On 3 June 1947, he announced his plan to transfer the power on the basis of Dominion Status for India and Pakistan. Ultimately, the British imposed 'partition' before we attained freedom. The Congress as well as the Muslim League accepted his plan.

Critical Appraisal

The momentous period began with Non-Cooperation and ended with Civil Disobedience. Gandhi involved the masses from every corner of the country. Their response also indicated how Gandhi was respected as a leader. His activities and response from the people made the Britishers realize that their stay could not be continued for long.

The aspirations of the Indians to acquire an independent entity remained unfulfilled till the second half of the 19th century. The real organized effort to achieve political, social and economic liberty was made only after several leaders joined the national movement. The Indian nationalism was developed in phases. The emergence of Moderates movement was recognized as the first phase. They believed in the gradual realization of their national goals. The repression of the moderates paved the way for the rise of extremists. Boycott, resistance and demonstrations were their political weapons. The third phase of the Indian National Movement was dominated by Gandhi's ideology and was regarded as the Gandhian phase. This phase included Non-Cooperation, Civil Disobedience movement and mass movements. All these efforts ultimately resulted in the freedom of the country in 1947.

Indian National Movement grew in phases as the political awareness, organisation and people's participation developed. A retrospective study of the Indian National Movement is marked by three phases namely, the period of Moderates, the period of the Extremists and the period of Gandhi.

SUMMARY

- Moderates fashioned the spirit of public service in the minds of the people and made them aware of the detrimental policies of the British.
- Extremists aimed at the all round development and upliftment of the people. In order to popularize the movement, they advocated boycott of foreign goods and use of Swadeshi goods. They also supported the Home Rule Movement, National Education and Passive Resistance.
- Gandhi's leadership and his strategy gave a new turn to the Indian National Movement. His non-violence and non-cooperation helped to hasten the transfer of power from the British without loss of life.
- The Wavell Plan, Cripps Proposals and Mountbatten Plan paved the way for the transfer of power to a divided country in 1947.

QUESTIONS

- Describe the ideological features and political contributions of Moderates in the Indian National Movement.

- **Discuss the nature of National Movement during the Gandhian era.**
- **How did the transfer of power to India take place in 1947? Discuss.**
- **What were the principles adopted for non-cooperation movement? Why was it withdrawn?**
- **What were the developments that led to the Civil Disobedience movement? What were the issues focused upon during Gandhian movement?**

2

Constitutional History

After reading this chapter, you will be conversant with:

- Indian Councils Act, 1909
- Government of India Act, 1919
- Government of India Act, 1935
- Constituent Assembly – Debates and Discussions

What is Constitution?

In simple terms Constitution of a nation lays down the basic structure of the political system under which its people are to be governed. It establishes the main organs of the state—the legislature, the executive and the judiciary—defines their powers, demarcates their responsibilities, and regulates their relationships with each other and with the people.

Constitution of a country may also be described as its foundational law which commands the fundamentals of its polity and on the altar of which all other laws and executive acts of the state are to be tested for their validity and legitimacy.

The Indian National Congress, which came into being in 1885, awakened the political consciousness of the Indians and received extensive support from the masses. Seven years after a fierce campaign had been carried out in the country, both inside and outside the Indian National Congress for greater participation of the educated classes in the affairs of the Government, British Parliament enacted another act known as the Indian Councils Act of 1892 for the governance of India. It made a marginal improvement over the Indian Councils Act, 1861. The Indian Councils Act of 1892 deprived the members of the Council of their power to submit or propose any resolution under the authority of the Act or the rules made there under. Moreover, educated Indians were not to be absorbed in high-level administrative posts.

THE INDIAN COUNCILS ACT, 1909 (MORLEY-MINTO REFORMS)

The failure of the Indian Councils Act of 1892 to fulfill the legitimate wishes of the people and Lord Curzon's imperialistic attitude, autocratic rule and lack of sympathy for India displeased the Indians. Ultimately, his administration witnessed rigorous agitations. The Universities Act of 1904, which removed the autonomy from the Indian Universities and the Partition of Bengal created further unrest.

The period between 1892 and 1909 was tumultuous. Lord Morley, the then secretary of state for India, piloted a Bill through the British Parliament. Lord Minto, the Viceroy witnessed severe agitation and discontentment in the country. He too suggested reforms to please the Indians. Hence, the Indian Council Act, 1909, otherwise called as Morely-Minto reforms was introduced.

REASONS FOR MAKING THE ACT

- India and its masses were adversely affected by the plague during 1896 followed by severe famine. The British provided inadequate measures. Dissatisfied with the measures taken by the British administration, people became resentful with the government and killed Mr. Rand who worked as the Commissioner-in-charge of the plague reforms.
- Lokmanya Tilak became very popular through his speeches and writings. He started the 'Kesari', a daily paper through which he educated the people about nationalism and also made them aware of the British policies.
- Lord Curzon became the Viceroy of India. He always underestimated the Indians and their administrative capabilities. He reserved all the executive posts, indisputably and exclusively for the British. He considered the Indians suitable only for the lower posts.
- Lord Curzon partitioned Bengal in 1905. In retaliation, Indians held widespread demonstrations. The moderates too realized that constitutional agitations alone were insufficient to counter the British Government.
- During the same period in 1905, two tiny countries, namely Japan and Abyssinia won sound victories over Russia and Italy, respectively. These two victories bolstered the confidence of the Indians that they could also drive away the British. The defeat of Russia and Italy exploded the myth of European superiority and their invincibility.
- The Indian economy was deteriorating day by day. Industries were neglected. The prices of necessary commodities were on the rise. The Indian nationalist leaders exposed the high handedness of the British government and the diminishing economic condition of the country through the press.
- The British adopted the 'divide and rule' strategy and encouraged communalism. As a result, the Muslim League was formed in 1906 under the leadership

of Aga khan. He made a representation to the British government for separate electorates which was immediately accepted.

- Indians living in South Africa too were subjected to humiliation. Tilak and other nationalist leaders brought their sufferings to the notice of the fellow Indians which caused further discontentment.

Provisions of the Act

- The strength of the additional members of the Governor-General's Council was increased to a maximum of sixty, whereas the strength of provinces like Bombay, Bengal, Bihar, Uttar Pradesh and Orissa were fixed at a maximum of fifty and those of Punjab, Burma and Assam at thirty.
- Lord Morley insisted upon retaining a substantial majority in the Imperial Legislative Council. Accordingly, the strength of the members in the Imperial Legislative Council was fixed to sixty, out of which the official members were thirty seven and non-official members, twenty three. Of the thirty seven official members, the Governor-General nominated twenty eight members and the remaining nine were ex-officio members. Out of the twenty three non-official members, the Governor-General nominated five members and the remaining were to be elected by the people.
- The Act did not insist upon any majority of the official member in the Provincial Legislative Councils. The non-official members were in majority. The Governor-General appointed some of the non-official members and the remaining were nominated members.
- There was no fixed term for the non-official members. The Governor-General at the Center and the Governor at the state level were given the powers to nominate and remove them.
- The Act provided separate electorates for communities, classes and interests. Limitations were also placed in utilization of the adult franchise.
- The functions of the Legislative Councils were increased. The Indian members were provided with the provision of raising questions and discussing the Budget and put forward any proposal to change the taxes. The Presiding Officer, however, could disallow these proposals if he felt they were undesirable.
- Members of the Council were also provided with additional provisions of raising questions on any of the administrative matters. The member in-charge of the department, could refuse to answer off-hand and was provided some time to do so.
- Members of the Council were also given the provision to move resolutions in the form of recommendations to the government. They had to be clear, precise and exact. The Presiding Officer could disallow the resolution or part of it without giving any reason.

- The Council allowed discussions subject to the condition that they did not affect any of the matters related to the Government or under adjudication by a court of law.
- The Act also raised the strength of the members in the Executive Council of the Governor at Bombay, Bengal and Madras to four. It also empowered the government to constitute the Executive Council for the Lieutenant Governor's provinces.
- The British imposed disqualifications on political offenders to debar them from seeking election. However, the heads of the Governments were given the power to remove those disqualifications.

Criticism

The reforms were not satisfactory and criticised on the following grounds:

- Indians expected a 'Self and Responsible Government'. But they received only a shadow of it because Lord Morley had no intention to oblige them.
- This Act created a rift between the Hindus and Muslims. It counter-posed natives against natives.
- Indirect method of election system was introduced and the number of voters was limited. In some of the constituencies, the voter strength did not exceed ten. Women were barred from voting.
- The method of indirect election created many problems in electing the representatives.
- The Act established separate electorates for the Muslims. This resulted in the 'Divide and Rule Policy'.
- The Indians resented the maintenance of British majority in the Imperial Council.
- The non-official members of the Provincial Legislature did not enjoy any powers as the nominated members dominated them.
- This Act established centralized administration. Provincial Councils were under the control of the Central government.
- The Act gave importance to the landlords, capitalists, and Chambers of Commerce who were considered to be loyal to the British.

THE GOVERNMENT OF INDIA ACT, 1919 (MONTAGUE-CHELMSFORD REFORMS)

The Act of 1909 was concerned with the setting up of representative form of government. It also dealt with the communal electorates. The British imperialists ensured that this Act would develop differences within the natives, result in infighting and diverting their spirit of nationalism. The National movement leaders were very conscious of this fact and took all measures to inculcate a sense of integrity within the people. During the First World War, the British insisted upon India's co-operation in the form of men, material and money against the Nazis to emerge victorious. In return, they promised constitutional reforms. Believing them, Indians participated in the war. The diehards in Britain also accepted that India made a significant contribution to Britain's victory. But, after the war, India witnessed Jallianwala Bagh Tragedy which shocked the entire country. This confirmed that the British government did not appropriately acknowledge their sacrifices. Concurrently, the moderates also felt dissatisfied with the 1909 reforms and the British attitude after the war. Therefore, the British felt the need to introduce some more reforms.

Montague, the then Secretary of State for India, and Chelmsford, the then Governor-General of India were entrusted with the task of formulating proposals for a policy and thus recommended the Government of India Act, 1919. Hence, this Act was named as Montague-Chelmsford Reforms.

Circumstances Leading to the Enactment of the Act

- The Morley-Minto Reforms of 1909 were not successful. Indians realized that this Act was passed not with the intention to establish Parliamentary Government in India, but to strengthen the British bureaucracy by aligning the moderates and Muslims.
- The Indian National congress also articulated its discontent at the British for the following reasons:
  - — The extreme and unlawful preponderant share of representation given to a particular religion.
  - — The undue, unpleasant and humiliating distinctions made between Muslims and non-Muslims in the matter of electorates.
  - — The illogical and irrational disqualifications and limits for candidates seeking election to the Councils.
  - — The general suspicion of the educated classes towards British administration.
- The inadequate composition of the non-official majorities in the Provincial Councils.
- The Muslims too were dissatisfied by British policies. British negative approaches towards the establishment of Aligarh Muslim University, its policies towards Turkey in the Turco-Italian War (1911-1912), and the revision of the Partition of Bengal in 1911 further fuelled their resentment.
- Mahatma Gandhi appealed to the Indians to come forward and help the British people during the First World War. Inspired by Gandhi's call, Indians

participated in the war. Even so, the British government did not take any measure to reconstruct the Indian economy. They did not even mention anything of self-rule.

- The war changed the conditions of the British in India. It's hope of victory vanished. It also led to further disillusionment among the Indians.
- The Indians thus demanded an effective share and control in the administrative, legislative and political spheres.

The Indians demanded the British to establish a government by giving them necessary representative powers in the legislature. The British government, however, found it unfeasible to accept the demand.

MAIN PROVISIONS OF THE ACT

The Act of 1919 was actually a comprehensive legislation. The Act considered the Governor-General as the Head of the entire administration. The administration of the State was performed only on his assent. He was assisted by a council to advise him in the matters of administration. The Act of 1919 did not make many changes at the central level. The Act introduced diarchy at the provincial level.
The other important provisions of the Act were:

Preamble

The Preamble of the Government of India Act 1919 declared it as a policy of the Parliament to provide for the increasing representations of Indians in every branch of administration and gradual development of self-governing institutions.

Secretary of State

The Act also incorporated changes in the post of Secretary of State. Formerly, his salary was to be paid out of the Indian money. According to the new changes, he was paid directly from the British revenues. Some of his powers were given to the High Commissioner to reduce his burden of administration.

Appointment of High Commissioner

The Act made a provision for the appointment of the High Commissioner. Some of the powers of the Secretary were removed and assigned to him. The Act made a provision that the salary of High Commissioner was to be paid by the Government of India. He acted as an agent of the Governor-General-in-Council. He was in charge of the stores department, the student department and others.

Bicameral Legislature

The Act of 1919 provided for a Bicameral legislature at the Centre. The Lower House was named as the Central Legislative Assembly and the Upper House was named as the Council of States.

The Central Legislature had very wide powers. As part of the services of the Crown, it was empowered to make laws for the entire British India and for the subjects of His Majesty. It also possessed the powers to amend the legislations, if necessary. For some of the Acts like abolition of High Courts, previous sanction of the Secretary of State was essential.

Adult Franchise

The adult franchise for both the Houses of Central Legislature was restricted.

Governor-General

The Act of 1919 increased the powers of the Governor-General as under:

- He could summon, prorogue and dissolve any of the Houses.
- His sanctions were essential to introduce the following bills in the Legislature:
  - — Bill concerned with public debt or revenues.
  - — Bill concerned with religion or religious rites.
  - — Bills concerning the maintenance of His Majesty's military, naval or air forces.
  - — Bills concerning the relation of states within British India and with foreign countries.
- He could abolish the High Court in consultation with the Secretary of State.
- He was given the power to prevent a bill from consideration if he felt that it would affect the safety or tranquility of British India.
- He could enact laws if he considered it essential for the safety, tranquility of interests of British India, even if the House refused to pass them.
- He could promulgate ordinance in times of emergency for the maintenance of administration. The ordinance could survived for six months.
- He could return the bill to the legislature for re-consideration.
- He was empowered to send the bill for the consideration of the Crown.
- All the financial bills had to be introduced in the Parliament only after his consideration.
- He had the power to veto the bills passed by the Legislatures.

Financial Powers

- Prior permission of the Governor-General was required to submit the national budget by the government and also to submit the proposals to the Legislature for appropriation in the form of demands for grants on voting in the Legislative Assembly.
- Non-votable items in the budget were allowed to be discussed only after the approval of the Governor-General.
- He could restore any grant even if it had been refused by the legislature.

Criticism

- The above powers prove that the Central Legislature was helpless before the Central Executive.
- The Executive had the power to over-ride the Legislature in almost all the respects.
- The members of the Executive Council were nominated members and so they could not be removed under normal circumstances.

Central Government

The Act also introduced some changes at the Central Government level. The Act envisaged that the Government was responsible for the Parliament. The Act provided limitations to the number of members of Executive Council of the Governor-General The Executive Council was responsible and accountable to the Secretary of State. The Governor-General was empowered to make ordinance as he enjoyed maximum powers of the state.

Powers of the Central Legislature

Central Legislature under the Act was a bicameral Legislature. It made laws for the entire country and possessed the power to amend them if necessary. It was also empowered to make the Budget. The Governor-General was empowered to prevent discussion on any bill in the Legislature, for the safety and tranquility of the country.

Change in Provincial Governments

The Act introduced the democratic system at the provincial levels. In view of this arrangement, subjects of administrative matters were clearly demarcated between the center and provinces. The subjects that covered entire India were included under the Central List. The Central List included defense, foreign and political relations, customs, currency, and post and telegraph. The Central Government was empowered to make legislations over these subjects. The subjects in the provincial list included local self governments, famine relief, and co-operative societies. Provincial governments were empowered to make legislations on this list. The residuary list included the items that were left over after the distribution of powers between Central List and Provincial List. Both the center and the states had equal powers over it.

The provincial subjects were again divided into reserved and transferred list. No separate staff was engaged to administer transferred list.

The Provincial Executive

The Governor was the Chief Executive of the Provincial governments. The Secretary of State appointed the Governor in consultation with the Governor-General. As the Secretary of State appointed the Governor, he was answerable to him for all his acts of omissions and commissions.

The Council of Ministers assisted the Governor. The Governor administered the transferred subjects with the help of his ministers and the remaining reserved subjects with the help of his Executive Council. The members of the Executive Council were appointed by the Secretary of State for five years and were responsible to him for all the administrative matters. The council decided the matters by the majority vote and in case of a tie the Governor could use his vote. He was empowered to override the decisions of the Council.

The Council consisted of four members of whom two had to be Indians, one should have served the Crown for twelve years and the other had to be appointed by the Secretary of State.

Administration of Transferred Subjects

The highlight of the 1919 reforms was division of administrative subjects into reserved list and transferred list. The Council administered the reserved list and the Governor and his ministry administered the transferred list. There were no such limitations regarding the strength of ministers. The Act provided diarchy and also a responsible government. According to this principle, each minister had to be appointed by the Governor and hold office during his pleasure. All the ministers were collectively responsible to the legislature. The Governor had the power to appoint and remove the ministers. The Governor was issued with an 'Instrument of Instructions' with which, he could, without the advice of the Council, take decisions of his own in all policy matters for the well-being of the people.

Powers and Functions of Governors

The Governor enjoyed the following powers and performed the following functions:

- He was responsible for the maintenance of safety and tranquility of all parts of the provinces.
- He solved religious and racial conflicts and established a peaceful administration.
- He promoted the welfare of those people who could not fully rely upon joint political actions of Hindus and Muslims.
- He looked into provisions of the civil servants employed in the state and was responsible for their duties.
- He ensured that no unfair discrimination was made in matters of commercial or industrial interests.
- He fulfilled the orders issued by the Secretary of State and the Governor-General.

Provincial Legislature

The Act also discussed the powers and functions of the legislatures. The strength of the Council was decided depending upon the size and population of the State. Members were elected by adult franchise. Separate provisions were made for certain communities. The voting right was provided if the citizen possessed the following qualifications:

- A person had to be a resident of that province for twelve years.
- He had to be an income-tax payer
- He had to be a graduate.

All the persons who had completed twenty five years of age were eligible to contest.

Meetings

The Council elected the Presiding Officer and a Deputy Presiding Officer. The Presiding Officer could be removed through a no-confidence motion. The members of the Council had the right to raise questions and supplementary questions on any of the administrative matters over the Presiding Officer.

Joint or Collective Responsibility

The Provincial administration was divided into reserved and transferred subjects. The ministers of the Legislative Council administered the transferred subjects. This evidently proved the question of 'Collective Responsibility' as these subjects were concerned purely with the provincial matters. All the ministers were collectively responsible and accountable to the Legislative Assembly.

Critical Appraisal

The leaders of the national movement considered diarchy as another wrong policy of the British because power was divided haphazardly. They believed that, "There could not be any worse division as that of 1919 Act."

The relationship between the civil servants and ministers was not clearly mentioned. The civil servants were under the direct control of the Secretary of State. The ministers were under the control of the Governor and Legislature. There was no integration and co-ordination between the civil servants and ministers. Civil servants did not care for the ministers and the ministers had no power to select suitable subordinates.

The ministers' position was also very weak. They had to serve the Governor and the Legislative Council. They served the Governor because he had the power to appoint as well as dismiss. Similarly, they were responsible to the Legislature for all the administrative matters. In case of inefficiency, the ministers were removed through a no confidence motion.

The ministers did not bother to promote the principle of responsibility. They lacked unity and were unable to work as a team. Surendra Nath Banerjee and Nawab Sahib openly canvassed against each other in case of the Calcutta Municipal Bill. The Governor also did not show any interest to protect the ministers from any disputes.

Another setback to the diarchy was the arrangement of Department of Finance. The powers of this department were given to the members of Executive Council. At the same time, the ministers of various departments were responsible for nation building. The minister had no power to utilize the money for the implementation of policies as he had to depend upon the will of the Finance Secretary. The Finance Secretary being a civil servant exhibited more interest towards reserved subjects than transferred subjects thereby delaying administration.

The division of subjects amidst the center and provinces were also defective. There was overlapping of items in the lists. And because of flexibility, subjects were changed according to their convenience.

There was confusion regarding the subjects in the provinces and their division. All the revenue earning departments were under the control of the Governor and departments concerned with spending were arranged under the ministers. The ministers were unable to satisfy the people due to lack of funds and consequently earned displeasure of the people.

The composition of the Legislative Council was also criticized. It included members belonging to all the communities. The members showed more interest towards their community rather than solving the existing problems.

Some of the subjects were divided over the self-interest of the British. For example, general education was included in the list of transferred subject and the education of

Anglo-Indians was included in the list of reserved subjects. The ministers, therefore were made responsible both to the Legislature and Governor.

THE GOVERNMENT OF INDIA ACT, 1935

The Reforms of 1919 did not come up to the expectations of the Indians. They were also introduced at an inappropriate time when all the major political parties were busy trying to restore peace after the First World War. The Indian National Congress, at its annual session in 1919, labeled these reforms as, 'inadequate, unsatisfactory and disappointing'. Some of the National Movement leaders too criticized this by stating that the existing system had to be replaced with a few modifications.

Reasons for enacting the Act of 1935

Some of the following issues were the reasons behind the promulgation of the 1935 Act:

- **Rowlett Act and Jallianwala Bagh Tragedy:** Based on the recommendations of Justice Rowlett, the British Government made oppressive laws which in turn provided extensive powers to the police to detain and arrest persons without conducting any trials. The Act armed the executive and police authorities to suppress the civil liberties of the Indians. Gandhi suggested the people to resort to Satyagraha to revolt against these iniquitous laws. Heeding his call, *Hartals* were arranged all over the country. As a result, Gandhi was arrested, but the movement spread throughout the country. In Punjab, Marshal Law was imposed to curb the *Hartals*. People became distressed and arranged public meetings. This resulted in the Jallianwala Bagh tragedy in which hundreds of the assembled were shot dead and thousands were wounded.
- **Turko-Italian War:** The Muslims developed a sense of animosity and hatred towards the British government and its allied powers on the defeat of Turkey. Gandhi espoused their cause and launched a non-violent and non-cooperation campaign in support of the Khilafat movement. The impact of the war, tragedy at Amritsar, and the Khilafat Movement helped to bridge the gap between the Hindus and Muslims.
- **Non-Cooperation Movement:** Gandhi started the Non-Cooperation Movement to protest against the Jallianwala Bagh tragedy. His movement gained mass acceptance. It is estimated that nearly fifty thousand people from all over India were arrested because of their participation in the non-cooperation movement. All public meetings were banned. The Congress, in its Ahmadabad session in 1921 determined to begin civil disobedience and decided to avoid paying taxes.

The incident of Chauri-Chaura resulted in the suspension of the non-cooperation movement. Gandhi felt that the movement had become unrestrained and therefore, turned violent.

- **Swaraj Party:** Some of the Congress leaders became distressed with Gandhiji's sudden decision to suspend the non-cooperation movement. They left the Congress party and started the Swaraj Party under the guidance of C. R. Das and Motilal Nehru. It gained maximum seats in the 1923 elections of the Central Provinces Council and became the single largest party in Bengal and some other provinces. It exposed the double standards behind the policy of diarchy adopted by the government.
- **The Simon Commission:** The British government appointed the Simon Commission in 1927 to investigate the failure of the Montague-Chelmsford Reforms. The Simon Commission consisted exclusively of English members. The Indians were determined to disallow this commission and observed a general *Hartal* all over the country on the day Simon landed in India.
- **Nehru Report:** While Simon Commission was carrying on its work, all the leading Indian political parties organized a meeting at Bombay on May 19, 1928. Dr. M. A. Ansari presided over this meeting and appointed a committee under the Chairmanship of Motilal Nehru to consider and determine the principles of Constitution. Report of this Committee confined itself to British India, as it envisioned a future link-up of British India with the Indian states on a federal basis. The report recommended joint electorates with reservation of seats for minorities (except in Punjab and Bengal) on population basis with the right to contest additional seats. Full protection was afforded to the religious and cultural interests of the Muslims, and even 'new provinces on linguistic basis were to be created'.
- On 2 December, 1928, the All Parties Conference met at Calcutta to consider the Nehru report and Mr. Jinnah, on behalf of the Muslim League, moved a number of resolutions.
- On 31 December, 1928, the Congress at its annual session adopted a resolution welcoming the All Parties Conferences report and affirming that if this Constitution was entirely approved by the British Parliament within a year, that is by 3 December, 1929, the Congress would accept it, but if it was rejected, then it would organize a campaign of non-violence, non-cooperation, non-payment of taxes and others. The Muslim League meeting at Delhi on 31 March, 1929 rejected the Nehru report and affirmed Mr. Jinnah's celebrated 'fourteen points' as the minimum condition acceptable to the Muslims for any political settlements.
- Meanwhile, in Britain the Labour Party formed the government under the leadership of Ramsay McDonald. This amplified the hopes of the Indians.

The Viceroy declared on 31 October, 1929 that the government accepted the suggestions of Simon Commission; however, it did not give any clear information on the Nehru Report. The Congress leaders were dissatisfied. Gandhiji's meeting with the Viceroy did not bear fruit either. Therefore, at the Lahore session under the presidentship of Pandit Nehru, the Congress resolved to boycott the Round Table Conferences and declared that the nation's aim was to win 'complete independence'. It also decided to launch a civil disobedience movement similar to Gandhi's historic Dandi March.

- **Round Table Conferences:** The British government arranged the First Round Table Conference in November 1930, which proved unsuccessful. After the Gandhi-Irwin Pact, Gandhi attended the Second Round Table conference in 1932. This conference was unable to settle the communal conflicts. The British government further arranged the third Round Table Conference on 17 November, 1932, which yet again proved to be a failure. The British government issued a White Paper in March 1933, on the basis of which a bill was introduced in the House of Commons in 1935, resulting in the Government of India Act, 1935.

MAIN PROVISIONS OF THE GOVERNMENT OF INDIA ACT, 1935

It was a lengthy and detailed document. The Act consisted of 321 Sections with 10 Schedules. It introduced diarchy at the center. The subjects at the Center were arranged as reserved and transferred subjects. Reserved subjects included defence, external affairs, and religious affairs. The Governor-General administered the transferred subjects with the help of his ministers. The British Parliament maintained complete supremacy over India through this document. It was partly implemented in 1936 and completely in 1937. The following were the main provisions of the Act:

- **The Home Government:** The Act of 1935 continued the position of the Secretary of State to exercise control over reserved subjects. He had the power to give instructions to Provincial Governors as well as the Governor-General, civil service personnel and through them the whole administrative machinery. He acted as the connecting link between Government of India and British Parliament. He vetoed the acts of the Parliament. His recommendations were essential for all the appointments made by the Governor-General office for the posts of Commander-in-chief and Judges of the Supreme Court. He controlled the recruitment of Indian Civil Services. The Advisory Council was appointed for a period of five years to advise the Secretary of State on its duties.
- The Act empowered the Governor-General to appoint the High Commissioner for India in his individual capacity rather than the advice of his council.

- **Federal Executive:** According to the Government of India Act, 1935, the Governor-General was the Executive of the federal state. A council assisted him. He represented the Crown and was the Head of the British India. The Crown appointed him for a period of five years. He enjoyed a dual post as the chief executive of the federal state and as the Head of the state.
- **Executive Powers:** The Governor-General exercised the following powers:
  — He appointed the Ministers.
  — He took advice of his ministers to run administration over the items in the transferred Subjects.
  — He allowed them to continue in the post till he was satisfied with their duties.
  — He was empowered to remove the following executives:
  Chairman and members of the Federal Service Commission.
  Commissioners of Delhi, Ajmer, Mewar and Baluchistan.
  Financial Advisor.
  Auditor General.
  Governor of Reserve Bank and its nominated Director.
  Governors of states.
- **Legislative Powers:** The Governor-General had the following legislative powers:
  — He could summon, prorogue and dissolve both the Houses.
  — He addressed both the Houses on certain occasions.
  — He issued ordinances. The ordinances issued by the Governor-General were known as 'Governor-General Acts'.
  — Only on the assent of the Governor-General a bill could become an Act.
  — He had the power to send any controversial bill for Royal assent.
- **Financial Powers:** The Governor-General exercised the following financial powers:
  — His assent was essential to introduce the financial bill in the Parliament.
  — He exercised his powers over eighty percent of the total amount of the budget.
  — He could give his consent to any bill which was rejected by the Legislature.
  — He could sanction a bill which was rejected by vote on account.
- **Emergency Powers:** The Government of India Act, 1935 provided emergency powers to the Governor-General: He had the power to impose emergency in the federal government at the state or national level.

- **Instrument of Instructions:** The Governor-General in India had very extensive powers. He exercised some of the powers on the advice of the ministers, some by his discretion and the remaining at the discretion of the Queen. The British government issued some guidelines to the Governor-General indicating the method of exercising his powers. Some of the important guidelines were as below:
  - — He must give preference to the minority community in the ministry.
  - — He must encourage collective responsibility among the ministers.
  - — He should consult the concerned minister in the matters relating to defence and finance.
- **Federal Legislature:** The Federal Legislature was composed of two houses. They were, the Council of States and Federal Assembly or Legislature. The Federal Legislature had the following powers and functions:
  - — It had the power to make legislation over Federal list.
  - — It chould make legislation over emergency declared provinces.
  - — The Federal Legislature prepared ordinances with the help of the Governor-General that could continue for six months.
  - — It provided freedom of speech and the freedom to criticize the government.
- **Relationship between the Federal Legislature and the Governor-General:**
  - — Federal Legislature could not control the members of the Executive Council of Governor-General.
  - — The executive members of the Governor-General were not the members of the Federal Legislature.
  - — To some extent, it could control ministers as they were members of the Federal Assembly.
- **Council of States:** The Federal Legislature had two houses: Upper House and Lower House. The Council of States was the Upper House. It was a permanent body. The members were elected for a period of nine years. One third of the Council members retired after every three years. The house had two hundred sixty members. Of these, one hundred fifty six represented British India and the Governor-General nominated the remaining one hundred four. The system of equal representation was not allowed in the Upper House.
- **Federal Assembly:** Lower House was called the Federal Assembly or House of Assembly. It consisted of three hundred seventy five members out of which two hundred fifty represented Indian provinces and the remaining represented Indian states. Seats were arranged according to the religious representations. The term of the house was for a period of five years. A person who presided over the house was elected as a Speaker.

- **Federal Courts:** The Government of India Act, 1935 made a provision for creating a Federal Court. The Crown appointed the Chief Justice and judges. The Federal Court consisted of one Chief Justice and six judges. The Crown decided the number of judges.

Powers and Functions of the Federal Court

— It exercised both original and appellate powers.

— Original powers of the court were protection and interpretation of the Act, and settlement of disputes between the provinces and between the Center and provinces.

— The appellate powers were pursuing the cases and decisions of High Courts or any other dispute whose value was more than Rs 50,000.

— It advised the Governor-General in all the administrative matters.

- **State Government:** The Government of India Act, 1935 dissolved the dual government policy and provided provincial autonomy. The diarchy that was introduced by the 1919 Act came to an end. The provinces were provided with executive and legislative powers. Provincial autonomy had the power to make legislations over the subjects of the state list. The Governor was the Chief Executive. All the states had the provision of self-rule. In case of emergency, the Governor-General would administer the state. According to the Prime Minister Ramsay Me Donald, the concept of 1935 Act was to provide self-rule at the state level and educate Indians about the concept of a responsible government. Based on this concept, the dual government at the state or provincial level was dissolved. But the Government of India Act, 1935 imposed some restrictions on the provincial government. The Governor and the ministers were not independent. No special importance was given to the ministers.
- **Governor:** According to the 1935 Act, the Governor enjoyed certain powers while exercising his duties. His salary and powers were fixed depending upon the State's conditions. The Governor was the Chief Executive of the State. Some of his powers were as follows:

Executive Powers

- He appointed the ministers and removed them.
- He looked after the salaries of ministers.
- He appointed the Chairman and members of the Public Service Commission.

- He took the advice of Governor-General in protecting the State.
- He appointed the officials of his office.

Legislative Powers

- He had the power to summon, prorogue and dissolve the Assembly.
- He sanctioned some bills which were very urgent.
- He could veto or reserve a bill for the consideration of the Governor-General.
- He could proclaim emergency when the state was under disorder.
- He could promulgate ordinance.
- He could stop discussion of a bill if he considered it necessary.

Ordinance Powers

The Governor had the powers to issue ordinances. Each ordinance survived for six months. The ordinances made by the Governor were named as 'Governor-made Act'.

Financial Powers

- The Governor's assent was essential to introduce any financial bill in the Assembly.
- All the financial transactions of the state were to be performed only on his assent.

Discretionary Powers

The Governor exercised certain discretionary powers:

- Prevent utter disorder in the province.
- Protect the interests of the minorities.
- Safeguard the rights of princely states.
- Protect the rights and liberties of civil service personnel.
- Execute orders issued by the Governor-General.
- Amend the rules that affect the defence services.

Appointment of Council of Ministers

According to the theory of 'Instruments of Instructions' Governor could appoint the leader of the majority party as the Chief Minister, and on his recommendations the

Council of ministers. The Governor had to follow the following conditions in appointing the ministers:

- Minorities had to be given an opportunity in the Ministry.
- The Council of ministers had to develop a 'responsible government'.

Removal

The Governor could suspend the Council of ministers; or the ministers could lose their posts when they faced any no confidence motion in the Assembly.

State Legislature

The Act of 1935 provided for bicameralism in the six-states of Assam, Bengal, Bihar, Bombay, Madras and United Provinces. In the small states, however, unicameralism was provided.

Bicameralism

The bicameralism provided two houses at the state level: 1. State Assembly; and 2. State Council. The State Assembly was a temporary House and the members were directly elected for five years. The members elected the Speaker and the Deputy Speaker.

Legislative Assembly

It prepared legislations on fifty four items mentioned in the state list and thirty six items in the concurrent list. All kinds of financial bills were to be introduced only in the Assembly with prior consent of the Governor. About seventy five percent of the budget was allowed for voting in the Assembly.

Legislative Council

The Legislative Council or the Upper House was a permanent house. Members were elected for a period of nine years. One-third members retired every three years. Special provision was made for minorities. All kinds of proposals could be introduced in this House. But it had no power to discuss financial bills. The Governor could arrange a joint meeting for the two houses whenever there was a dispute.

Reserve Bank of India

The Act also setup the Reserve Bank of India to manage and control India's currency and credit. The Governor, assisted by the Deputy Governor, headed this bank. The Governor-General appointed the Governor and Deputy Governor on the recommendations of his council. Twelve directors were also appointed to assist them in the administrative matters.

Federal Railway Authority

The Act made arrangements to establish a Federal Railway Authority to administer the railways. The authority had seven members of whom the Governor-General appointed three. Each member had experience in industry or agriculture or finance administration.

Drawbacks of the Act of 1935

The Act of 1935 was the last Act enacted by the British Government. It reflected a federal setup for India, but could not be implemented because the Kings or Princes of several Princely States in India did not co-operate. The Act had some drawbacks as follows:

- The system sowed the seeds for communal disharmony.
- The system tried to setup an unnatural federal setup.
- The Governors gave abundant discretionary powers to the civil servants by which they became unresponsive and selfish.
- Civil servants did not develop good relations with the political executives because of their excessive powers.
- They were reluctant to implement the policies of the ministers, as they were not dependent on ministers.
- The diarchy arranged at the center was also strongly criticized as 'pseudo federalism' as most of the policies were left to the discretion of the Queen.

In spite of all these defects, the conventions established by the Act were recognized as a major step towards a new system. Indians were made to learn about the political education, voting system, and federal system of government. The elected representatives came to learn about technicalities of the government and administration. The Act provided good training to Indians to learn about democratic values.

CONSTITUENT ASSEMBLY

Mahatma Gandhi, in early 1922 called upon Indians to determine India's political destiny. According to him, "Swaraj will be a free gift of the British Parliament; it will be a declaration of Indian's self expression. That, it will be expressed through the Act of Parliament but it will be merely a courteous ratification of the declared wish of the people of India, even as in the case of Union of South Africa."

The Indian National Congress once again stressed the word 'constitution'. In 1933, Pandit Jawaharlal Nehru formulated his demand for a Constitutional Assembly. The working committee of the Congress reiterated this.

The British government published a white paper in 1933 outlining the proposals for constitutional reforms. The paper did not satisfy Indians as it was short of their expectations. The Congress working committee then resolved that, "The only satisfactory alternative to the white paper is to draw up a constitution by a Constituent Assembly elected on the basis of adult franchise or, as near to it as possible, with the power, if necessary to important minorities to have their representatives elected exclusively by electorates belonging to such minorities."

M. N. Roy in 1934 itself suggested to the Indians for having a Constituent Assembly. The Swaraj Party endorsed this proposal. Thus, the Congress decided to have a constitution most appropriate to the conditions of India. It also demanded an individual constitution and agreed to provide seats to religious minorities. In 1936, the Congress presented a Constitution for India as its election manifesto. Pandit Nehru supported this by calling it as the 'Congress party Franchise'. The Simon Commission was set up with the objective to find solutions to the constitutional problems of India. The Indians rejected this commission and started the 'Quit India Movement'. In 1946, the cabinet mission proposed to arrange Constituent Assembly. It recommended that each province could have specific number of seats. The number of seats in each province was to be allotted according to proportional representation. The total number of seats was fixed at three hundred eight nine. The princely states consisted of ninety three Constituencies. The seats allocated to the various provinces were to be divided into three sections: General, Muslims and Sikhs.

The Congress won the majority of the seats and formed the Government. The Muslim League was displeased and therefore decided not to participate in the Constituent Assembly elections. Jinnah blamed the Viceroy for having shown partiality towards the Hindus. Jinnah also requested the Muslims not to join the assembly.

Assembly Meetings

The Constituent Assembly met on 9 December, 1946 without Muslim League representatives. Prof. J. B. Kriplani, the President of the Congress party invited the eldest philosopher of the session, Dr. Sachidananda Sinha to be the temporary President of the Constituent Assembly. Out of the two hundred ninety six members, only Congress members attended the meeting. On 11 December, 1946, Dr. Rajendra Prasad was unanimously elected as the President of the Constituent Assembly.

Nehru's Objectives Resolution

On 13 December, 1946, Pandit Jawaharlal Nehru moved the Objectives resolution. He pointed out that India should be sovereign. Main provisions of this resolution were as follows:

- The Constituent Assembly declared its firm and solemn resolve to proclaim India as an Independent Sovereign Republic and to draw up a Constitution for her future governance.
- The territories now comprised British India, territories that formed the Indian states, and such other parts of India as were outside British India and the states as well as such other territories as were willing to be constituted into the Independent Sovereign India, would be a union of them all.
- The said territories, whether with their present boundaries or with such others as may be determined by the Constituent Assembly, and thereafter according to the law of the Constitution, would possess and retain the status of autonomous units, together with residuary powers and exercise all powers and functions of government and administration, except such powers and functions as were vested in or assigned to the Union; or as were inherent or implied in the Union or resulted in there from.
- All powers and authority of the Sovereign Independent India, its constituent parts and organs of government were derived from the people;
- Fundamental Rights: justice, social, economic and political, equality of status, of opportunity, and before the law; freedom of thought, expression, belief, faith, worship, vocation, association and action, subject to law and public morality would be guaranteed and secured to all the people of India.
- Adequate safeguards would be provided for minorities, backward and tribal areas, and depressed and other backward classes;
- The integrity of the territory of the Republic and its sovereign rights on land, sea and air according to justice and the law of civilized nations would be maintained.
- This ancient land would attain its rightful and honoured place in the world and make its full and willing contribution to the promotion of world peace and the welfare of mankind.

Working of the Constituent Assembly

The Constituent Assembly started preparing a Constitutional document. It reflected the wishes of the people and sovereignty of the nation. The Assembly adopted a committee to look into various issues that were essential for the preparation of the Constitution. Some of the Committees constituted by the Constituent Assembly were:

- Fundamental Rights Committee.
- Committee on Supreme Court.
- Union Powers Committee.
- Steering Committee.
- Advisory Committee on minorities.

The Drafting Committee consisted of the following members:

S. No.	Name	Designation
1	Dr. B. R. Ambedkar	Chairman
2	N. Gopala Swamy Iyengar	Member
3	Alladi Krishnaswamy Kyer	Member
4	K. M. Munshi	Member
5	Mohammad Saadullah	Member
6	N. Madhava Rao (He replaced Sri B. L. Mittre)	Member
7	T. T. Krishnamachari	Member

This Committee analyzed the reports of all the committees and then prepared a draft of the Constitution. The Committee thoroughly went through all the proposals. The President of the Constituent Assembly took utmost care to see that the draft of the Constitution was prepared at the earliest. In the primary session, that was held on 20-26 January 1947, the Assembly adopted the objective resolution prepared by Jawaharlal Nehru. It was decided that India should be 'sovereign and democratic'. Other issues discussed were:

- The powers of the Union Government.
- The Justifiability of Fundamental Rights.
- Whether to write Constitution in English or Hindustani or both.
- Report of the Union Constitutional Committee.

Dr. Rajendra Prasad being the President of the Constituent Assembly presided over the meeting. He expressed his satisfaction over the work of the Assembly.

The Constituent Assembly assembled for eleven times to discuss the draft of the Constitution that was submitted by the Drafting Committee. The discussion commenced on 9 December 1946 and continued up to 26 November 1949. The time taken by the Constituent Assembly to discuss Constitution was two years eleven months and eight days.

CHRONOLOGICAL EVENTS IN ADOPTING THE CONSTITUTION

- The Drafting Committee submitted its report to the Constituent Assembly on 21 February 1947. The Assembly made a thorough discussion on the draft from 4 November 1948 to 15 October 1949.
- The Constituent Assembly made a continuous discussion on the draft for two years eleven months and eight days.
- The Drafting Committee proposed 7,635 proposals and the Assembly accepted only 2,473.
- The total expenditure made in framing the constitution was Rs sixty four lakhs. Finally, the Drafting Committee proposals were accepted on 15 October 1949 and adopted on 26 January 1950. Another important feature of the Constituent

Assembly was the election of Dr. (Babu) Rajendra Prasad as the first President of India.

- The Constitution of India was adopted on 26 November 1949 and the Hon'ble members appended their signatures on 24 January 1950. In all, two hundred eighty four members actually signed the Constitution.
- The Constitution of India came into force on 26 January 1950.

DEBATES AND DISCUSSIONS ON THE CONSTITUTION

The Constitution is the steel framework of the nation and it reflects the wishes and ambitions of its people. It is also recognized as the embodiment of the desires of the people and the intention of the nation to achieve developmental objectives. It also indicates the method of governance of the people, structure of the government, its powers and functions. The philosophy of rule of a state is the basis for the formation of a constitution.

Some of the issues that were discussed in the Constituent Assembly were as follows:

- **The Forms of Government:** The primary problem of the Constituent Assembly was to make a decision over the form of the government. The only two options were the Parliamentary and Presidential form of government. India was new to both these forms. Conditions were developed for both the types of Governments in India. National Leaders like Mahatma Gandhi, Pandit Jawaharlal Nehru and Maulana Abdul Kalam Azad were in favour of Parliamentary government as they opposed concentration of power and authority in one single hand. They also believed that the Presidential system of Government might once again lead to dictatorship.
- At the same time, the constitution makers felt that India's prevailing problem of illiteracy might not enable the people to use proper discretion to elect their own representative on the basis of merits. It might not be possible for the people to understand the policies of the Government, so essential for national building. There was another apprehension that the elites and capitalists might exploit the illiterates. The urban elites could occupy the Government and control the Parliament for a long time. Elections could also be influenced by caste and religion. The constitution makers decided that all these problems could be resolved by educating the people and having a sound governance policy. The power of people to elect their government on broader basis was considered as paramount and hence parliamentary form of government was chosen.
- There was a controversy about secularism. Some of the Congress leaders in the Assembly firmly believed that India should be a secular state. According to them, the whole freedom movement was made on secular principles. The Muslim patriots believed that in free India they would enjoy equal rights as that of Hindus. A vast majority of the Muslims had also participated along with the

Hindus for independence of India. It was also said that India had the glorious tradition of being the land of religious tolerance. Thus, the concept of democracy overcame all the theocratic policies. All the persons in the society were to be respected and honoured on the basis of their abilities and capabilities. It was also argued that after the independence crores of Muslims living in India might not co-operate for development of the country, if they were treated as secondary citizens. There was a possibility of internal disputes which could hamper administration. A strong argument was made on how the secular countries were prospering. Finally, it was decided that India should be a secular state.

- **Democratic Socialism or Communism:** Democracy or capitalism was anotherissue for discussion. When India became independent the world was divided into two blocks: Capitalist Bloc and Socialist Bloc. It was for India to decide as to what type of economic theory it wanted to adopt. Capitalism was favoured by some because of the moral support given by the United States during the national movement. At the same time it could not forget the prosperity of Russia after the 1917 Revolution and impact of Socialist theory on it. Most of the Congress leaders were very much impressed with the Socialistic theory. The socio-economic conditions of India were not favourable to adopting the capitalistic concepts and total socialistic ideals. It was felt that the country would find it difficult to bear the consequences of free entrepreneurship under capitalism. At the same time it would be politically not possible to shift to socialistic pattern of society as prevailed in Russia. The assembly at the end decided in favour of a democratic socialistic state rather than an authoritarian socialistic state. Therefore, the country chose the midway between capitalism and socialism and established a 'Mixed Economy State'.
- **Unitary and Federal System:** India is a big country with vast geographical area and large population representing diverse religions, castes, languages and cultures. However, the nationalism of the citizens is displayed by unity in defending the country from foreign invasion. The transformation of the erstwhile semi-federal setup of British Rule in to unitary system of governance in post-independence period was considered from different view points. The questions of national security and sharing of natural resources by different regions were debated at length. Finally, it was decided to have a unitary country, i.e. Indian Union with federal features of governance for the states.
- **Reservations and its problems:** The reservation issue was an additional and specific issue for drafting in the Constitution since the early period of 19th Century. The demand for reservations was based on the economic and social inequalities meted out to certain sections of the society. It was strongly advocated that the tribes which formed the disadvantaged sections specifically needed the constitutional guarantee of opportunities for betterment of their lives. The Constituent Assembly, thus decided to incorporate statutory reservations in electorate, education and employment for disadvantaged sections of people under

categories of scheduled castes and scheduled tribes. The objective of providing the reservations was to provide for equalization of social and economic status of SC/ST's within certain time and to integrate them in to national main stream. The British government policy of providing special representation to Muslim minorities made the policy of reservations more problematic. It gave a fillip to the national movement. Communal awards, during Ramsay McDonald's time, did not satisfy the Indian community. The British politics of reservations ultimately resulted in the partition of India.

The British had imposed their own political system in India where Indians had very little choice to enjoy liberty and participate in administrative matters of the country. The people had a limited choice to elect their representatives and these elected bodies had limited powers. The British administrative methods did not satisfy the Indians. Hence, the British made the 1909, 1919 and 1935 Acts in the name of reforms. These Acts ultimately proved the British imperialism over India. After the Second World War, the Labour Party assumed power in Britain and decided to give independence to India. The Constituent Assembly worked over the controversies that arose for governing the country. It became a herculean task to solve and settle the controversies to satisfy the needs of all sections of India. The towering personalities of the Assembly contributed their efforts for a suitable and amicable constitution.

SUMMARY

- The failure of the British to provide adequate relief to the people suffering from severe famine caused discontentment to the Indians. The Nationalist leaders realized that agitations alone were insufficient to counter the British government. To satisfy the wishes of the Indians, British passed the Morley-Minto Reforms (Indian Council Act, 1909). This Act provided the representative form of government and communal electorates.
- After the First World War, Indians realized that the British government had not appropriately acknowledged their sacrifices. To please the Indians, the British enacted the Montague-Chelmsford Reforms (The Government of India Act, 1919). This Act introduced the diarchy at the provincial level and considered the Governor-General as the Head of the entire administration.
- The failure of the Round Table Conference led to the enactment of the 1935 Act. Though this Act did not satisfy the Indians, the British Parliament, however, maintained complete supremacy over India.
- The Simon Commission recommended that in the Constituent Assembly each province must have specific number of seats and the number of seats in each

province must be allotted according to proportional representation. The total number of seats was fixed at three hundred eighty nine.

- The Indian Constitution cleared all the existing problems to build a bright future for the Nation.

QUESTIONS

1. Discuss the main provisions of the Act of 1935 which paved the way for further constitutional development.
2. What were the reasons for formulating the Act of 1909? Analyse its main provisions.
3. Why was Morley-Minto Reforms introduced? Discuss the main features of the Act of 1919.
4. Critically analyse the working of the Constituent Assembly.
5. What were the main issues discussed in the Constituent Assembly? Discuss.

3

Salient Features of Indian Constitution

After reading this chapter, you will be conversant with:

- Meaning
- Constitutional Law and Constitutionalism
- Sources of the Constitution
- Salient features of the Constitution
- Criticism of the Constitution

MEANING

The 26 January, 1950 was one of the most memorable days in the history of modern India. That day announced the birth of a new nation as a republic to the entire world. A new Constitution was brought into force. It was in fact, a rebirth of an ancient country after centuries of dire vicissitudes.

The legacy of two hundred years old British rule came to an end and there was complete transfer of political authority to the Indian leaders on 15 August, 1947. However, attainment of Independence is not an end in itself. It was the beginning of another new struggle of establishing a democracy based on ideas like justice, equality, liberty and fraternity. It is a struggle to live as an independent nation from times to come. The paramount importance at that time was the need for a new Constitution that forms the basic law of the land. Therefore, one of the first tasks undertaken by independent India was to frame the Constitution.

Constitution of a country may also be described as it's foundational law which command the fundamentals of its polity and on the altar of which all other laws and executive acts of the state are to be tested for their validity and legitimacy.

Every Constitution represents the vision and values of its founding fathers. It is based on the social, political and economic ethos, faith and aspirations of the people. It is wrong to regard a country's Constitution as a mere inert document. It is not just a written text. Every Constitution gets its meaning and content from the manner in which and the people by whom it is operated. The effects it acquires from how it is interpreted by courts of the land and the conventions and practices that grow around it in the actual process of its working.

In a democracy, sovereignty rests with the people and people govern themselves. But with the growth of nation states and complexities involved in the administration, direct democracy is no longer feasible. In modern day representative democracies, people decide as to by whom they should be governed through their inalienable right to vote. The first and the most fundamental application of people's sovereignty is giving themselves a Constitution which outlines the ground rules under which certain powers are transferred to different organs of the state and are to be exercised by them. In a federal polity, Constitution delineates, delimits and distributes powers between organs of the state, both at the central and state level.

CONSTITUTIONAL LAW

A Constitutional law connotes the fundamental law of the land as per the provisions of the Constitution. It is concerned with the basic features of the framework of the distribution of powers between the organs of the state and between the unions and the units. In modern representative democracy, Constitutional law lays emphasis on human rights and the relation between the individual and the state.

CONSTITUTIONALISM

The concept of Constitutionalism is that of a polity governed by a Constitution that prescribes a limited government and rule of law that is completely opposed to arbitrary, authoritarian or totalitarian rule. Constitutionalism is also associated with written Constitution as a written Constitution is definite and delimits the powers and functions of various organs of the state and the government. However, there are countries, though, that have a written Constitution, as they are not democratic in true sense. It's only that they have Constitutions but not Constitutionalism.

SOURCES OF INDIAN CONSTITUTION

The Constitution of India was derived from diverse sources. The founding fathers, the authors of the Constitution made conscious attempt not to make a complete departure from the past but to build the existing structure and institution. Indian Constitution otherwise evolved out of interactions between various demand representatives, responsible for independence and small reforms grudgingly granted by the British from time to time. In fact, the fundamental source of some of the provisions of the Constitution can be traced to that of East India Company and the British rule in India.

It is remarked that Constitution of India was prepared after "ransacking all the known Constitutions of the world" and most of it were substantially borrowed from others. Though borrowed, the framers took great care in gathering best features of the Constitutions by avoiding all the faults and adapting them to the existing needs and conditions of the nation. To begin with, the chapter on Fundamental Rights was based upon the model of Bill of Rights enshrined in the American Constitution. The Parliamentary form of Government was adopted from the Westminster model of the United Kingdom. The concept of Directive Principles of State Policy was borrowed from the Irish Constitution. Provisions relating to that of emergency powers were adopted from the German Reich. The provision that makes the President the executive head of the State and the supreme commander of armed forces and the Vice-President the *ex-officio* chairman of the Rajya Sabha or the Upper Chamber of the Parliament were based on the US model. The federal structure and provisions relating union-state relations and the distribution of powers between the union and the states was adopted from the Canadian Constitution. From the Australian Constitution, the framers of the Constitution adopted the Concurrent list in the Seventh Schedule, and the provisions regarding trade, commerce and industries and other parliamentary privileges. Finally, nearly seventy five percent of the Constitution was the replica of the Government of India Act, 1935 though with suitable modifications and adaptation. The basic structure of the polity and provisions regulating union-state relations, declaration of Emergency, by and large, are based on Government of India Act, 1935.

SALIENT FEATURES OF INDIAN CONSTITUTION

The salient features of the Indian Constitution can be discussed as follows:

WRITTEN CONSTITUTION

The Republic of India has an enacted and a written Constitution, one of the most comprehensible in nature. The framers of the Constitution did not want to leave any matter under doubts, difficulties and controversies in near future. The original Constitution contained 395 Articles and 8 Schedules. Today, the Constitution has 442 Articles divided in to 22 Parts and 12 Schedules. It was remarked, "Like the Constitution of United States of America, Canada and France, India too has a written Constitution, though it differs from those documents in many respects". (Dr. B.L. Fadia, *Indian Government and Politics*, p. 21).

THE LONGEST KNOWN CONSTITUTION

The Indian Constitution has been distinguished as one of the lengthiest and detailed Constitutional document in the world. This extraordinary bulk of the Constitution is due to several reasons as underlined below:

The framers of the Constitution sought to incorporate the accumulated experiences gathered from all the Constitutions of the world and avoid all defects and loopholes thereof. Moreover, Indian Constitution has embodied the modified results of judicial decisions made elsewhere, interpreting comparable provisions in order to minimize uncertainty and litigation.

- In addition to the Union, it also includes the Constitutions of the state. The American Federal Constitution covers only the organizations of national government, leaving the state Constitutions to be framed by the states themselves. The Constitution has special provisions for different classes of states: like Part B states (representing the former Indian states), Part C states (the Centrally-administered areas) and some smaller territories in Part D.
- It has a detailed list of administrative provisions. Though, most of the provisions were based on the Government of India Act, 1935, the authors had an apprehension that if the provisions are not enumerated in a detailed manner, the present conditions of the country might pervert the form of administration. It was also believed that the smooth functioning of nascent democracy would be jeopardized if things were left to ordinary legislation. It is for this reason the Indian Constitution has a detailed provision about the organization of the Judiciary, the Public Services Commissions, Elections and others.
- The peculiar problems with regard to the Scheduled Castes and Scheduled Tribes and other backward classes, matters relating to Official language and also relating to Emergency provisions have contributed to the bulkiness of the Constitution.
- The Constitution has provided a special status to the state of Jammu and Kashmir and special provision to make its own state Constitution as per Article 370. Any provision of the Constitution of India does not apply to Jammu and Kashmir but depends on the order of the President in consultation with the Government of the state. (Wadhwa Nagpur, p. 34)
- The vastness and the certain specific problems to be solved have also contributed towards the bulk of Constitution. Special provisions have been incorporated to meet the regional matters and demands of certain states like Nagaland, Assam, Manipur, Andhra Pradesh, Maharashtra, Gujarat, Sikkim, and Mizoram.
- The Constitution not only provided provisions with regard to states but also the relation between the center and the states with reference to legislative or administrative relations in order to minimize conflicts between the two. Further, elaborate explanation is provided with regard to inter-state relations, co-ordination and adjudication of disputes amongst the states.
- The detailed explanation of the Fundamental Rights and the Directive Principles of State Policy enshrined in Part III and IV respectively, adds to the vastness of the Constitution. The Fundamental Rights were made justifiable while the Directive Principles are not justifiable. The list of Fundamental Rights became bulkier because the framers of the Constitution also included new

matters of concern like untouchability, preventive detention and so on. At a later stage, a special chapter on Fundamental Duties was incorporated in Part IV A, Article 51 A.

The main reason for vastness of the constitution, according to lvor Jeanings is largely the legacy of the past. The Constitution, which is based on the Government of India Act, 1935 itself was one of the longest measures ever passed by the British. In fact, it was the British who set the fashion by framing lengthy and detailed Constitution for the Indians. The new Constitution of India is like a new law or a detailed code dealing with all important aspects of the Constitutional and administrative system of the country. (Fadia, p. 22)

PARTLY FLEXIBLE AND PARTLY RIGID

The Indian Constitution is partly rigid and partly flexible. The procedure laid down by the Constitution for its amendment is neither easy as in England, nor very rigid as in the United States. England has no written Constitution; there is no difference between a Constitutional law and an ordinary law. Both Constitutional laws and ordinary laws are amended or passed in a similar manner. In United States, however, the procedure for Constitutional amendment is highly rigid. Amendments can be brought only if two-thirds majority of the Congress agree and subsequently ratified by at least three-fourths of the states. The Constitution of India is a combination of extremely flexible British Constitution and highly rigid United States Constitution.

The amendments for certain provisions in India require the ratification of the state legislatures and for some ratification by only half of them would suffice. The rest of the Constitution may be amended by a special majority of the Union Parliament, however, not less than two-thirds of the members must be present and vote.

Parliament also has the power to modify or alter many of the provisions of the Constitution by a simple majority. For instance, (a) Changes in the names and boundaries, areas, amalgamation and separation of the states (article 4); (b) Abolition or creation of the second chamber of a State Legislature (article 69); (c) Administration of scheduled areas and scheduled tribes; and (d) Creation of legislatures and council of ministers for certain Union Territories [Article 239A (2)].

The flexibility of the Constitution is manifested through the power given to Parliament to supplement the provisions of the Constitution by legislation. Some of the principles, wherein the Parliament is empowered to supplement by laws are related to that of citizenship. Articles 5-8 lay down the conditions for acquisition of citizenship and article 11 provides plenary powers to legislate on this subject. As a result of this power, Parliament in 1955 enacted Citizenship Act. Similarly, the Parliament is empowered to legislate on some subsidiary matters relating to that of Preventive Detention under article 22(7). Again, Parliament, in order to protect the civil rights of the people, proclaimed that untouchability is an offence and punishable in accordance with law according to article 17. Finally, though the Constitution specified provisions relating to election of the President and the Vice President as per article 71(3), the Parliament however can supplement these provisions with legislations (Wadhwa Nagpur, p. 36).

Preamble

The Preamble to a Constitution is expected to embody the fundamental values and the philosophy on which the Constitution is based, and the aims and objectives which the founding fathers strived to achieve.

The Preamble of the Constitution begins with:

"We the PEOPLE OF INDIA, having solemnly resolved to constitute India in to a SOVEREIGN, SOCIALIST, SECULAR, DEMOCRATIC, REPUBLIC and secure to all its citizens, **JUSTICE**: social, economic and political.

LIBERTY of thought, expression, belief, faith and worship;

EQUALITY of status and of opportunity, and to promote among them all;

FRATERNITY, assuring the dignity of the individual and the unity and integrity of the nation;

IN OUR CONSTITUENT ASSEMBLY, on this twenty-sixth day of November 1949,

We do **HEREBY, ADOPT, ENACT AND GIVE TO OURSELVES THIS CONSTITUTION."**

One of the most important amendments to the Preamble was the 42nd amendment in 1976. Two significant changes were made to the Preamble. Firstly, for the words 'Sovereign, Democratic, Republic', the words 'Sovereign, Socialist, Secular, Democratic, Republic' were substituted and secondly, for the words 'Unity of the Nation' the words, 'Unity and Integrity of the Nation' were included.

A Preamble has certain essential elements through which the purpose of it will be clear to one and all. The major ingredients of a Preamble are: (i) The source of the Constitution, (ii) Type of the government, (iii) Objectives of the political system, and (iv) The date of its adoption and enactment. A brief explanation of each of the element is as follows:

The source of the Constitution: The Preamble opens with words "We, the people of India, adopt, enact and give to ourselves this Constitution" suggests that people of the country are supreme. It is the Constituent Assembly that enacted and adopted the Constitution in the name of the people of India. Commenting on the validity of the Constitution, the chairman of the Drafting Committee once stated on the floor of the Constituent Assembly in 1949, "I say that this Preamble embodies what is the desire of every member of the House that this Constitution should have its roots, its authority, its sovereignty from the people that it has." (Fadia, p. 32)

Type of Government: The polity or the type of government promised to the people was well described in the Constitution as a Sovereign, Socialist, Secular, and Democratic, Republic.

The expression ***Sovereign*** clearly signifies that India is a free nation and ceased to be dependent on the British Empire with the passing of Indian Independence Act, 1947. From 15 August 1947 to 26 January 1950, India's political status was that of a Dominion in the British Commonwealth of Nations. But with the commencement of the Constitution, India became a 'Sovereign Republic' like that of United States or the Swiss republic. However, India still continues to be a member of Commonwealth of Nations. Perhaps, India categorically claimed that its voluntary association with Commonwealth does not affect her sovereignty in any manner and India can cut off its association as easily as it had been declared. (Pylee, p. 48) The Constitution, as specified, derives its powers and authority from the people. Legal sovereignty is therefore with the people and political sovereignty is distributed between the union and the states with greater powers vested with that of the Union. Finally, the state does not possess absolute sovereignty.

The framers of the Constitution never desired to align with any specific ideology, or a limited economic doctrine. The term Socialist, incorporated in the Constitution can be identified as a theme which aims to secure people from all forms of exploitation, social economic or political, and also elimination of inequality in income status, and standard of living. Further, it aims to provide its people justice in social, political and economic fields as well. However, the inclusion of the term Socialist was not readily accepted. It was criticized that the term is very vague and means different things to different people. The term Socialism was defined only during the 45th Constitutional Amendment.

The term ***Secular*** had been added to the Constitution by the 42nd amendment in the year 1976. It is put forward that the state have no religion of its own and all persons shall be equally entitled to freedom of conscience and right to freely profess, practice and propagate religion. The 42nd Amendment Act, though inserted the term secular was never defined. The 45th Constitution Amendment Bill defined 'Secular Republic' as a 'Republic in which there is equal respect to all religions'.

The founding fathers of Constitution envisaged a nation that transcends all diversities of religion, caste and creed. They were not hostile to religion but hoped that it would be possible to forge political unity. The Constitution envisaged a new social order free from communal conflicts. It visualized a polity under which laws would not discriminate between citizens on the grounds of religion, caste, etc. The Constitution aimed at the establishment of a secular order under which majority of the population does not enjoy any special privileges or preferential treatment at the hands of the state and the religious rights of the minorities were protected in different ways.

The term ***Democracy*** is derived from two Greek terms namely, Demos which means the people, and Kratia meant rule. So, in simple terms, democracy implies the rule of the people. Democracy is a complete negation of aristocracy and dictatorship. The main fundamentals of democracy are that the sovereign power resides with the people irrespective of religion, race, caste, sex, place of birth, and economic, educational or professional background. Furthermore, all are equal in the eyes of law and the individuals are capable of self-governing and manage affairs in their own way.

The term democracy can be understood in two senses. In a narrow political sense, it is a form of Government which is both responsible and responsive system under which, the representatives are chosen by the electorate for a fixed term. In broader sense it implies social as well as economic democracy apart from political democracy. Democracy further believes in methods of discussion and persuasion than going for outright war or armed conflict. The ballot substitutes bullet.

In the ancient Greek city states, people participated in the political affairs directly and decided matters of the polity. This system of democracy was called direct democracy. However with the changing times and increase in population and territory, it became difficult to directly participate in the political affairs of the state. This gave way to indirect democracy in modern state systems. Under an indirect democracy, government is carried on and laws are made by the representatives elected by the people.

The Constitution of India provided for a representative parliamentary democracy. Maximum representation is provided to the vast population of the country without any conditions. Another important aspect of India's democracy is that it provides for universal adult franchise to all the citizens who cross the age of eighteen.

The term *Republic* implies an elected head of the state. The Preamble declared that the source of all authority under the Constitution is the people of India and that there is no subordination to any external authority. While Pakistan remained a British Dominion until 1956, India ceased to be a Dominion as she declared herself a Republic (Wadhwa Nagpur, p. 21). A democratic state may have an elected or a hereditary head. One of the best examples of a hereditary head is Britain. As long as the real power vests with the people, there is no harm to the very existence of the people either with a monarchical or a hereditary ruler or head. In most of the republican countries, the head of the state is elected for a prescribed number of years. For example, in USA, the President is elected for a term of four years. In Switzerland, a group of seven members are elected for a period of four years which constitutes the executive. India, by virtue of being a republic has chosen the system of electing one of its citizens as the head of the state for every five years.

Objectives of the Political System: The Preamble defined four different objectives of the political system. These *are Justice, Liberty, Equality* and *Fraternity.*

The term *Justice* implies a harmonious reconcilement of the individual conduct with the general welfare of the society. The attainment of common good is the essence of justice. The Preamble proclaims that justice embraces the entire social, political and economic spheres of human activity.

Social justice implies that all citizens are treated equally irrespective of their status in the society. Access to public places is not denied to anybody. The state also thrives to promote welfare of all the individuals in the society. With regard to economic justice, the state makes provisions for human conditions of work, maternity relief, leisure, reduction in disparities, and ensuring a decent standard of living for the workers, weaker sections and backward classes. Economic justice aims at reducing the gap between the haves and have-nots. In fact, various articles in Part IV of the Constitution are directed towards securing a new social and economic order imbued with justice. Thus, there are provisions for right to work, to education and public assistance, in certain cases promotion of economic interests of the people, especially the weaker sections. With reference to political justice, it means equal rights to all citizens to participate in the political process without any discrimination on the basis of caste, colour, creed, sex, etc. Founding fathers claimed that political justice is meaningless without economic justice.

The term *Liberty* is derived from Latin term *Liber,* which means freedom from captivity, imprisonment, slavery, serfdom or despotism. The Preamble provides two different aspects of liberty. It signifies not only absence of any arbitrary restraint on the freedom of the individual but also the creation of conditions that provide the essential elements necessary for the overall development of personality of the individual.

The leaders of the French Revolution were strong believers in the concept of equality and professed that all men are equal in the eyes of law. There must be no discrimination based on the place of birth. Further, all citizens were eligible to public offices and honour and position strictly according to their capacities, virtues and talent only.

The term *Equality* does not mean that all individuals are equal mentally and physically. It signifies equality of status, the status of free individuals and equality of opportunity. Equality of status is provided by prohibiting artificial restriction like religion, race, caste, etc. It is further enhanced by the prohibition of untouchability and also abolition of conferring titles. Moreover, equality of opportunity is provided by guarantee of rule of law. Equality is granted in social, political and economic spheres as well. All citizens are entitled to participate in political affairs without any restrictions. In the economic field, equality means, for the same ability and same labour, the salary would also be the same. Further, one or more class would not exploit other men or classes.

Finally, the Preamble emphasizes on the objective of *fraternity* to ensure dignity of the individual and the unity of nation. By *fraternity* we mean a spirit of brotherhood, the promotion of which is absolutely essential in our country that comprises of people of many races and religions. Dignity is a word of moral and spiritual importance and imposes a moral obligation on part of the Union to respect personality of the citizen and to create conditions of work which will ensure self-respect (Fadia, p. 34). The terms 'unity and integrity' are included in the Constitution to save the country from the influences of tendencies like regionalism, linguism, communalism and also secessionism and separatist activities in order to achieve national integration.

The objective of *fraternity* is to improve the quality of life of the individual by guaranteeing the Fundamental Rights. It also issues guidelines to the state in the form of Directive Principles of State Policy that makes sure adequate means of livelihood, just and humane conditions of work and a decent standard of living. Moreover, fraternity is given more stress because unless and until there is unity and integrity of the nation, it is not possible to take the country economically forward. It cannot hope to preserve either democracy or independence of the country and the honour of the countrymen.

Date of Adoption and Enactment: The last part of the Preamble mentions the date on which the Constituent Assembly was adopted, enacted and given to the nation as 26 November, 1949. The Preamble, however, came into force only on 26 January 1950.

In conclusion, the Preamble of the Constitution can be regarded as one of the best of its kinds ever drafted. It embodies the spirit of the Constitutions, the determination of the Indian people to unite them in a common adventure of building up a new and independent nation which will ensure the triumph of justice, liberty, equality and fraternity (Pylee, p. 50).

FUNDAMENTAL RIGHTS

There is always a longstanding conflict between the state and the individual which, in fact is as old as human history. In spite of various attempts to resolve the competing claims between the state and the individual, a solution seems to be far off. This situation is primarily because of dynamics of human nature, values, ideas that constantly change making space for new ones. If the individual is given complete freedom, it invariably results in chaos, uncertainty and anarchy. If the state was provided with absolute powers it would result in tyranny. Hence, there is a need to bring about a compromise between the two. This problem is more obvious in a democratic country because the civil liberties enjoyed by the people determine the very existence of democracy. Democracy aims at maximum personality development of the individual in a free society that finally helps in the advancement of human welfare. In order to achieve this, a common device has been adopted, namely. Fundamental Rights.

India's Fundamental Rights reflect Western ideas and also the political freedom that people were denied during the British rule. The Fundamental Rights were incorporated in Part III of the Constitution. Fundamental Rights are not a distinctive feature of Indian Constitution. Almost all the countries with a written Constitution have these rights. The French Declaration of Rights, the Bill of Rights of the US, Universal Human Rights Charter is all a similar list of rights provided in various Constitutions of the world. All these documents provide the necessary guidance to the framers of the Constitution in selecting those rights that are suitable to the socio-economic and political conditions.

The Indian desire for civil rights was deep rooted and became more prominent with the formation of Indian National Congress (INC) in 1885. The Indian National Congress, its members, the Liberals, Moderates and religious minorities like Muslims, the Christians and the Sikhs expressed the need for rights that provided protection to these minorities and infused confidence in majority communities. Indians wanted the same kind of privileges and rights the British enjoyed in India and also a complete end to discrimination practiced by them. The first ever demand for Fundamental Rights was the India Bill of 1895. Article 16 of this Bill laid down a variety of rights including those of free speech, imprisonment only by competent authority, and free state education (Fadia, p.45). A series of resolutions were adopted by Congress between 1917 and 1919 that constantly demanded civil rights and equality of status with that the Englishmen. In 1925, seven Fundamental Rights were drafted called Mrs. Besant's Commonwealth of India Bill that laid emphasis on individual liberty, freedom of conscience, free expression of opinion, free assembly, and equality before the law. The Government of India Act, 1935 also emphasized on rights but was out rightly rejected by the Simon Commission and the Joint Parliamentary Committee in the year 1942. The next major development on the issue of rights was that of Sapru Report published in the year 1945 that made a categorical distinction between justiciable and non-justiciable rights.

Rights can be defined as those conditions of social life without which no man can seek to be himself at his best. The term Fundamental Rights imply that they have been incorporated in the fundamental law of the land, i.e. Constitution and they are enforceable by a court of law in case of any violation. Further, Fundamental Rights are binding on the central government, state government and even the local bodies.

Salient features of the Fundamental Rights

The Fundamental Rights are guaranteed by the Constitution of India and have certain specific features. A brief description of the features is as follows:

Firstly, Fundamental Rights cannot be altered or taken away by ordinary legislation as they form the integral part of the Indian Constitution. Even if any particular law is passed by the legislature that jeopardizes the rights, then that law is declared null and void.

Secondly, the chapter on Fundamental Rights in Part III of the Constitution is considered to be the most detailed and comprehensive in nature. It clearly enumerates each of the Fundamental Rights granted to the Indian citizens along with clauses and sub-clauses.

Thirdly, the Fundamental Rights enshrined in our Constitution have two different aspects, positive and negative aspect. These rights restrict the negative character of the state without conferring special privileges to the citizens, while the positive aspect of rights confers privileges on the people. For example, article 18 of the Constitution abolishes special titles to be given to the citizens. Similarly, article 17 abolishes untouchability.

Fourthly, Fundamental Rights are justifiable in nature. This means that if any individual rights are affected, he or she can move to a court of law for protection and enforcement of the same. The Supreme Court has the power to declare any law as null and void if they are found to be inconsistent with the rights guaranteed by the Constitution. The Judiciary plays the role of a guardian of the Constitution. .

Fifthly, Fundamental Rights are not absolute which suggests that there are certain limitations or restrictions on them in the interest of the entire community. In some cases, restrictions are imposed by the Constitution itself. Though freedom of speech is provided to all in the country, the citizens are expected not to utter anything that is likely to affect the security of the state, public order or the country's relations with a foreign power.

Sixthly, Fundamental Rights are suspended during emergencies. The President of India is authorized to suspend the Fundamental Rights of the people and also their right to move to courts.

Seventhly, Fundamental Rights are applicable to the citizens as well as aliens though only with some exceptions. Rights like protection of life, freedom of religion, right against exploitation are guaranteed to all without exceptions. This suggests that the Constitution draws a clear-cut distinction between citizens and aliens.

Eighthly, Fundamental Rights do not believe in the theory of natural rights.

Finally, Fundamental Rights are amendable but cannot be subject to abrogation because the later will amount to violation of the basic structure of the Constitution.

Classification of Fundamental Rights:

The Fundamental Rights incorporated in part III of the Constitution are more elaborate than any other written Constitution relating to Fundamental Rights. The Fundamental Rights are classified into seven groups. They are as follows:

1. Right to Equality.
2. Right to Freedom.
3. Right against Exploitation.
4. Right to Freedom of Religion.
5. Cultural and Educational Rights.
6. Right to Property.
7. Right to Constitutional Remedies.

Of these, the 44th Constitutional Amendment Act eliminated Right to Property from the list of Fundamental Rights in 1978. Subsequently, Right to Property has become a legal and a civil right. As such, there are only six Fundamental Rights now stands guaranteed by the Constitution.

The following is the explanation of each of the right:

Right to Equality (Articles 14-18):

Articles 14-18 of the Constitution deal with right to equality. Equality is one of the important tenet upon which democracy was build and therefore it is given utmost importance in a democratic country like India.

Article 14 of the Constitution provides that "State shall not deny to any person equality before law or the equal protection of the laws within the territory of India".

The terms 'equality before law' and 'equal protection of laws' though sound similar, they are two separate entities and the expressions owe their origin to English Common Law and American Constitution, respectively. Equality of law implies absence of any special privileges in favor of any individual and equal subjection of all classes. Equal protection of the law signifies equality of treatment in equal circumstances.

Another simple interpretation of equality before law is related to that of A. V. Dicey's concept of Rule of Law which means that no man is above the law and that every person whatever be his rank or status is subject to the ordinary law. Equal protection of the law on the other hand denotes that among equals the law should be equal and equally administered. To simplify further, this means right to equal treatment in similar circumstances, both in the privileges conferred and in the liabilities imposed by the laws. Thus, it does not mean that every person must be taxed equally, but that persons under the same character should be taxed by the same standard.

Article 15 states, "The state shall not discriminate against any citizen on the grounds of religion, race, caste, sex, place of birth or any of them. Further, on the basis of these a citizen cannot be denied access to shops, public restaurants or the use of wells, tanks, bathing ghats, roads and places of public resort maintained wholly and partly out of state funds or dedicated to the use of the general public."

Article 15 (i) prohibits discrimination based on place of birth; it cannot be read as prohibiting discrimination based on residence. Residence, as a qualification for certain purposes, such as employment may not be dealt with discrimination based on caste and place of birth. The significance of this article is that it is a guarantee against every form of discrimination by the state on the basis of religion, race, caste or sex. It attacks the root of provincialism by prohibiting discrimination based on place of birth.

However, there are certain exceptions to this article. Special provisions are made for the benefit of women and children. Further, special arrangements are provided for the advancement of socially and economically backward classes of the society, as they require special protection.

Article 16 of the Constitution states, "There shall be equality of opportunity for all citizens in matters relating to employment or appointment to any office under the state." Furthermore, the article specifies, "No citizen shall, on grounds only of religion, race, caste, sex, descent, place of birth or any of them, be ineligible for any office under the state."

This article, however is not free of certain exceptions. These are:

- Residence within the state may be laid down by the Parliament as a condition for particular classes of the employment or appointment under any state or other local authority.
- The state may reserve any post or appointment in favour of any backward class of citizens, who, in the opinion of the State, are not adequately represented in the services under the State.
- The claim of the members of the Scheduled Castes and Scheduled Tribes shall be taken into consideration in the matter of appointment to services and posts under the union and the states, as long as consistent with the maintenance of efficiency of the administration.

Article 17 of the Constitution states, "Untouchability be abolished and its practice in any form is forbidden. The enforcement of any disability arising out of untouchability shall be an offence punishable in accordance with law."

However, the term untouchability has not been defined either in the Constitution or in the Untouchability Offences Act passed by the Parliament in 1955. It is usually referred to as a social practice that looks down upon the depressed classes primarily on account of their birth and hinder them in having any interaction with the people of upper classes or castes.

The 1955 Act prescribed punishment for certain specific actions defined as offences. These are:

- Refusing admission to any person to a public institution, such as hospital, dispensary, educational institutions, etc.
- Preventing any person from worshipping or offering prayers in any place of public worship.
- Subjecting any person to any disability with regard to access to any shop, public restaurant, hotel or public entertainment or with regard to the use of any reservoir, tap or other source of water, road, cremation ground or any place, where services are rendered to the public.

Furthermore, in 1976, the Act was enlarged wherein it was stated that the following will also be punishable offences:

- Insulting a member of a Scheduled Caste on the ground of untouchability.
- Preaching untouchability, directly or indirectly.
- Justifying untouchabilty on historical, philosophical or religious grounds or on the ground of tradition of caste system.

The punishments awarded for a person convicted of practicing untouchability ranges from one to two year imprisonment and shall be disqualified for election to the union or a state legislature.

Article 18 abolishes all titles and the state is prohibited from conferring titles on any person.

The British government conferred upon a number of titles, mostly on their political supporters and government officers and thus created a special class of nobility among the people. It was difficult for independent India to recognize and accept these titles apart from considerations of the merit of those who held them. Thus, Article 18 abolishes all titles to ensure equality. The only exception is in giving titles in favour of academic or military distinctions. However, the Constitution made it clear that:

- The state does not prevent other public institutions, such as universities, to confer upon titles or honours on their leaders or men of merit.
- The state is not debarred from awarding military or academic distinctions, even though they may be used as titles.
- The state is not prevented from conferring any distinction or award, say, for social service, which cannot be used as a title, that is, as an appendage to one's

name. Thus, the award of *Bharat Ratna* or *Padma Vibhushan* and *Padma Shri* cannot be used by the recipient as a title and does not accordingly come within the Constitutional prohibitions.

In 1954, Government introduced the *Bharat Ratna, Padma Vibhushan* and *Padma Shri* usually given to those who excelled in the field of art, literature, social service, or rendered service to the Government. Though these awards were not to be used as appendages to the names of persons, Article 18 was vehemently criticized by some sections of the society. Critics pointed out that these titles tend to make distinctions according to rank, contrary to Preamble that promised equality of status. It was also stated that there is ambiguity involved or there is no clarity if the title can be used as an appendage or not.

Right to Freedom (Articles 19-22)

Article 19 itself provides six different freedoms to the citizens. This article, in fact is considered as the core of the entire chapter on Fundamental Rights. Before the 44th amendment, there were seven freedoms guaranteed under Article 19. One article, namely. the right to acquire, hold and dispose off property was removed from the Constitution. The following is the list of six freedoms granted to the citizens:

i. freedom of speech and expression.

ii. freedom to assemble peacefully without arms.

iii. freedom to form associations or unions.

iv. freedom to move freely throughout the territory of India.

v. freedom to reside and settle in any part of the territory of India.

vi. freedom to practice any profession, or to carry on any occupation, trade or business.

Limitations upon Freedoms

- These rights are not absolute. The Constitution itself has conferred upon the power to state to impose reasonable restrictions if necessary, in the larger interest of the country. The Constitution, though guaranteed the freedom of speech and expression, there are certain circumstances wherein restrictions have to be imposed. Few such situations are- (a) defamation, (b) contempt of court, (c) decency or morality, (d) security of the state, (e) friendly relations with foreign states, (f) incitement to an offence, (g) public order, and (h) maintenance of sovereignty and integrity of India. Decency and morality are not confined to sexual morality alone. It indicates that the action must be taken in conformity with the current standards of behaviour. Hence, seeking votes at an election on the grounds of the candidate's religion in a secular state is against the norms of decency and propriety of the society. It is also evident that the freedom of speech and expression cannot act as a license to commit illegal or immoral activities or incite others to overthrow an established government by force. No one must exercise his right to speech in such a manner that violates another man's right.

- The state has the power to impose restrictions with regard to freedom of assembly of the individuals in order to maintain public order.
- Though citizens have the right to move freely throughout the territory of India, state can impose restrictions in the interest of public or for the protection of any scheduled tribes.
- Again, any citizen has the power to practice any profession or occupation, or business or trade but subject to restrictions imposed upon by the state or subject to any law laying down qualifications for carrying out any profession or technical occupation.

Freedom of Press: There is no special provision in our Constitution guaranteeing the freedom of press but implies in the broader 'expression' that was guaranteed under Article 19. Freedom of expression means the freedom to express not only one's views but also the views of others by any means, including printing. Since freedom of expression is not absolute it is subjected to the restrictions imposed by the state in order to maintain the security, integrity and sovereignty of the country. But it is also reaffirmed that absolute, unlimited and unfettered freedom of press at all times would lead to disorder and anarchy.

Article 19(1) (a) of the Constitution has enumerated the following provisions:

The press is not immune from:

- Ordinary forms of taxation.
- The application of general laws relating to industrial relations.
- The regulation of conditions of service of the employees.

But in view of guarantee of freedom of expression, it would not be legitimate for the state to:

- Subject the press to laws which take away the freedom of expression or which would curtail circulation and thereby lessen the scope of dissemination of information;
- Impose excessive and prohibitive burdens that would restrict the circulation of the matter; and
- Impose a specific tax upon the press, deliberately calculated to limit the circulation of information.

Article 20 of the Constitution affords protection against arbitrary and excessive punishment to any person who commits an offence. There are four such guaranteed protections:

- A person can be convicted of an offence only if he has violated a law in force at the time when he is alleged to have committed the offence.
- No person can be subjected to a greater penalty that might have been given to him under the law that was prevalent when he committed the offence.
- No person can be prosecuted and punished for the same offence more than once.
- No person accused of an offence can be compelled to be a witness against himself.

Article 21 of the Constitution provides, "No person shall be deprived of his personal liberty except according to the procedure established by law".

This implies that no man can be subjected to any physical coercion that does not permit legal justification. Therefore, when the state or any of its agencies deprive an individual of his personal liberty, such action must be justified by a law. However, no country can provide an absolute freedom to the individuals. The underlying principle is that the elected representatives have to determine the rights of the individuals and for the collective interest or for the security of the state, the freedom of the citizens can be curtailed as per the exigencies of time. This was the explanation given by the Constitution of India in saying that life and personal liberty are subject to the 'procedure established by law'.

The 44th Amendment Act declared that right to liberty and life cannot be violated. Whether there is an emergency or no emergency, the Fundamental Right to liberty and life will continue in all circumstances. Thus, Article 21 made an exception to the general rule laid down in Article 359 that the President has the power to suspend the enforcement of Fundamental Rights during an emergency. But after 59th Amendment Act in 1990, Article 21 can be suspended by the President.

Recently, Article 21 A has been inserted by the Constitutional 86th Amendment Act in the year 2002 which reads as follows: "The State shall provide free and compulsory education to all children of the age of six to fourteen years in such a manner as the state may, by law, determine".

Article 22 safeguards against arbitrary arrest and detention. It provides three guarantees:

- No person who is arrested shall be detained in custody without being informed the reasons for his arrest.
- No person shall be denied the right to consult and to be defended by a legal practitioner of his choice.
- Every person who is arrested and detained in custody shall be produced before the nearest magistrate within a period of twenty four hours of arrest excluding the time necessary for journey from the place of arrest to the court of the magistrate and no person shall be detained in custody beyond the said period without the authority of a magistrate.

The above safeguards, however, are not applicable to an enemy or alien and a person arrested or detained under a law providing for preventive detention.

The Constitution of India authorizes the Legislature to make laws on matters related with preventive detention as it is connected with the security of the state, maintenance of public order, or maintenance of supplies and services essential to the community. The term 'preventive detention' means detention of a person without trial. This is different from 'punitive detention'. While punitive detention punishes the person for whatever crime he has committed, preventive detention aims at preventing the person from doing something wrong. For instance, acts prejudicial to the security of the state, public order, maintenance of supplies and services to essential communities, defense, foreign affairs or security of India. If a person is arrested under a law of preventive detention, then:

- The government is entitled to detain him only for three months. If it seeks to detain the arrested person for more than three months, it must obtain a report from an Advisory Board who will examine the papers submitted by the government and by the accused, as to whether the detention is justified.
- The person so detained may, as soon, be informed of the grounds of his detention excepting the facts which the detaining authority considers to be against the public interest to disclose.
- The person detained must have the earliest opportunity of making a representation against the order of detention.

A law which violates any of the conditions imposed upon by Article 22, as stated above, is liable to be declared invalid and in order of detention, which violates any of these conditions will, similarly, be invalidated by the Court, and the detenue shall be set free.

The Preventive Detention Act, 1950 was passed by the Parliament which constituted the law of Preventive Detention of India. The Act of 1950 came to an end in the 1969. In 1971, a new act was passed called Maintenance of Internal Security Act (MISA). In 1974, Parliament passed the Conservation of Foreign Exchange and Prevention of Smuggling Activities Act (COFEPOSA) as an economic addition of the MISA. Though, MISA was repealed in 1978 but COFEPOSA still remains. Further in 1980, National Security Act (NSA) was enacted. According to the NSA, the maximum period for which a person may be detained shall be six months from the date of detention. Further, with the increase of terrorist activities by mid1980's, the government had to pass a new act called the Terrorist and Disruptive Activities Act in 1985, also popularly called TADA, in order to ensure the security of the country. In the recent times, a new act called Prevention of Terrorist Activities, also known as POTA was passed in 2002.

Preventive Detention attracted a large amount of criticism when India was under emergency at the time of war with Pakistan in 1971 and again in 1975 due to internal disturbances that had an adverse impact on the freedom of individuals. It was strongly felt that continuation of Maintenance of Internal Security Act would curb the liberties of the people. In the name MISA, a large number of people were taken in to custody and kept in detention without the due process of law. Though, vigilance is necessary to safeguard the hard earned freedom, unless and until each person, each party adopts constitutional means to achieve its objectives, provisions like preventive detention and TADA are essential for India.

Right against Exploitation (Articles 23-24)

In order to guarantee personal liberty and the prohibition against discrimination, the Constitution of India laid down certain provisions to prevent exploitation of weaker sections of the society by unscrupulous individuals of the society or the state.

Article 23 of the Constitution states:

- Traffic in human beings and beggars and other similar form of forced labour are prohibited and any contravention of this provision shall be an offence punishable in accordance with the law.
- Nothing in this article shall prevent the state from imposing compulsory service for public purposes, and in imposing such service the state shall not make any discrimination only on grounds of religion, race, caste or class or any of them.

The Constitution of India instead of using the term slavery used a more comprehensive expression in the name of traffic in human beings which includes prohibition, not only of slavery but also of traffic in women or children or the crippled, for immoral or other purposes. The Constitution of India also prohibits forced labour of any form wherein landlords at times used to compel their tenants to render free service.

Article 24 of the Constitution states, "No child below fourteen years of age, shall be employed to work in any factory or mine or engaged in any other hazardous employment."

The prohibition imposed by this article is absolute and does not admit any exception for the employment of a child in a factory or a mine or any other hazardous employment. The Supreme Court directed that the children must not be employed and positive steps must be taken for the welfare of such children in improving the quality of their life. Even if the children are employed, the employers must comply with the provisions of the Child Labour (Prohibition and Regulation) Act providing for compensation, employment of their parents or guardians and their education.

Right to Freedom of Religion (Articles 25-28)

Indian Constitution has proclaimed to be a 'Secular State' which observes an attitude of *neutrality and impartiality towards all religions.* A secular state is concerned with the relation between man and man, and not man and God which is a matter of individual conscience. The attitude of impartiality towards all religions is secured by the Constitution by certain provisions from article 25 to 28.

Article 25 enacts that all persons are equally entitled to freedom of conscience and the right to freely profess, practice and propagate religion. There are, however, three restrictions to the freedom of religion, namely public order, morality and health. Further, the state can impose restrictions relating to economic, financial, political or other secular activity which may be associated with religious practice, but do not really appertain to the freedom of conscience.

Article 26 guarantees the freedom to manage religious affairs. According to this article, every religious denomination is given the right to:

- establish and maintain institutions for religious and charitable purposes.
- manage its own affairs in matters of religion.
- own and acquire movable and immovable property.
- administer such property in accordance with the law.

Article 27 prohibits compulsory payment of taxes by individuals towards the promotion or maintenance of any particular religion or religious denomination.

Article 28 prohibits religious instructions in any educational institutions wholly maintained out of state funds, whether such instruction is given by the state or by any other body.

Even though religious instructions are given in any educational institution recognized by or receiving aid from the state, no person attending such institution shall be compelled to receive that religious instructions without the consent of himself or of his guardian (in case of a minor). Thus, while the secular character of the state is demonstrated by all the state educational institutions, private or denominational institutions, even when they receive state aid, are given freedom to maintain their religious character,

Cultural and Educational Rights (Articles 29-30)

Article 29 of the Constitution of India provides that "A minority shall have the right to converse in its own language, script, literature and culture. Admission to any state aided educational institution shall not be refused to anybody on grounds of religion, race, caste or language".

Article 30 provides that "All minorities, whether based on religion or language, shall have the right to establish and administer educational institutions of their choice".

The state shall not grant aid to educational institutions, discriminate against any educational institution on the ground that it is under the management of a minority, whether based on religion or language. With the guarantee of these rights, the Constitution opens a new era of rights for the minorities. The Constitution further aims at securing the unity and integrity of the nation. Religious and cultural freedom is guaranteed to minorities in order to ensure them justice, freedom of thought, expression, belief, faith and worship.

Right to Constitutional Remedies (Article 32)

Declaration of Fundamental Rights in the Constitution is useless unless they are effective. Constitutional experience in all countries shows that the reality of the existence of such rights is tested only by the courts. The power of courts to enforce, however, depends upon the impartiality and independence of judiciary. Under Anglo-American system, the courts are empowered to issue directions or orders or writs in the nature of *habeas corpus, mandamus, prohibition, quo warranto* and *certiorari.*

The Constitution of India has laid down certain provisions for the enforcement of the Fundamental Rights. The following is a list of the same:

- The Supreme Court is empowered to declare any law as null and void if they take away or abridges the rights of the individuals. The Supreme Court has the power to enforce the Fundamental Rights against private bodies and individuals and award compensation for violations of the Fundamental Rights. It can exercise *suo moto* or on the basis of Public Interest Litigation or PIL.
- The judiciary, apart from declaring laws as null and void, has the power to issue writs.
- The rights so guaranteed shall not be suspended except during a Proclamation of Emergency.

Article 32, in fact is considered as a cornerstone of the entire set of Fundamental Rights, and the Constitution of India rightly described it as Constitutional remedy for the enforcement of Fundamental Rights included in Part III of the Constitution. The following is a brief description of the nature of writs and Constitutional guarantees, and the scope of each of the writ.

i. ***Habeas Corpus:*** This is an order calling upon the person who was detained and produce him before the court and let the court know on what ground he has been confined and to set him free if there is no legal justification for the imprisonment. The word 'habeas corpus' literally mean 'to have a body'. It is a direction of the court to a person who is detaining another, commanding him to bring the body of person in his custody at a specified time to a specified place for a specified purpose. The main aim of the writ is to set a person free if detained without any legal justification. The writ is issued to not only against state authorities but also to private individuals or organizations, if necessary.
ii. ***Mandamus:*** It is an order of the higher court commanding a person or a body to do their duty. Usually, it is an order directing the performance of ministerial acts. A ministerial act can be described as one in which a person is obliged by law to perform under given circumstances.
iii. ***Prohibition:*** This writ is issued by the higher court to an inferior court forbidding the latter to continue proceedings there in excess of its jurisdiction or its jurisdiction or to usurp a jurisdiction with which it is not legally vested. In other

words, the main purpose of this writ is to compel inferior courts to keep themselves within the limits of their jurisdiction.

iv. ***Certiorari:*** This writ orders the removal of a suit from an inferior court to a superior court. It may be used before trial to prevent an excess or abuse of jurisdiction and remove the case for trial to a higher court.

v. ***Quo warranto:*** A proceeding where by the courts enquire in to the legality of the claim which a party assents to a public office and to oust him from its enjoyment if the claim is not well founded. The fundamental basis for proceedings of quo warranto is that the public has an interest to see that an unlawful claimant does not usurp a public office.

Thus, Article 32 provides a guaranteed remedy for the enforcement of Fundamental Rights in case of any violation.

Right to Property (Article 31)

One of the most controversial articles of the entire list of Fundamental Rights was right to property under Article 31. This article, though removed from the list of Fundamental Rights, experienced most number of amendments. The First, Fourth, Seventeenth, Twenty-fifth, Forty-second and finally Forty-fourth amendments tried to modify the right in some form or the other.

Article 31 of the Constitution provides the following provisions:

Guarantees every citizen the right to acquire any property by any lawful means, such as inheritance, personal earning or otherwise, to hold it as his own and to dispose of it freely; limited only by (a) reasonable restrictions to serve the exigencies of public welfare and (b) any other reasonable restrictions that may be imposed by the state to protect the interests of any Scheduled Tribe.

- If the state wants to acquire private property of an individual or to requisition that to take over its possession for a temporary period, it could do so only on two conditions, (a) that acquisition or requisition is for public purpose, (b) that when such a law is passed, it must provide for payment of compensation or by specifying the principles upon which it is to be determined and given.
- No law made by the Legislature of a state has effect unless such law has received the assent of the President.
- If the state enacted not more than eighteen months before the commencement of the Constitution, may, within three months from such commencement, be submitted to the President for his certification, thereupon, if the President by public notification so certifies, it shall not be called in question in any court on the ground that it contravenes the provisions of the article.

But, as of today, the right to property is not a Fundamental Right but a legal right. The removal of this right from the list of Fundamental Rights was welcomed as it created frictions between the Judiciary and the Parliament. Its removal made it easy for the governments to pursue socialistic philosophy and inclinations.

AN ASSESSMENT OF FUNDAMENTAL RIGHTS

Fundamental Rights enshrined in Part III of the Constitution of India is, however, not free from criticism, be it in India or abroad. The critics of Fundamental Rights can be broadly classified into three categories. According to the first group, certain rights like right to work, and right to education have been ignored. The second group expressed the opinion that much of the spirit and substance of the rights is taken away by extraordinary provisions like preventive detention, suspension of the right to Constitutional remedies, etc. They criticised that they have taken away what was actually guaranteed. Third group ascertained that even those rights that are expected to safeguard are full of exceptions and explanations and sometimes it is difficult to understand what exactly is available to the individual by way of Fundamental Rights (Pylee, p. 126).

It is certainly true that right to work and education, or right to leisure and rest, and material security are not included in the list of Fundamental Rights. Further, most of the rights are justifiable in nature. The main reason for not including these rights in the list of Fundamental Rights was that it was impossible for the government to build thousands of schools all over the country and also provide jobs to a large number of people because of the conditions prevailing at the time of framing the Constitution. These rights could have been included only in course of time which was unfortunately not done.

Provisions like preventive detention and suspension of Constitutional remedies also needs attention. It was categorically stated that restrictions on individuals is necessary in the interest of the society. The framers of the Constitution of India were, in fact unaware of the dangers a republic has to encounter. Moreover, the country had gone through difficult times which became evident with the assassination of Gandhi. Various groups formed that threatened the very foundations of democracy which prompted the framers of the Constitution to enact a law of preventive detention. In India, however, it was only in 1975 that for the first time preventive detention laws were put into practice when national emergency was declared wherein large number of persons were taken into custody. The government justified the action in the name of protecting the country from anarchy and chaos. Fortunately, the situation did not last long. When Parliamentary elections were announced in 1977, the central government ordered for the release of political prisoners under the Maintenance of Internal Security Act. However, in 1978, MISA was abolished. Under Preventive Detention Act the government can impose restrictions, short of detention, regulating the conduct in any particular matter as may be specified in the order or employment, association or communication with other persons or against propagation of opinion.

Another criticism levelled against the Fundamental Rights is that the language used is too complex with exceptions and explanations unlike the one used in American Bill of Rights. The American Constitution framers have entrusted to the courts the job of interpreting. The Indian Constitution framers however took up the responsibility of expressing the laws in a compendious manner in the Constitution. Moreover, it is not the language alone that is making the Constitution difficult to understand but the unfamiliarity of a new Constitutional system that requires a close study and deep understanding along with common national heritage.

A close examination of the chapter on Fundamental Rights suggests that it is not a product of consistent philosophy. This, to an extent, is more prominent because of heterogeneity in languages, cultures, religions, etc.

Finally, we can say that Fundamental Rights though protected by court of law, is the public opinion that has much more crucial role to play. Public opinion can act as the best safeguard of Fundamental Rights provided the people are well organized. In the absence of public opinion it can be stated with confidence that the Fundamental Rights will be in danger if left to the discretion of executive authorities or legislative majorities.

FUNDAMENTAL DUTIES

A duty can be described as an obligation that humans owe to others as a part of the society. A person's right of living involves his duty to fellowmen to allow them the same conditions of life. A right to one person is a duty to others. Enjoyment of rights involves certain obligations as well. Rights and duties are correlative. They go hand-in-hand. Laski described the relation between rights and duties in three different aspects. Firstly, it is the imperative duty of a citizen to use his rights in such a way that contributes to social richness. Secondly, the enjoyment of his rights by an individual enjoins upon him the duty to let others enjoy the same rights. Thirdly, since the state protects ones right, therefore it is ones duty to perform his/her obligations towards it.

The need for fundamental duties was emphasized during the internal emergency declared in 1975. Accordingly, a committee was appointed under the chairmanship of Swaran Singh. The committee recommended for inclusion of a chapter on fundamental duties in the Constitution so that people become more conscious that in addition to the rights, they also have certain duties to perform as well.

As a result the 42nd Amendment of the Constitution of India in 1976 incorporated ten fundamental duties of the citizen under Article 51A as suggested by the committee. The main purpose of enumerating these duties is to provide a code of conduct which the citizens are expected to follow in their actions and conduct. The following is the list of fundamental duties:

- To abide by the Constitution and respect its ideals and institutions, the National Flag and National Anthem.

- To cherish the noble ideals which inspired our national struggle for freedom.
- To uphold and protect the sovereignly, unity and integrity of India.
- To defend the country and render national service when called upon to do so.
- To promote the harmony and common brotherhood amongst all the people of India transcending religious, linguistic and regional or sectional diversities; to renounce practices derogatory to the dignity of women.
- To value and preserve the rich heritage of our composite culture.
- To protect and improve the natural environment, including forests, lakes, rivers and wild life, and to have compassion for living creatures.
- To develop the scientific temper, humanism and the spirit of inquiry and reform.
- To safeguard public property and abjure to violence.
- To strive towards excellence in all spheres of individual and collective activity, so that the nation constantly rises to higher levels of endeavour and achievement.

Article 51A has recently been amended according to the 86th Amendment Act in 2002 and one more clause has been inserted to the above list. Clause (K) inserted after Clause (J) imposes a duty on a parent or guardian to provide opportunities for education to his child or ward, as the case may be, between the age of six and fourteen.

In 1998, the Supreme Court of India issued a notice to Government of India to enquire about the Government's plan to operationalize the suggestion to teach Fundamental Duties to the citizens of the country. The court issued the notice after a complaint which it received wherein a general sense of deterioration in human behaviour in the society was expressed. Consequently, the Government of India set up a committee in order to operationalize fundamental duties for an effective society. The committee submitted its report in 1999, wherein it emphasized on the following:

The committee suggested for "Seven Principles of Public Life". The following is a brief description of each of the same:

1. **Selflessness:** Holders of the public offices must take decisions solely in the interests of the public. They should not do so in order to gain material or financial benefits for themselves or their families or friends.
2. **Integrity:** Holders of public office should not place themselves under any financial or other obligation to outside individuals or organizations that might influence them in the performance of their official duties.
3. **Objectivity:** In carrying out public business, including making public appointments, awarding contracts, or recommending individuals for rewards and benefits, holders of public office should make choices on merit.
4. **Accountability:** Holders of public office are accountable for their decisions and actions they take and must submit themselves to whatever scrutiny is appropriate to their office.

5. **Openness:** Holders of public office must be open to all decisions and actions they take. They must be able to give reasons for their decisions and restrict information only when wider public interest clearly demands.
6. **Honesty:** Holders of public office have a duty to declare any private interests relating to their public duties and to take steps to resolve any conflicts arising in a way that protects the public interest.
7. **Leadership:** Holders of public office should promote and support these principles by leadership and example.

Though fundamental duties are not justifiable in nature, the courts certainly take into consideration while interpreting a law which is amenable to be interpreted in more than one sense. In making people more duty conscious, educational institutions and voluntary organizations have a great role to play.

DIRECTIVE PRINCIPLES OF STATE POLICY

Part IV of the Constitution of India from Article 36-51 deal with the Directive Principles of State Policy. These principles are classified into three different groups: (a) Certain ideals which according to the framers of the Constitution, state should strive for; (b) Certain directions that describes the relation between the legislature and the executive; (c) Certain rights of the citizen which shall not be enforceable by the courts like Fundamental Rights, but which the state shall nevertheless aim at securing by the regulation of its legislative and administrative policy. The framers of the Constitution were influenced by the Irish Republic. Further, the French Declaration regarding rights of man, American Declaration of Independence and The Charter of United Nations also had an influence over these principles. However, it cannot be stated that Directive Principles have an excessive foreign borrowings. In fact, a number of principles are entirely Indian and Gandhian in nature.

MEANING AND NATURE

Directive Principles of State Policy are described as directions or instructions to the State. They embody the objectives and ideals which the Union and State Governments must bear in mind while formulating policies and making laws. These principles laid down a code of conduct for the administrators of India while they discharge their responsibilities as agents of sovereign power of the nation. They enable the people of India to realize the noble ideals set in the Preamble of the Constitution viz., justice—social, political and economic, liberty, equality and fraternity, unity and integrity.

Directive Principles of State Policy are not enforceable by any court of law and the state cannot be compelled through courts to implement them. Dr. Ambedkar observed, “If any Government ignores them, they will certainly have to answer for them before the electorate at the election time.” These principles are also a weapon in the hands of the opposition to harm the reputation of the Government on the ground that any of its executive or legislative acts is opposed to the Directive Principles. If Fundamental Rights enshrined in part III of the Constitution of India laid the foundations of political democracy in India, the Directive Principles incorporated in Part IV of the Constitution of India spell out the norms of social and economic democracy in the country.

Classification of Directive Principles of State Policy

The Directive Principles of State Policy are divided into three categories, viz., Socialistic, Gandhian and Liberal Intellectual principles. The following is the explanation of each of the principles:

1. **Directive Principles aiming at the establishment of a Welfare State:**

   India committed itself to the establishment of a welfare state as proclaimed in the Preamble of the Constitution. Thus,

   Article 38 of the Constitution provides that state shall strive to promote the welfare of the people by securing and protecting a social order in which justice—social, political and economic shall inform all the institutions of national life.

   Furthermore, one more clause has been added to this Article by the Constitution's 44th Amendment Act in 1978, according to which the state shall strive to minimize inequalities in income and endeavour to eliminate inequalities in status, facilities and opportunities, both among individuals and groups irrespective of their residence and vocation. Thus, **Article 38** is an omnibus clause ensuring social and economic justice.

   Article 39 emphasized that state shall direct its policy towards securing:

   - Adequate means of livelihood to all citizens.
   - A proper distribution of material resources of the community for the common good.
   - The prevention of concentration of wealth to the common detriment.
   - Equal pay for equal work for both men and women.
   - The protection of the strengths and health of the workers and avoiding circumstances that force citizens to enter vocations unsuited to their age or strength.
   - The protection of childhood and youth against exploitation or moral and material abandonment.

   Article 41 seeks to, within the limits of economic resources and capacity, ensure the right to work, right to education and to public assistance in cases of unemployment, old age, sickness and disablement and in other cases of undeserved want.

Article 42 declares that State shall make provisions for securing just and humane conditions of work and for the maternity relief.

Article 43 declares that the state shall endeavour to secure to all workers a living wage, a decent standard of life, leisure and social and cultural opportunities for the people.

Article 46 lays down an obligation on the part of state to promote with special care the educational and economic interests of weaker sections of the people, and in particular, of the scheduled castes and scheduled tribes and to protect them from social injustice and all forms of exploitation.

Article 47 declares as a primary duty of the state to raise the level of nutrition and improvement of the public health.

2. **Directives relating to culture and educational matters:** Another group of directive principles that relates to the obligations of the state in educational and cultural matters are discussed as under:

   Article 45 declares that the state shall endeavour to provide early childhood care and education for all children until they complete the age of six years.

   Article 49 enumerated protection of monuments and places or objects of the artistic or historical interest as an obligation on the part of the state.

3. **Directive Principles aiming to implement Gandhian Principles:**

   Article 40 claims that state shall organize village Panchayats as units of self government.

   Article 43 claims that state shall try to promote cottage industries.

   Article 45 provides that state shall promote with special care the educational and economic interest of the weaker sections of the people.

   Article 47 states that state shall try to secure the improvement of public health and the prohibition of consumption of intoxicating drinks and drugs except under medicinal purposes.

   Article 48 ensures that state shall preserve and improve the breeds and prohibit the slaughter of cows, calves and other milch and draught cattle. It also emphasizes the need to organize agriculture and animal husbandry on modern and scientific lines.

4. **Directive Principles relating to International Peace and Security:**

   Article 51 A declares that the state shall endeavour to:

   - promote international peace and security.
   - maintain just and honorable relations between nations.
   - the settlement of international disputes by arbitration.

5. **Miscellaneous:** Some other important directive principles are:

   - **Article 50** suggests separation of the judiciary from the executive.

- **Article 44** aims to secure a uniform civil code applicable to the entire country.
- **Article 48** aims to organize agriculture and animal husbandry on scientific lines.

6. **The 42nd and 44th Amendment:** The 42nd amendment introduced certain changes that have been incorporated in Part IV of the Constitution. A set of new directives were included to highlight the socialistic bias of the Constitution;
    - **Article 39A** enjoins the state to provide 'free legal aid' to the poor and to take other suitable steps to ensure justice to all, which is offered by the Preamble.
    - **Article 43A** has been incorporated to direct the state to ensure the participation of workers in the management of industry and other undertakings. This is a positive step in advancement of socialism in the sense of economic justice.
    - **Article 48A** is inserted in order to direct the state to protect and improve the environment and to safeguard the forests and the wild life of the country.

Implementation of Directive Principles of State Policy

One of the most Herculean tasks that were taken up by the government was the implementation of the directive principles of the state policy just after they were incorporated in the Constitution of India. Nevertheless, some of the outstanding achievements of the Government are worth mentioning. The following is a brief description of accomplishments of the government.

One of the achievements in carrying out the directives was when the state could secure the ownership of and control of the material resources of the community. In an agrarian society like India, since the pre-independence days, the land was an important source of wealth and was largely appropriated by proprietors referred to as *zamindars, jagirdars* or *inamdars* at different places and other intermediaries. These landlords took control of the lands and impoverished the tillers. The intermediaries exploited the tiller by extracting rents from them. The Planning Commission at this juncture recommended the abolition of these intermediaries in order to provide land to the tiller which was systematically implemented throughout the country. Furthermore, legislation has been undertaken to improve the conditions of cultivators in terms of the security of tenure, fair rent and others. In order to eliminate concentration of wealth by the landlords, the government imposed a ceiling, by fixing the amount of land to an individual owner.

A large number of laws have been enacted to implement village panchayats throughout the country. Though the functions and structure of the panchayats differ from state to state, generally speaking, the panchayats are elected by the adult population in the villages and are eligible to take care of the civic administration such as medical relief, maintenance of village roads, streets, tanks and wells, provision of primary education, sanitation and the like. Besides this, panchayats also exercise judicial powers. They try cases whose value does not exceed five hundred rupees and also other minor offences. The 73rd and 74th Amendments Acts have given the power of self-governance to the panchayats.

For the promotion of cottage industries, the central government has established several boards that help state government in matters of finance and marketing, etc. Boards like All India Khadi and Village Industries Board, Small scale Industries Board, Silk Board, Coir Board, All India Handloom Board, and Small Industries Corporation has been set up with certain functions for the development of khadi and village industries.

In order to improve the standard of living, especially of the rural populace, the Government of India launched programmes like Community Development Programme (CDP) way back in 1952 itself. Later, Integrated Rural Development Programme (IRDP) in 1978-1979, National Rural Employment Programme (NERP), Rural Landless Employment Guarantee Programme (RLEGP), Drought Prone Area Programme (DPAP), Desert Development Programme (DDP) etc. were launched.

Legislation relating to prohibition of intoxicants, though launched much before the Constitution was framed, nothing substantial could be done till the same was included in the Directive Principles of the State Policy. The Planning Commission took up the issue and adopted a scheme through Prohibition Enquiry Committee. From then on, prohibition has been successfully introduced in many states.

Uniform Civil Code was introduced in 1973 which placed the function of judicial trial in the hands of the judicial magistrate who is completely under the control of the High Courts. With this, there is clear cut demarcation of powers between the executive and judiciary.

Further, the state has taken up adequate measures to provide primary education to children of religious minorities in their mother tongue. The Union government has taken up the task of promoting the spread of Hindi language as a medium of expression of all the elements of the composite culture of India.

Failures in the Implementation of Directive Principles of State Policy

Though Article 45 stated that all the children below fourteen years of age will be provided free and compulsory education, it is unfortunate that there is still a high rate of illiteracy. With the increase in population of the country, there was also an increase in illiterates. In fact, India can be regarded as having the largest concentration of illiterate population. Secondly, the state has failed in providing care and consideration towards women, children and the handicapped. Though some progress has been achieved in improving the conditions of women in urban areas, the conditions of rural women remain dismal. Children, particularly, are neglected in the society. There is an increasing trend of child abuse in the society. Child labour still prevails and the government is unsuccessful in abolishing the same. Children today do not have opportunities and facilities to grow in a healthy manner and live a life of dignity. Youth are not protected against exploitation and against moral degeneration.

Right to work, right to adequate means to earn livelihood and public assistance in cases of unemployment, old age, sickness, disablement and other cases still remain problematic. Though reasonable and just humane conditions of work have been provided to organized industrial sector, the government failed miserably in providing the same to unorganized sectors or landless agricultural labour. Bonded labour, beggars and trafficking in human beings is still widely in practice.

The main reasons for the failure in proper implementation of Directive Principles of State Policy to an extent depend upon the inherent criticism within these principles. The foremost criticism of Directives is that they lack legal force. Though directives are fundamental for the governance of the country, the state must apply these principles in making laws, they however are non-justiciable. It means that courts, including Supreme Court have no power to enforce these principles which is in stark contrast to Fundamental Rights which are justiciable in nature. There are no legal obligations on the part of state to implement these principles. K. C. Wheare described them as a "manifesto of aims and aspirations". Secondly, these principles have been criticized as vague and repetitive. They are neither properly classified nor logically arranged. According to Srinivasan, "The formulation of the directives of state policy can hardly be considered inspiring". Thirdly, they are just moral percepts. Mr. Nasiruddin, member of the Constituent Assembly stated that they are just like "new year resolutions that are broken on the second January."

The above criticism of the directive principles of state policy gives rise to an important question, whether it is worthwhile to incorporate them in a Constitution of the twenty first century. India still needs to reach in many spheres of economic activity. A standard comparable to that exists in Europe. Moreover, it is not correct to characterize these principles as borrowings from abroad. In fact, there are many provisions that are suitable to the conditions that prevail in India.

Under any circumstances, the Directive Principles of State Policy have become outmoded; they can be easily modified or amended or altogether abolished as the process of amendment is simple. If amendments are needed, then one can say with conformity that the principles will become a part and parcel of Indian heritage. These principles have great educative value. They instill in the minds of the youth some fundamental values of a stable political order and dynamic economic system. A Constitution is primarily concerned with the present. It is quite unnecessary therefore, to think of the distant future with reference to certain provisions of a Constitutional document.

PARLIAMENTARY FORM OF GOVERNMENT

The Constitution declared that India would follow a parliamentary form of government based on the British model. The main reason to adopt the British model is that the Indian leaders gained some experience in administration before the pre-independence period. Perhaps there are two other reasons that justify the parliamentary form of government as explained by Dr. Ambedkar. He stated, "A democracy and executive must satisfy two conditions: stability and responsibility". In non-Parliamentary governments, the assessment is done by the electorate through periodic elections. However, in a parliamentary government, the assessment is almost daily, and periodic as well. The daily assessment is carried out by the members of parliament through questions, resolutions and motions, while periodic assessment is done by the electorate after every five years. Secondly, a parliamentary system is more likely to accommodate various groups and sections in the decision making process.

Though India adopted the British system, the former differs from the latter in two important aspects. In Britain, the Parliament is supreme and no court can question the validity of any law passed by the Parliament. In India, the Constitution is supreme and not the Parliament. The Indian courts are given the power to adjudicate on the validity of any law passed by the Parliament. Secondly, in Britain the head of the state is a non-elected hereditary, while in India, the head of the state is indirectly elected.

In recent years, however, the Parliamentary form of government has been criticized for not achieving progress in socio-economic field and transformation as well. The main reason attributed to this criticism is that the executive depends upon the support of the legislature, its tenure is uncertain and susceptible to the pressures of the legislature, and it makes the government weak and unstable and also takes strong measures for development. Another strong argument is that if a Presidential form of government is followed, the elected executive is likely to usurp all the power and act as a real dictator.

CABINET GOVERNMENT

The Constitution of India established a Cabinet form of government both at the centre as well as at the state level. The cabinet comprises the Prime Minister at the apex assisted by senior colleagues, who occupy other important portfolios. All the ministers share the responsibility of formulation and execution of the policies of the government. In a cabinet form of government, the Head of the State or the President possess a position of dignity and honour but in practice, all authority is in the hands of the Prime Minister and his colleagues. The President is nominal executive while the Prime Minister is the real executive. All the activities are performed in the name of the President. The cabinet system thrives on the principle of collective responsibility which stands on the ideal of 'one for all, all for one'. The Prime Minister is considered as the 'kingpin of the cabinet arch'. The actions of the executive are constantly watched over by the legislature that makes the executive act responsibly. The moment the government proves unsuccessful in any particular set of actions, it is removed from the office by passing a non-confidence motion.

SECULAR STATE

The Preamble of the Constitution clearly stated that India is a Sovereign, Socialist, Secular, Democratic, Republic. In fact, the term 'secular' is added to the preamble during the

42nd amendment act in 1976. A secular state can be described as a state that provides freedom to religious worship, religious tolerance and communal harmony. It allows all the existing and new religions to flourish wherein the state act with neutrality, in the sense, not showing any favours to any particular religion. Commenting on the concept of secularism, Nehru once stated, "Where religious diversity existed in the country, secularism was essentially a practical approach for maintaining social stability and harmony". A secular state guarantees to religious minorities the right to maintain their own language and to establish educational institutions of their choice. An important manifestation of secularism in India is the abolition of communal electorate and the adoption of the provision that elections are to be held on the basis of universal franchise and joint electorate. However, politicians in their urge to acquire power, make religion as their base and mobilize people for elections. This trend is resulting in the growth of religious fundamentalism and rise of anti social elements that has serious effects on socio, economic and political development.

FEDERAL SYSTEM WITH UNITARY BIAS

The framers of the Constitution, keeping in view the multi-cultural, multi-lingual and multi-ethnic society mentioned in the Preamble that the main objective is to promote fraternity among citizens and assure dignity of the individual. These were operationalized by the incorporation of Fundamental Rights. The Constituent Assembly also declared its firm resolves to constitute India into a Federation in which states shall possess and retain the status of autonomous units as also the residuary powers and functions of the government. Article 1 of the Constitution of India states that 'India is a union of States'. This statement was clearly explained by the Chairman of the Constituent Assembly, Dr. Ambedkar in two terms. First, the Indian Federation was not the result of an agreement among the units, and second, the component units had no freedom to secede from the Union.

By federal polity we mean a clear division of the country into states or units with their set of functions as mentioned in the Constitution. India has a written Constitution which is rigid in nature, a dual polity and division of powers between the centre and the states. Further in order to resolve the disputes between the centre and the states, the Constitution provided for a Supreme Court to settle the matters. A brief explanation of each of the federal features of Indian Constitution is described as follows:

- *Written Constitution:* A written Constitution is considered necessary for a federation so that both the states and the centre can refer to it, whenever required. Indian Constitution is the most elaborate document with 441 articles and 12 Schedules that fulfils the basic needs of a federal government.
- *Supremacy of the Constitution:* In a federation, Constitution is regarded as the supreme law of the land, and any law passed either by the state or the centre

should be in conformity with the Constitution. The courts are entrusted with the responsibility of maintaining the dignity of the Constitution and if any state violates any provision of the Constitution the courts deal with such states.

- *Rigid Constitution:* A rigid Constitution can be described as one which cannot be changed easily. This rigidity is essential, so that the centre cannot make amendments to the lists that suit it the best. Amendments to the provisions of the Constitution relating to centre-state relations can be done only by a joint action of the State Legislatures and Union Parliament with not less than two thirds of members present and voting and ratified by at least one half of the states.
- *Division of Powers: A* federation needs a clear cut division of powers wherein units as well as the centre enact laws with their sphere of activity without disturbing the other states or encroach upon the others. Accordingly, the Constitution made provisions for three different lists, viz., the Union list, State list and Concurrent list incorporated in the Seventh Schedule of the Constitution. The Union list consists of ninety seven items of national importance over which only the Union government has the power to make laws. Some of the items of this list are defence, foreign affairs, railways, posts, telegraphs, currency, etc. The State list has sixty six items upon which the state government has the power to make laws. Items like public order, education, police, justice, health and agriculture are included. Finally, concurrent list consists of fourty seven items in which criminal law, marriage, divorce, trade unions, electricity, economic and social planning and bankruptcy, are included. It is the centre that has the overriding power to legislate, though the states also have the power to legislate. In case of any deadlock the opinion of the centre will always prevail over that of the state.
- *Independent Judiciary:* In a federation the judiciary is entrusted with the duty of acting as a custodian of the Constitution of India. The Supreme Court has the power to declare any law as unconstitutional or *ultra vires* if it is against the provisions of the Constitution. Furthermore, in a federation there is every possibility of friction or differences between the states and the centre on any specific matter. Here again, it is the responsibility of the Judiciary to act accordingly.
- *Bicameral Legislature:* The Constitution of India provided for a bicameral legislature at the centre consisting of two houses, viz., Lok Sabha and Rajya Sabha. While the lower house or Lok Sabha represents the elected representatives of the people, the upper house or Rajya Sabha consists of representatives elected by the state legislative assemblies. Even at the state level some states have two houses.

Some of the unitary features of the Indian Constitution can be described as follows:

- *Strong Centre:* Though there is clear cut division of powers between the centre and the states, the Union government is certainly more powerful than the state.

Under certain circumstances, the centre over-powers the state governments and has the residuary power over the whole country.

- *Power of the Centre to change names and boundaries of the States:* In a conventional federal system, the centre has no power to change the boundaries of states. But in India, centre has the power to change the boundaries or create a new state all together. States like Andhra Pradesh and Chennai were an outcome of this power of the centre. Once the States Reorganization Committee was established, a series of events were unfolded.
- *Unitary in Emergencies:* The Constitution of India made it clear that during normal times, India will be a federal government and during emergencies, India will work as a unitary government. If it is an emergency in the political field, it suggests that the administrative machinery cannot be carried out in accordance with the Constitution. It means, there is political instability and complete breakdown of Constitutional machinery. If it is an emergency in financial field, it implies there is a grave fiscal crisis. Once an emergency is declared, the state administration comes under the grip of the centre.
- *Common All India Services:* The Constitution in order to maintain administrative standards and common administrative system, created All India Services like Indian Administrative Service, Indian Police Service and then placed these members in key administrative positions in the States.
- *Appointments by the President:* The President is empowered to appoint the Governor, Judges of High Courts, Comptroller and Auditor General and the Election Commission that is responsible for holding elections to the entire country. This enables the Central government to exercise control over the state administration.
- *Control over State laws:* Sometimes, the laws passed by the state government cannot be put in to effect till they are approved by the President. Thus, laws related to property, laws on items of the concurrent list which are contradictory to the laws passed by the Parliament, laws with regard to sales tax on essential commodities, etc. need the approval of the central government. Further, it is the Governor who reserves these bills for the consideration of the President who may or may not give his approval.

Thus, the above mentioned features strongly suggest that the centre has an overriding power over the states in spite of the states having their own powers. Further, the power of the centre is enhanced with programmes on economic planning and development, social reforms, etc. In addition, the nature of party system and the style of leadership at the centre have also created an ever increasing process of centralization and interference by the centre in state matters. This excessive involvement is resulting in new tensions or conflict in the centre-state relations. At this juncture, it is highly essential to revamp the federal values in order to bring about more understanding and harmony between the centre and the states.

UNIVERSAL ADULT FRANCHISE

One of the vital steps that were ever taken up just after attaining Independence was the adoption of the principle of universal adult franchise in a country dominated by vast cultural and lingual differences, and more importantly highly illiterate populace. The Constitution of India provided franchise to all the citizens who crossed the age of eighteen without any discrimination on the basis of caste, colour, sex, religion, race, etc. The right to vote enhances the power of the people or popular sovereignty.

SINGLE CITIZENSHIP

The Constitution of India provided a single citizenship unlike the U.S. Constitution that guaranteed double citizenship. All the citizens of the country, irrespective of their domicile enjoy single citizenship in India. The Constitution provided single citizenship in order to build a strong social and political unity among the people of the country who were hitherto divided on racial, lingual, religious and cultural grounds.

The Constitution of India, from Articles 5 to 8 clearly mentions as to who constitute the citizens of India:

- A person born as well as domiciled in the territory of India, irrespective of the nationality of his parents.
- A person born and domiciled in the territory of India, either of whose parents was born in India, irrespective of the nationality of his parents or the place of birth of such person.
- A person who or whose father or mother was not born in India, but who (i) had his domicile in the territory of India, and (ii) had been residing within the territory of India for not less than five years immediately preceding the commencement of the Constitution. In this case also, the nationality of the person's parents is immaterial.

The Constitution also prescribed certain ways or methods of acquiring citizenship. Citizenship Act of 1955 mentioned the following ways of acquiring citizenship:

- *Citizenship by birth:* Every person born in India on or after 26 January, 1950 becomes the citizen of India.
- *Citizenship by descent:* A person born outside India on or after 26 January, 1950 shall be the citizen of India by descent, if either of his parents is a citizen of India at the time of the person's birth.
- *Citizenship by registration:* Indian citizenship can be acquired even by registering themselves to the prescribed authority after having resided in the country for more than 5 years or if a person has married a citizen of India.
- *Citizenship by naturalization:* A foreigner can acquire Indian citizenship on application for naturalization to the Government of India.

- *Citizenship by incorporation of territory:* If a new territory becomes a part of India, the Government of India shall specify the persons of that territory who shall be the citizens of India (Wadhwa, p 76).

INDEPENDENT AND INTEGRATED JUDICIARY

The framers of Constitution were more concerned with the idea of providing justice in various aspects, be it Fundamental Rights, Directive Principles or protection of minorities, etc. Furthermore, having experienced totalitarian and arbitrary nature of state during the colonial rule, made the authors of the Constitution more cautious with regard to legal matters. Therefore, in order to make sure the freedoms of the individuals more meaningful, the framers of the Constitution opted for an independent judiciary. This independent judiciary has four different functions to perform:

- Protect and guarantee the Fundamental Rights.
- Maintain federal equilibrium.
- Act as a check on the executive and legislature and enforce rule of law.
- Interpret the Constitution of India.

Constitution in order to maintain this independence of judiciary separated the executive and the judiciary. This independence is maintained by certain conditions as in the case of appointment of judges, the Chief Justice of India must be consulted before appointing the judges of Supreme Court or the High Court. Judges are provided with high salaries and their conditions of work cannot be altered to their disadvantage. Their conduct does not come under the purview of the legislature for discussions. They can be removed from office only on the grounds of proved misbehaviour. For removing the judge from office, both houses of the Parliament must pass a resolution with not less than two-thirds majority present and voting against the concerned Judge. The Constitution of India also specified that India has an integrated judiciary. The term integrated refers to clear hierarchy in the judicial system. At the apex we have the Supreme Court followed by High Courts at the state and district courts at the district level. The judgment of the Supreme Court is final and it is the highest court of appeal.

JUDICIAL REVIEW

The term 'judicial review' describes the power of the courts to pronounce upon the Constitutional validity of the acts of public authorities, both executive and legislature. It means that any law that is inconsistent with the basic law of the land is declared null and void. In other words, it is the power exerted by the courts of a country to examine the actions of the legislature, executive and administrative arms of the government and to ensure such actions confirm to the provisions of the Constitution. The concept of Judicial Review is borrowed from Constitution of United States.

However, the power of judicial review is limited because in India, the judiciary is not as powerful as the US system. The scope of judicial review is confined to the examination of Constitutional validity of an impugned law or executive action on two accounts: (i) whether it falls within the competence of the authority that has framed it, and (ii) whether it is consistent with Part III of the Constitution dealing with the Fundamental Rights.

Though the power of judicial review is limited in India, its significance is pronounced by certain principles. The following is the description of each principle:

- *Principle of severability:* While interpreting the impugned law, the Court sees if some parts of the law are unconstitutional or the entire law itself. If the entire law is defective, then it is declared *ultra vires;* it can declare so even in case of a part of the law and allow the rest as operative. The court will decide such matters on the construction of the provisions of the law in question.
- *Principle of progressive interpretation:* There is always some amount of confusion if the provisions of the Constitution should be understood in the light of the changing times and changing socio-economic conditions of the country or should they be fixed at the time of framing the Constitution. Fortunately, the judiciary in India is provided with the power of progressive interpretation wherein changes can be incorporated as per the changing times that suit the conditions.
- *Principle of dynamism:* The Courts in India are not bound by the earlier affirmation. They may change their views or precedents from time to time while making a dynamic interpretation of the provisions of the Constitution. The Supreme Court reiterated that interpretation of law should be done in a dynamic way so that it may reconsider its earlier rulings and also depart from them, if necessary.
- *Principle of spirit of the Constitution:* It has been clearly mentioned in the Constitution that any law that is likely to put the Fundamental Rights in jeopardy shall be declared void. However, Fundamental Rights are not absolute and are subject to certain restrictions in the interests of morality, order, public health, national security, etc. Perhaps, it is the function of the courts to examine whether the restrictions imposed by law are in consistent with the tenor of the provisions of Part III or not. It is by virtue of this special arrangement that Supreme Court has invalidated several important laws made by the union as well as the state government.
- *Principle of empirical adjudication:* Courts, while exercising the power of judicial review, do not entertain hypothetical cases. It is essential that a matter brought before the court must be specific and not ambiguous. Moreover, the court must confine itself in giving a practical decision within narrow limits of the controversy between the concerned parties in a particular case.

- *Principle of indirect judicial review:* Sometimes, it so happens that an impugned law can be understood in both positive and negative aspects. At this juncture, the court will consider the positive aspect of the law and tries to interpret the law.

In the end, although the Indian Constitution does not assure great scope in judicial review as guaranteed by the U.S. Constitution, still the Supreme Court has rendered a large number of decisions clarifying various provisions of the Constitution. In cases like Golaknath vs State of Punjab Case, Privy Purse Case, Keshavananda Bharathi vs State of Kerala Case, etc., a great amount of judicial creativity was clearly displayed.

AMENDMENT PROCEDURE

The Constitution is regarded as the fundamental law of the land. It is a document that defines the powers and functions of the three different organs of the state, viz., Legislature, Executive and Judiciary. The Constitution at the same time also mentions the limitations imposed on these organs because an absolute authority of these organs can jeopardize the rights of the people. So, such a fundamental document must not undergo frequent changes as it would undermine the confidence of the citizens in the Constitution itself. However, the Constitution at the same time is a dynamic document that has to grow and suit the changing times and people. Sometimes, it so happens that the social, political and economic situations make changes to the pattern of government as well. If the Constitution stands as a stumbling block to desirable changes, a day is inevitable when it has to be destroyed.

Article 368 of the Constitution clearly describes the procedure for amending the same. According to this article, an amendment may be initiated only by the introduction of a bill for the purpose in either of the House of Parliament. When the Bill is passed in each House by a total membership or majority of not less than two-thirds of members both present and voting, the bill is sent to the President for his assent. When the President gives his assent, the bill is said to be passed and the Constitution can be amended in accordance with the terms of the Bill. But in some cases, the ratification of the state legislatures is also required before the bill is sent to the President for his assent. Some provisions that fail under this category are:

- Election of the President (Article 54), Method of election of President (Article 55), Extent of executive power of the Union (Article 73), Extent of executive power of the state (Article 162), High Courts for Union Territories (Article 241).
- Chapter IV of Part V (Union Judiciary), Chapter V of Part VI (High Courts in the State), Chapter I of Part XI (Legislative relations between the Union and the States).
- Any of the lists in the Seventh Schedule.
- The representation of States in the Parliament.
- Provisions dealing with the amendment of the Constitution.

During the first sixteen years of framing of the Constitution, it was amended twenty times which drew a lot of criticism that suggested the weakness of the Constitution. Some opined that there must not be much scope for making amendments to the Constitution which is true to an extent. But, in certain compelling situations, say the period of consolidation and stabilization of political freedom just after Independence, led to Constitutional amendments. In other cases, amendments became necessary to overcome the difficulties in the working of political system.

Apart from Article 368, there are some other articles in the Constitution and by invoking them the Parliament can amend some of the important provisions of the Constitution through legislative enactment. For example, Articles 2, 3, 4 may be amended by the Parliament with simple majority.

Of all the amendments that were made to the Constitution of India, two amendments had a tremendous influence on the socio, political and economic scenario. They are the 42nd and the 44th Amendment Acts passed in 1976 and 1978 respectively. Recently in 2000, the Government of India set up a Constitutional Review Commission consisting of eleven members with former Chief Justice of Supreme Court, M.N. Venkatachalaiah as Chairperson to review the Constitution. In the same year, amendments were passed that declared the creation of three new states of Jharkhand, Chattisgarh and Uttaranchal.

CRITICISM OF THE CONSTITUTION OF INDIA

The various outstanding features of the Constitution certainly distinguish it from other Constitutions of the world. However, it is not free from criticism. In fact, the members within the Constituent Assembly criticized the Constitution which they have adopted for the entire country. They condemned the Constitution as a 'slavish imitation of the west' or 'not suited to the genius of the people'. Another member of Constituent Assembly charged that this Constitution will not prove suitable and will breakdown soon after being brought in to operation. The main criticisms levelled against the Constitution of India are as follows:

- The Constitution of India is criticized on the grounds of being the most lengthiest and detailed Constitution in the world. Ivor Jennings stated that "the provisions borrowed were not always well selected and that the Constitution, generally speaking, was too long and complicated".
- The Constitution of India is called as a carbon copy of Government of India Act 1935 because the framers have borrowed a large number of provisions from the act and incorporated the same in the Constitution.
- Another serious complaint against Constitution of India was that it was a lawyer's paradise. Commenting on the Constitution, one member stated, "the Draft tends to make people more litigious, more inclined to go to courts, less truthful and less likely to follow the method of truth and non-violence. If I may say so,

the draft is really a lawyer's paradise. It opens up vast avenues of litigation and will give our able and ingenious lawyers plenty of work to do." (Pylee). The main reason for the complexity of the document is the problems that framers encountered at the time of making the Constitution. They also attempted to embody solutions for them within the Constitution. It is also because of the detailed and elaborate language used in drafting, which only courts of law can follow. Further the numerous exceptions, qualifications and explanations of various provisions make it extremely difficult to understand for a layman. Only an experienced lawyer, well versed in Constitutional Law, will be in a position to interpret the legal language in which the provisions were couched. This justifies the expression Lawyer's Paradise.

- A small section of activists criticized the Constitution as being un-Gandhian in its outlook. The Constitution does not reflect the principles of Mahatma Gandhi and the ideology of Indian National Congress. Others thought that the Constitution should have been raised and built upon village panchayats and district panchayats. Further, there is no part of the Constitution that mentions ancient polity of India, its genius and spirit of its hallowed and glorious traditions.
- Some critics pointed out that the Constitution made Centre more powerful than the States. There is too much of centralization and states are reduced to mere municipalities.
- Finally, the Constitution is criticized with regard to the chapter on Fundamental Rights. It is stated that each right mentioned has exceptions which sometimes tend to swallow the rights itself. Rights like right to life and liberty are in most cases at the mercy of the government and there is hardly any protection against tyrannical laws.

SUMMARY

- Constitution is the most essential document that is absolutely necessary for a sovereign country in the world. The Constitution of India aimed at providing best of the conditions for taking the country forward in all respects.
- The Fundamental Rights, the Directive Principles as well as the Fundamental Duties were all incorporated in order to provide security to the people against arbitrary rule, to provide directions to the governments in making the lives of the people more comfortable and meaningful, and finally to imbibe a feeling of respect and honor towards their country.
- Moreover, the Parliamentary form of government with a cabinet system provides a scope for more grass root participation in political matters because the people themselves are the real sovereigns.

- Perhaps the independent and integrated judiciary lessens the amount of conflicts between the centre and the state. The concept of judicial review further enhances the power of the courts to declare any law null and void that is likely to harm the interests of the people.
- The amending procedures of the Constitution have been made slightly stringent that assures safety of the law of the land and at the same time approves to make amendments as per the changing times.
- India has parliamentary form of government with some variations from the British Model.
- The Constitution provides for indirect election, qualifications, term of office, emoluments and allowances, and impeachment of the President of India who is constitutional Head of State.
- The President of India has legislative, executive, financial, judicial military, diplomatic and emergency powers. These powers are normal as the president acts on the advice of the cabinet headed by the Prime Minister.
- Vice-President of India is an indirectly elected office, who is also the chairperson of the Rajya Sabha.
- Real executive power is exercised by the PM, who is the leader of the majority in the Lok Sabha.
- Functions of the PM: Head of the government, leader of the Cabinet, communicates with the President, leader of the Parliament, chief spokesperson of foreign relations, chairman of Planning Commission.
- The dynamics of the party system, evolution of the PM's office and charismatic personality of the Prime Ministers like Nehru, Mrs. Gandhi, Rajiv Gandhi and Vajpayee have led the analysts to describe Indian political system as prime ministerial system.

QUESTIONS

1. The Indian constitution has been distinguished as one of the lengthiest and detailed constitutional document. In the light of this statement enumerate salient features of the Indian Constitution.
2. It is remarked that Constitution of India was prepared after ransacking all the known constitutions of the world. In the light of this statement, mention how Indian constitution has derived many salient features from diverse sources?
3. Write short notes on:

   a. Amendment procedure

   b. Judicial Review

c. Directive Principals of State Policy

d. Fundamental Duties

4. Discuss the Fundamental Rights in the Indian constitution. What are the features of fundamental rights in India?
5. What is the significance of Directive Principles of State Policy? To what extent has the government been able to implement them?

4

Union Executive

After reading this chapter, you will be conversant with:

- President – Election, Powers and Position
- Vice President – Election, Qualification and Functions
- Prime Minister – Method of Appointment, Powers
- Prime Minister's Office (PMO)
- Council of Ministers – Features of Cabinet System
- Comptroller and Auditor General–Appointment, Removal and Functions

The framers of the Constitution provided for a Parliamentary form of government based on Westminster model of Britain. However, there are some differences between the British model and Indian Parliamentary system. Firstly, in Britain the Constitutional head is hereditary monarch, whereas in India, the Constitutional head is indirectly elected. Secondly, Britain neither has a rigid nor a written constitution, while India has a written, as well as a partly rigid Constitution. Third, in Britain, Parliament is a sovereign and supreme institution and its laws are not subjected to judicial review. In India, Parliament is neither supreme nor sovereign and the legislations passed are justifiable in the Supreme Court. Finally, England has a unitary model while India has a federal system.

PRESIDENT OF INDIA

President is considered as the constitutional head of the state. He is the embodiment of ultimate authority of the Constitution. His oath of office compels him to 'preserve, protect and defend the Constitution and the law' and 'to devote himself to the service and well-being of the people of India'.

Qualifications: Some of the essential qualifications required to become the President of India are as follows: (a) He must be a citizen of India having completed 35 years of age; (b) He should be qualified for election as a member of the House of the People (Lok Sabha); and (c) Must not hold any office of profit under the Government of India or the

Government of any State or under any local or other authority subject to the control of any of the said Governments.

Election Procedure: According to Article 54 of the Constitution, President is elected by an electoral college consisting of: (a) the elected members of both the Houses of the Parliament, and (b) the elected members of the Legislative Assemblies of the State. The nominated members of Parliament and Assemblies have no place in Electoral College. The President is elected by the system of proportional representation by means of a single transferable vote. The Constitution prescribed two principles for the election.

The framers of the Constitution adopted a system wherein the President is elected indirectly. The justification provided for indirect election of the President is as follows:

- In a cabinet system of government, direct election of the constitutional head, as is the case with the Presidential elections in US, was considered neither necessary nor advisable. However, it was thought desirable to have the President elected by a popular body. Both these purposes have been realized under the present system.
- The Electoral College consists of not only members of both Houses of Parliament but also the members of State Legislative Assemblies. In an election of the Head of the Nation, it was believed that if the members of the Parliament alone are allowed to participate, then there is every possibility that the party in power can easily see to it that its candidate is elected as the President. But, when the members of State Assemblies are also allowed to participate in the election, it is possible that the party in power at the centre may be a minority in some states. Under such circumstances, the party supported by a majority of members in Parliament will not by itself be able to elect its candidate to office.
- The election of the President is made indirect in order to make sure that the President is both a representative of States as well as Union (Fadia, p 214).

Term of Office: The term of office of the President is five years from the date on which he enters upon his office, but is eligible for re-election. However, the President's office maybe terminated within the term of five years in two ways:

- By resignation in writing under his hand addressed to the Vice-President of India.
- By removal for violation of the Constitution by the process of impeachment according to Article 56.

Emoluments and Allowances of the President: The President is entitled for a rent-free accommodation and also other privileges and emoluments and allowances as determined by the law of the Parliament. In 1998, by passing President's Emoluments and Pension Act by the Parliament, the emoluments were raised to Rs. 50,000/- per month. Article 59 (3) provides that the emoluments and allowances of the President shall not be reduced during his term of office. The Amendment Act also provided for the payment of an annual pension of Rs 3,00,000 to a person who held the office as President, on the expiry of his term or on resignation, provided he is not re-elected to the office.

Vacancy in the Office of the President: Vacancy to the office of the President may occur in any of the following ways:

- Expiry of his term of five years.
- On death.
- By resignation.
- Removal by impeachment.
- Setting aside of his election as President.

The following is the explanation of the above cases:

- Article 62(1) of the Constitution states that if a vacancy is going to be caused by the expiry of the term of the President, an election must be held to fill up the vacancy before the expiry of the term. But, in order to prevent an 'interregnum' due to any delays, the outgoing President must continue to hold office even after the expiry of his term until a new successor takes charges as the President.
- In case of vacancy arising by the death of a person who holds the post, an election has to be held as soon as possible within six months from the date of occurrence of the vacancy. Article 65(1) specifies that in case of death of the President, till a new President is elected, the Vice-President shall act as the President.
- In some cases, the President may not be in a position to discharge his functions due to his absence from India, illness or any other reason. In such a case, article 65(2) maintains that it is the responsibility of the Vice-President to discharge the President's functions till the date on which the President would resume his duties.

Procedure for Impeachment: The process of removal of President from office is called impeachment procedure. This procedure is more or less similar to that of the United States, though with one difference. In India, any house of the Parliament can charge the President for violation of the Constitution for treason, bribery, etc. But in US, it is only the House of Representatives that has the power to try for an impeachment. The impeachment procedure of President of India is well described in Article 61 of the Constitution.

Impeachment is a quasi-judicial procedure in the Parliament. The President can be impeached only for the violation of the Constitution which covers crimes, such as treason, bribery and other crimes. Usually, either of the houses may prefer the charge of violation of the Constitution before the other House which then investigates the complaints. But a charge cannot be investigated unless certain conditions are meted out:

- a resolution containing the proposal is moved after a fourteen day notice in writing, signed by not less than one fourth of the total number of members of the house
- the resolution is then passed by a majority of not less than two-thirds of the total membership of the House.

If the charges levelled against the President are proved, then a resolution must be passed by not less than two thirds of the total membership of the House. Then the President ceases to hold office of the President of India from the date of passing such a resolution.

Conditions of President's Office: Article 59(1) of Constitution states that the President shall not be a member of either House of the Parliament or of a House of the legislature of any State, and if a member of either House of the Parliament or a House of the Legislature of any State be elected President, he shall be deemed to have vacated his seat in that House on the date on which he enters his office as President. The President shall not hold any other office of profit.

Powers of the President

The Constitution of India under Article 53 states that the executive power of the Union shall be vested in President. Thus, the President is the head of all executive power of the Union. All the executive action is taken in the name of the President. However, in a Parliamentary form of government, it is the Council of Ministers headed by the Prime Minister which exercise actual powers. The President in most cases acts on the advice of the Prime Minister and Council of Ministers. Commenting on the role of President, Dr. B. R. Ambedkar once stated, "Under the Constitution, the President occupies the same position as the King under the English Constitution. He is the head of the state but not the executive. He represents the nation but does not the rule the nation. He is the symbol of the nation. His place in the administration is that of a ceremonial device on a seal by which the nation's decisions are made known." (Fadia, p. 219)

The powers of the President can be broadly classified into seven categories, viz.,

- Executive powers.
- Legislative powers.
- Financial powers.
- Judicial powers.
- Military powers.
- Diplomatic powers.
- Emergency powers.

EXECUTIVE POWERS

The executive power of the Constitution is vested in the President. The term executive power in simple terms, means the execution of the laws enacted by the legislature and the power of carrying on the business of Government or the administration of the affairs of the state. All executive action is taken in the name of the President. Though not the actual head of the administration, all executives of the Union are subordinate to him and has the right to be informed about the affairs of the Union.

The executive power of the President enable him to appoint and remove the high dignitaries of the State. The President appoints: 1. The Prime Minister of India, 2. Other Ministers of the Union, 3. The Attorney General of India, 4. The Judges of the Supreme Court, 5. The Judges of the High Court of States, 6. The Governor of the State, 7. Comptroller and Auditor General of India, 8. A commission to investigate interference with water supplies, 9. The Finance Commission, 10. Union Public Service Commission (UPSC) and Joint Commission for a group of States, 11. Chief Election Commission and other members of the Election Commission, 12. A special officer of Scheduled Castes and Scheduled Tribes, 13. A commission to report on the administration of scheduled areas, 14. A commission to investigate into the condition of the backward classes, 15. A commission on official language, and 16. A special officer for linguistic minorities. In making appointments, the President is required to consult persons other than the ministers like the Judges of Supreme Court and High Courts, if necessary.

The President has the power to remove: 1. Ministers, 2. The Attorney General of India, 3. The Governor of the State, 4. The Chairman or the members of UPSC and State Public Service Commission based on the report of the Supreme Court, Judges of the Supreme Court and High Court, or the Election Commissioner.

LEGISLATIVE POWERS

President is considered as the integral part of the entire legislative process. In legislative field also, he has certain important powers exclusive to his post. A brief explanation of the legislative powers of the President is as follows:

- The President has the power to summon or prorogue the House of Parliament and to dissolve the Lower House. He can also summon a joint sitting in case of a deadlock between both Houses of Parliament.
- The President addresses the first session of both Houses of Parliament after each general election to the House of the People and at the commencement of the first session of each year and informs Parliament of the reasons of its summons.
- President has the power to address either House or a joint sitting, at any time.
- President has the power to nominate a certain number of members to both the Houses of Parliament in case of any inadequate representation at the time of elections. He can nominate 12 members to the Council of States and not more than two members to House of People from the Anglo-Indian community.
- A Bill cannot become an Act until it receives the assent of the President. Once the bill is passed by both the Houses, it is sent to the President for his assent. At this juncture, the President is entitled to take any of the following three measures: (i) declare his assent to the Bill; or (ii) withhold his assent to the Bill;

or (iii) return the Bill for reconsideration in case the bill is other than Money Bills, with or without messages suggesting amendments. A Money Bill cannot be sent for reconsideration. Finally, if the Bill is passed by both the houses of the Parliament with or without amendments, and presented to the President, then it becomes obligatory on the part of President to give his assent.

- Article 123 of the Constitution empowers the President to promulgate ordinances when both Houses of Parliament are not in session, if the circumstances demand for such an action. The ordinance of the President is as powerful as an Act of Parliament. However, such ordinances must be placed before the Parliament within six weeks of re-assembly. Failure to comply with this condition or Parliamentary disapproval within six weeks period will make the ordinance invalid. These ordinances can be withdrawn by the President at anytime.

FINANCIAL POWERS

The President has the power to introduce the annual financial statement before the Parliament at the beginning of the financial year. No Money Bill can be introduced in Parliament without his prior recommendation. He distributes the shares of all Income Tax receipts between the Centre and the States and allocates grants-in-aid to the states of Assam, West Bengal, Bihar and Orissa in lieu of their share in export duty on jute (Fadia, p. 221).

JUDICIAL POWERS

Article 72 of the Constitution has bestowed upon the President the power to grant pardon, reprieve, respite, suspension, commutation or remission in respect of, i) all cases of punishment by a court martial; (ii) offences against laws made under the Union and Concurrent lists; and (iii) all death sentences. He appoints the judges of the Supreme Court and High Courts after consultations with the other judges of Supreme Court and High Court. Any matter of Constitutional law can be referred to the Supreme Court by the President. However, the advice of Supreme Court is not binding on the President.

MILITARY POWERS

The President is the Supreme Commander of all the three forces, viz., Army, Navy and Air force. He has the power to declare war or peace. However, the Constitution clearly specified that the exercise of these powers is regulated by law.

DIPLOMATIC POWERS

The President of India represents the nation during his visits to other nations. He appoints Indian diplomats to other nations and receives ambassadors and representatives of other countries.

EMERGENCY POWERS

The President has wide powers during emergencies. The Constitution of India provided three categories of emergency powers to deal with different situations. The Emergency Provisions are mentioned in Part XVIII of the Constitution. The 42nd and 44th Amendments Acts in 1976 and 1978 respectively, have extensively modified these provisions and finally gave the shape that is now under use. The following is the explanation of each emergency power:

National Emergency (Article 352)

The Constitution of India under article 352 specifies that the President, at any time, if satisfied that the security of India or any part is threatened by war, external aggression or armed rebellion, then he can proclaim national emergency. The 44th Amendment Act in 1978 substituted the term armed rebellion with that of internal disturbance because it was felt that the term is too vague and broad. The 44th Amendment Act also specified that the President of India cannot proclaim an emergency unless, the Union Cabinet, headed by Prime Minister communicates to the President in writing that a situation has arrived wherein it is necessary to impose an emergency.

A proclamation must always be put before each House of the Parliament. It ceases to operate if the Parliament does not approve the resolution within a period of one month. Before the 44th Amendment Act, the time for approval of emergency was two months, but was reduced to one month in 1978. However, if at the time of the issue of proclamation, Lok Sabha is dissolved without approving the proclamation, and Rajya Sabha approves it, then Proclamation ceases to operate thirty days after the Lok Sabha sits again after fresh elections, unless in the meantime the new Lok Sabha passes a resolution approving the proclamation. The amendment also specified that the resolution of approving proclamation of emergency must be passed by each house with a majority of not less than two-thirds present and voting.

Once approved by the Parliament, the emergency remains in force for six months and if the situation demands, it can be extended for another six months only after the approval of the Parliament again. The 44th Amendment Act also stated that if not less than one tenth of the total membership of the Lok Sabha express their disapproval to the proclamation of emergency to the Speaker and if the House is not in Session, then a special sitting has to be convened within fourteen days to discuss the plan of action. During emergencies, the legislature and the executive has extraordinary powers.

Effects of Proclamation:

- The union executive has all the power in giving any directions to the state executive during emergency.
- The Parliament has the power to make laws on the items included in the State list also.

- The Parliament by law can extend the life of Lok Sabha for a period of six months, but must not exceed more than a year.
- The federal provisions of the Constitution cease to function in the areas affected by an emergency.
- The President can restrict or prohibit the distribution of revenues that are assigned to states under normal conditions.
- The emergency also has an effect on the Fundamental Rights. Article 19 of the Constitution is restricted. The right to move to Courts for the implementation of such Fundamental Rights, except article 20 and 21 that guarantee right to life and personal liberty, can be suspended by the President during an emergency.

Use of the Emergency Powers:

Emergency was first proclaimed as per the provisions of Article 362 by the President on 26 October, 1962 during Chinese aggression. The proclamation was revoked by the order of the President on 10 January, 1968. The second proclamation of emergency was made on 3 December, 1971, when Pakistan invaded India. Though, a ceasefire was agreed upon between India and Pakistan by signing of Shimla Agreement, the proclamation continued for a longer period of time owing to the hostile attitude of Pakistan. The third proclamation was made in the year 1975 on the grounds of internal disturbance.

Failure of Constitutional Machinery in a State (Article 356)

Article 356 of the Constitution of India stated that if the President of India is satisfied that the State government cannot be carried out in accordance with the provisions of the Constitution, either on the report of the Governor, he is empowered to issue a proclamation. Apart from this, the President is also empowered to issue a proclamation, if the State has failed to comply with, or to give effect to, any directions given by the Union in the exercise of its executive power. This is popularly known as President's Rule (Wadhwa Nagpur, p. 351).

Once a proclamation is issued, then (i) the President assumes all the powers or may vest all or some of the functions in the Governor or any other executive authority; (ii) President may declare that powers of the State Legislature may be performed by the Parliament; and (iii) President may make any other consequential provisions necessary to give effect to the proclamation.

Any proclamation has to be approved by both the houses of the Parliament within two months of its operation. If it is not approved, it ceases to function. Usually, proclamation remains in force for a period of six months, which can be extended for another six months, but must not exceed more than one year. If situations demand for the extension of proclamation even after a year, then two conditions have to be satisfied: (i) a proclamation of emergency is in operation, in the whole of India, as the case may be, in the whole or any part of the state at the time of the passing of such resolution, and (ii) the Election Commission certifies that it is necessary to extend the proclamation on account of difficulties in holding general elections to the Legislative Assemblies of the state concerned.

Use of Article 356

A proclamation of emergency can be declared only when there is a failure of constitutional machinery and not when there is an external emergency or an armed rebellion. In most cases, Article 356 is considered as a coercive power in the hands of Union government to maintain the democratic form of Government and also to prevent the factional strifes that have a tendency to paralyze the governmental machinery. However, it must be kept in mind that Article 356 was used more than one hundred eight times during the last fifty years of the working of the Constitution. On some occasions, Article 356 is used as a mechanism to completely put down the State government, though there is no tendency of any breakdown in the Constitutional machinery. This article was used a number of times during the reign of Mrs. Gandhi who, in the name of maintenance of law and order, unleashed great amount of tyranny. Press was curbed, and the Parliament passed laws that were suitable to the ruling party. All the opponents of Mrs. Gandhi like Jaya Prakash Narayan, Morarji Desai and others were put behind bars in 1975. At this juncture, it is equally important to know as to under what conditions an emergency would not be proper to use (Wadhwa Nagpur, p. 355).

- A situation of maladministration in a state, where a duly constituted ministry enjoys the support of the Assembly.
- When a ministry resigns or is dismissed on losing majority support and when the Governor recommends imposition of President's rule without exploring a possibility of installing an alternative government.
- When a ministry has not been defeated on the floor of the House, the Governor on his subjective assessment recommends suppression and imposition of President's rule.
- During the general elections to the Lok Sabha, when the ruling party in the state has suffered a massive defeat.
- When there is a situation of internal disturbance but possible to contain the situation by the Union promptly.
- When no prior warning is given to the state government to correct itself in case of directives issued under article 256 and 257.
- When the power is resorted to solve the intra-party problems of the ruling party.
- Emergency cannot be proclaimed because of financial exigencies of the state.
- Emergency cannot be imposed on the grounds of corruption charges on the ministry.

The appropriate occasion to use this emergency power is when a ministry resigns after the defeat in the Legislature and no other ministry commanding a majority in the Assembly can be formed. Another similar situation wherein emergency can be used is when the party having a majority declines to form a ministry and the governor fails in his attempt to find a coalition ministry.

Financial Emergency (Article 360)

Article 360 of the Constitution of India states that if the President is satisfied that a situation has arisen whereby the financial stability or credit of India or of any part of the territory of India thereof is threatened, he may proclaim an emergency to that effect.

Consequences of financial emergency:

- When a financial emergency is declared, the Union has the power to issue directions to any state to observe rules of financial propriety as specified in the directives.
- Any direction may include the following:

  Reduction of salaries and allowances of persons serving in connection with the affairs of the state.

  Money bills and other bills are reserved for the consideration of the President, though passed by both the houses of the Parliament.
- The President is empowered to issue directions for the reduction of salaries and allowances of the Judges of the Supreme Court and the High Court.

A proclamation usually remains in force for not less than two months, once approved by both Houses of Parliament. Till date, Article 360 has never been put into practice.

Assessment of the Emergency Powers

The emergency provisions of the President are not free from criticism. K. T. Shah, member of the Constituent Assembly, once stated, "I notice distinct currents of thoughts underlying these provisions, (i) To arm the centre with special powers against the Units, and (ii) To arm the Government against the people. An observation of these provisions suggests that only the name of liberty and democracy remains under the Constitution" (Fadia, p. 224). After a thorough discussion on the emergency powers, it can be stated that the federal character of the Constitution is destroyed with these powers. Once article 352 is proclaimed, the centre completely takes over the matters that are otherwise under the purview of the State. This is complete negation of the concept of division of powers between the Centre and the State. Secondly, these provisions are regarded as incompatible with the spirit of democracy. Thirdly, the most undemocratic act is the suspension of fundamental duties and denying the right to move to the court for the enforcement of the same. Finally, the freedom of the states is curbed to a great extent when any of the these emergency powers is proclaimed.

Position of the President

The Constitution of India adopted a Parliamentary form of government based on the British model wherein the President acts only on the advice of the cabinet. In such a case, the President has all the power only in theoretical sense and in practice, it is the Prime Minister and his Council of Ministers who exercise all the powers. In fact, the framers of the Constitution themselves were divided into three different schools of thought in defining the role and position of the President. The first school of thought with scholars like Granville Austin, C.H. Alexandrowics and M.C. Setalvad believe that the framers of the Constitution deliberately opted for a Parliamentary form of government and President as a mere constitutional head of the state. The second school of thought contends that the President, according to the Constitution, is not a mere figure head and has the power to act independently without violating the Constitution. Commenting on the position of the President, Justice P.B. Mukherjee in 1966 once stated, "an independent institution with independent authority and independent functions" (Fadia, p. 225). The third school of thought was dominated by K. Santhanam and A. Appadoria who were of the opinion that though the President is the Constitutional head of the state and acts on the advice of the Prime Minister, he still has certain unspecified reserve powers which can be used at his discretion. However, the statement passed by the Chairman of Drafting Committee of the Constitution made it clear that President is a mere figurehead and the actual powers resides with the Council of Minister headed by the Prime Minister. Ambedkar once asserted that the President of the Indian Union will be generally bound by the advice of his ministers. He can do nothing contrary to the advice, nor can he do anything without their advice.

Though, it is undoubtedly stated that President has to go by the advice of the Ministers, yet under certain delicate situations, it becomes imperative on the part of the President to act independently when no political party gains a requisite majority. The burden then falls upon the President to exercise his discretion and he can favour some party or person. Some incidents, wherein the President had to act decisively were as follows:

- In 1979, President Neelam Sanjeev Reddy took a decision wherein he did not allow Morarji Desai to form a new government as the leader of the single largest party. Secondly, the President did not consider the request of Janata Party leader Jagjivan Ram to form the ministry but instead dissolved the Lok Sabha. This act was however done on the advice of Charan Singh who after his installation as the Prime Minister decided not to face the Lok Sabha. The President justified his decision on the grounds of obtaining support from all groups, except the one led by Jagjivan Ram.

- In 1984, just after the assassination of the then Prime Minister Mrs. Indira Gandhi, President Zail Singh immediately appointed Rajiv Gandhi as the Prime Minister. It was later that the Congress leaders met at the party meeting and chose Rajiv Gandhi as their leader. However, critics pointed out that by appointing Mr. Gandhi as the Prime Minister and giving him all powers, the President made it *fate accomplice* for the Congress Parliamentary Party.
- In 1991, the position of the President once again acquired attention. President Venkataraman's invitation to Chandra Sekhar to form the ministry after the fall of V.P. Singh's Government, his reluctance to dissolve the Ninth Lok Sabha, the subsequent constitutional developments in Tamil Nadu, Bihar and Assam, the opposition parties warning to the President that they would not co-operate in passing the crucial bills in Parliament if the former does not dissolve the Lok Sabha and order fresh elections, were some unhealthy developments that forced the Presidency under public scrutiny.

There were also occasions when the Presidents did not function on the advice of the Council of Ministers between 1985 and 1991. For example, President Zail Singh did not give his assent to the Postal Bill though passed by both the Houses of the Parliament. There were serious differences between the President Venkataraman and the Government of Chandra Sekhar in 1991 when it was functioning as a caretaker government. In 1996, President Shankar Dayal Sharma refused to promulgate ordinances on two specific subjects, viz., introduction of job reservations to Dalit Christians and shortening of campaign period for Lok Sabha polls. In the year 1997, President K. R. Narayan rejected the proposal of imposing President's rule as suggested by Prime Minister I. K. Gujral in Uttar Pradesh and dismissed the Kalyan Singh Ministry, in spite of the report sent by the Governor of the State. In 1998, the President declined the proposal of Vajpayee Government to declare constitutional emergency and dismissed Rabri Devi Government in Bihar as advised by the Governor.

Finally, from the above discussion it becomes clear that the framers of the Constitution visualized the President as the constitutional head. But India being a Federation and a Republic, wherein the Head of the State is elected, has created confusions. Further, the nature of party system, and the decline in political values has made the position of President a highly discussed issue. Though, the President has to listen to the advice of the Prime Minister, yet in some cases he is the master in himself. In fact, the very nature of the President cannot be definite. It varies with the changing social, political and economic conditions, and also the stature of the person holding the highest position in the country.

VICE-PRESIDENT OF INDIA

The Constitution of India provides for the office of the Vice-President, who to a large extent occupies a position that is insignificant. His position is similar to that of the American Vice President as a superfluous a entity. In United States, if the President dies in office or is removed from office or resigns before the expiry of the term, then the Vice President takes over as the President. But in India, in case the President dies or if he resigns then the Vice President will act as President only for a maximum period of six months.

Article 66(1) of the Constitution states that the Vice-President is elected by an electoral college consisting of members of both Houses of the Parliament. The election of Vice-President is indirect, in accordance with the system of proportional representation by means of a single transferable vote.

The Constitution of India also specified certain qualifications required for the Vice-President. The person contesting for the post of the Vice-President must be:

- A citizen of India.
- over 35 years of age.
- not hold any office of profit.
- a member of the Council of sates.

The term of office of the Vice-President is five years. His term can be terminated before the expiry, either by his resignation or removal from office. A resolution of the Council of States passed by a majority of its members and accepted by House of People can lead to the impeachment of the Vice-President. He is eligible for re-election.

As regards the functions of Vice-President, he acts as the ex-officio Chairman of the Council of States. Secondly, he acts as the President in case of death or resignation or any other cause by which the President is unable to perform his functions. When the Vice-President acts as the President, he is entitled to get the emoluments of the President. When the Vice-President acts as the President, he shall cease to perform the duties of the chairman of the Council of states and it is the Deputy Chairman of the Council of States who acts as Chairman.

Finally, though the Constitution has not provided great powers to the Vice-President, it is a great honour and dignity to act as the Vice-President of a diverse country like India.

PRIME MINISTER AND COUNCIL OF MINISTERS

A Parliamentary form of Government can be described as a system wherein the power of the representatives of the people forms the real executive and the Head of the State is the nominal executive. As per the provisions of the Constitution, the nominal executive is the President, while the real executive is the Prime Minister and his Council of Ministers. Though all the actions are performed under the name of the President, it is the Prime Minister and his ministers who actually constitute the government.

The office of Prime Minister was originated in England which was later borrowed by the framers of Indian Constitution. The Constitution of India, under Article 74 stated that there shall be a Council of Ministers with the Prime Minister as the head to aid and advice the President who shall exercise his functions and act in accordance with his advice. Furthermore, Article 74(1) also stated that Prime Minister is the head of the Council of Ministers who suggests that the other ministers cannot exercise their functions without him. There are, in fact two approaches to understand the office of the Prime Minister. Lord Morley described the PM as *primus inter pares* (first among equals) and the other approach was suggested by Sir William Vernon called him *inter stellas tuna minores* (moon among the stars). Harold Laski called the PM as "the pivot of the whole system of government".

As regards the appointment of the Prime Minister, the Constitution of India under Article 75(1) stated that the Prime Minister is selected by the President of India. The President invites the leader of the majority party in the Parliament to form the Council of Ministers. Sometimes the President uses his discretionary powers if no party gains a clear majority in the Lok Sabha. In such a situation, the President requests the single largest party to form the government or he may allow a coalition Government to be formed. If the party has a clear majority and an able leader, then the President has no choice but to invite the leader to from the government.

Once the Prime Minister is selected by the President, the other ministers are appointed by the President on the advice of the Prime Minister. However, it is the Prime Minister who decides and allots portfolios to the Ministers. The number of members in the Council of Ministers is, however, not mentioned in the Constitution of India. The number of members in the Council of Minister to a large extent depends upon the exigencies of time. The number of members is usually the discretion of the Prime Minister. Generally, the Prime Minister makes sure that people of various areas, states and communities are represented in the Council. For administrative convenience, the Ministers are classified into three categories: (a) Cabinet Ministers, (b) Ministers of State, and (c) Deputy Ministers. While Cabinet Ministers have an independent ministry under them and have the right to call a meeting as and when they need, Ministers of State are not members of the Cabinet and they attend meeting only when invited. The last category is the Deputy Ministers who assist the Minister-in-charge of a department or a ministry and do not participate in Cabinet meetings. Article 88 of the Constitution further states that the ministers may be chosen from among the members and a minister who is a member of one House, has the right to take part in the proceedings of the other House but has no right to vote in which he is not a member. (Wadhwa, p. 180). Apart from the above provisions in the Constitution of India, there is no hard and fast rule that a minister must be a member of the Legislature. But he cannot continue as minister for more than six months unless he obtains a seat in any of the House of the Parliament. [Article 75 (5)]

As regards the ministerial responsibility, Article 75(3) of Constitution of India specifies that the Council of Ministers shall be collectively responsible to the House of the People. The concept of collective responsibility plays a crucial role in a Parliamentary democracy. In simple terms, it means that all the members of the Council of Ministers act in unison. Collective responsibility has two meanings: all ministers of a government unanimously support the policies and display unanimity in public occasions though differing in their cabinet meetings. Secondly, the ministers are personally and morally responsible for the success and failure of the Government. The entire ministry is under a

Constitutional obligation to resign as soon as it loses the confidence of the House of the People even though some members belong to the House of Representatives.

With regard to the salaries and allowances of the ministers, they are determined by the laws of the Parliament as specified in the Second Schedule. Each minister gets a sumptuous salary based on their ranks, and a rent-free residence. The Constitution of India also made provisions for a constant relationship between the Council of Ministers, and the President made it mandatory on the part of the Prime Minister to communicate all the decisions regarding the affairs of the administration To the Council of Ministers (Article 78). If the President does not agree with the decisions of the cabinet, he may persuade the cabinet to revise their decision on any matter. If he does not succeed, he has to accept the advice of the Council of Ministers.

Functions of the Prime Minister

The Prime Minister is described as one of the most vital entity in the entire political system. He is the undisputed leader of the cabinet. The personality of the Prime Minister also determines the nature of authority that he exercise. Sometimes his charisma makes the cabinet system more like Prime Ministerial system. The Prime Minister has to perform an innumerable number of tasks, especially in a country that thrives in ensuring welfare to the people. He is the Head of the Government and the chief executive of the entire nation. The first Prime Minister of India, Jawaharlal Nehru, described the role of Prime Minister as, "The Linch-Pin of the Government" (Fadia, p. 231). Brief explanations of certain important functions of the Prime Minister are as follows:

- *Head of the Government:* The President is the Head of the State while the Prime Minister is the Head of the Government. He is the chief executive of the nation and works as the head of the Union Government. All the major appointments are made by the President only on the advice of the Prime Minister. All the major decision making bodies like Union Cabinet, Planning Commission, and Cabinet Committees function under the supervision and direction of the Prime Minister.
- *Leader of the Cabinet:* In a Parliamentary form of Government, the relation between the cabinet and the Prime Minister is important. It is in fact the good relation between the two that sustains the Government. The Prime Minister is the focal point in a cabinet system. Article 74 of Constitution of India mentions that there shall be a Council of Ministers headed by the Prime Minister. In the words of Ivor Jennings, he is the sun around which other ministers revolve like planets. The various ministers in the cabinet remain in office during the pleasure of the President. But in actual practice, it is the Prime Minister who decides their stay in the cabinet. He has the power to change the portfolio of any minister or demand his resignation or even dismiss him from the cabinet. He has the power to reshuffle the entire government ministers. No major decision of the Cabinet is taken without the presence of the Prime Minister. There is

more emphasis on consensus than on voting. It is the responsibility of the Prime Minister to sum the various opinions expressed by the cabinet members and then come to a conclusion that is acceptable to all the members. Resignation of the Prime Minister implies resignation of all the ministers. Laski once described that Prime Minister is central to the formation of Council of Ministers, central to its life and central to its death. However, there were occasions when the Prime Ministers acted in an authoritarian manner that sidelined the entire concept of collective responsibility. This change in the behavior of the Prime Minister is certainly due to ever increasing number of functions to be carried out. There is also a problem of co-ordination and proper care within the various cabinet committees which try to pass the buck to the Prime Minister in the name of leader and co-ordinator. The increase in his responsibilities is because of the increasing complexities within the cabinet form of government.

- *Prime Minister and the President:* In a Parliamentary form of Government, the President is the constitutional head who acts in accordance with the aid and advice of the Council of Ministers headed by the Prime Minister. But the President uses his discretionary powers when no party commands majority in Lok Sabha. The Constitution stipulated that it is the duty of the Prime Minister to communicate all the major decisions of the cabinet to the President relating to the administration of the affairs of the state. This suggests that the Prime Minister acts as the link between the cabinet and the President. The President also has the power to ask the Prime Minister to submit any decision taken by the cabinet but has not been discussed by the Council.
- *Leader of the Parliament:* The Prime Minister is the leader of the Parliament because he leads the majority party in the Parliament. He decides the meetings and also the programmes for sessions. He is empowered to prorogue and dissolve the House. As the chief-spokesperson of the Government, he informs the various motives of the Government to the House. He announces the various policies taken up by the Government and answers queries. He makes sure that no minister in his Government commits any mistake. But, if committed, he corrects them, and in some cases even rebukes them and reprimands them. He represents the cabinet as a whole unlike any other member of the Government.
- *Chief Spokesperson of Foreign Relations:* The Prime Minister plays a crucial role in maintaining good relations with his counterparts in other countries. He initiates policies that are likely to build friendship between two nations. He speaks on behalf of the entire nation in any international conferences.
- *Chairman of the Planning Commission:* Planning Commission is an extra constitutional body headed by the Prime Minister. It takes into consideration all the activities that have to be taken up for both the Centre and the States. All the important decisions regarding the economy of the country are taken care of by the Planning Commission under the Chairmanship of Prime Minister.

It becomes clear that Prime Minister is certainly the most powerful person in the entire gamut of politics. He has the right to form ministry, increase the size of the council or remove anybody, and more importantly, the power to make his party colleagues listen to his views and ideas. However, the compliance of his colleagues also depends upon his caliber, charisma, the strength of the party in national politics and also the socio-economic and political conditions of the times.

PRIME MINISTER'S OFFICE

The Indian Prime Minister occupies a place of eminence and authority in the Indian politico-administrative system and his functions and duties are myriad. They cannot be described in few pages of a legal or statute order of the Government. The constitution of India bestows her/him with vast authority in legislative and executive matters and makes him the person occupying position of preeminence in the Government. She/he heads the council of ministers and leads his team in the legislative proceedings in the Parliament. She/he is the primary spokesman of the governmental policies. She/he carries the confidence of the Parliament which is the law making body for the country. She/he instills confidence among citizens towards a brighter and prosperous future and commands respect from his political party or coalition members who support him in his functions as the head of the ruling party. She/he is the chief executive of the whole executive branch of the Government and also a part of the Indian parliament. She/he boosts the civil servants towards the accomplishment of public policies formulated by the council of ministers. To coordinate the activities of the Prime Minister and his council of ministers one finds the existence of cabinet secretariat and central secretariat. Besides, one finds the existence of Prime Minister's office to support secretarial service to the chief executive. Since the beginning of the office of the prime minister, it was a location of authority and a centre of prestige.

As regards the evolution of Prime Minister's office, it came into existence on 15 August, 1947 when India gained independence. The office was created for the purpose of taking over the functions performed by the secretary to the Governor-General. The functions carried by the office of the Governor-General were assigned to the Prime Minister's office, which assists the Prime Minister in his multifarious roles. Considering the importance attached to the office of Prime Minister in the Indian constitution, his office too assumed importance depending upon the individual personalities of prime minister and certain external factors like coalition politics. The position of the Prime Minister's office waned in case of weak prime ministers and multi-party coalitions.

With regard to functions of the Prime Minister Office, it provides secretarial services to the Prime Minister and is headed by the principal secretary to advice the Prime Minister. The Prime Minister's office also deals with anti-corruption unit and also certain grievances and requests from the people. The majority of the cases which come to the Prime Minister's office are related to policy matters, issues having wider ramifications, major appointments, inter-departmental issues, etc. The files usually referred to by the Prime Minister's office are the ones related to certain ministries and departments whose independent charge is held by the Prime Minister. In case junior ministers are given independent charge of the ministry, then the role of the Prime Minister's office is to inform the Prime Minister about the activities of the ministry. It is observed that usually the Prime Minister's office looks after the following issues:

- Atomic energy.
- Space.
- Ministry of personnel and grievance.
- To deal with references which come to his office under Rules of Business.
- To provide assistance to the Prime Minister in discharging his responsibilities as the chief executive of the Government.
- Keeping liaison with other central ministries.
- Helping the Prime Minister in discharging the duties of the Chairman of the Planning Commission and National Development Council.
- Act as Prime Minister's public relations office.

Some of the important matters that require Prime Minister's personal attention include the following:

- Important defense-related issues.
- Decorations, both civilian and defense, where Presidential approval is required.
- All important policy issues.
- Proposals for appointment of Indian Heads of Missions abroad and requests for grant of agreement for foreign Heads of Missions posted to India.
- All important decision relating to the Cabinet Secretariat.
- Appointments to the State. Administrative Tribunals and the Central Administrative Tribunal, UPSC, Election Commission, appointment of members of statutory/constitutional committees, commissions attached to various ministries.
- All policy matters relating to the administration of civil services and administrative reforms.
- Special packages announced by the Prime Minister for states are monitored in the Prime Minister's office and periodical reports submitted to the Prime Minister.
- All judicial appointments for which Presidential approval is required.

Apart from the above functions, the Prime Minister's office is also entrusted with taking up certain projects for the benefit of the people all over the country. One such project was The National Highways Development Project envisaged by the Prime

Minister and was dedicated to the nation in 1998. The aim of the project was to connect all the corners of the country and all major cities as well. In independent India, it is the most ambitious project undertaken by the government for the prosperity and rapid development of the country. Connecting the major cities of India paves way for the integrated development of India. The golden quadrilateral—Delhi, Kolkata, Chennai and Mumbai are also covered under this program. Although the scheme had been divided among many departments and states, the overseeing is the responsibility of Prime Minister's office.

Besides, another developmental project undertaken by the government is the Pradhan Mantri Gram Sadak Yojana (PMGSY). The objective of the project is to improve the infrastructure of rural India and was launched by the Prime Minister in the year 2000. The initiation of the project paved way towards the connectivity of many rural areas having a population of more than 500 people. This in turn led to the increase in access to the market for rural entrepreneurs. Since the Prime Minister directed the constitution of a task force towards expediting the project, it is the responsibility of the Prime Minister's office to keep the Prime Minister informed about its progress.

Furthermore, Prime Minister's office is also responsible to ensure the relief to the victims of natural calamities or man-made calamities. One such venture undertaken by the Prime Minister's office is Prime Minister National Relief Fund intended to provide relief to people in distress. This fund is entirely based on the donations from people for the assistance of people in distressing conditions. The families, whose members die in natural calamities like floods, cyclones, earthquakes, etc. get benefits under this scheme. The families affected by communal riots or major disturbances, accidents, etc. get benefits under the scheme. Besides, the persons can apply for financial assistance to the Prime Minister's office for certain health considerations like heart operations, kidney transplantation, and cancer treatment. It is the responsibility to check the veracity of the petitions and applications for help.

National Development Fund (NDF) was set up for the welfare of members of the armed forces affected by war under the aegis of Prime Minister's Office. The fund came into existence after the Chinese aggression in 1962. The beneficiaries are identified by an executive committee headed by the Prime Minister and the Prime Minister's office has to oversee its implementation. The fund is primarily meant for the rehabilitation of orphans and widows of defense personnel killed in war. The fund is utilized for the promotion of National Defense efforts and for the promotion of various schemes for the welfare of the personnel of Armed Forces and Central Paramilitary Forces like the following:

- Ex-gratia payment to personnel who are invalid or out of service due to injury sustained during action.
- Ex-gratia relief for dependent parents.

- Grant for the education of children.
- Grant for acquiring dwelling units.
- Relief and rehabilitation of civilian population displaced as a result of cross-border shelling in Border States.
- Construction of schools & hospitals.
- Assistance for augmenting the corpus of welfare funds under the Ministry of Defense, Armed Forces Headquarters and paramilitary forces like the Central Reserve Police Force, Border Security Force, etc.
- Purchase of books/reading material for defense personnel.

Furthermore, the Prime Minister's Office has a close relation with the Parliament as well. The Prime Minister's office looks after the issues of the Prime Minister pertaining to his charge and assists him in discharging his duties towards the Parliament. It collects the data regarding the questions to be answered in the legislature. Even if the minister is assigned the Parliamentary functions of the Prime Minister, i.e. answering the questions of the parliamentary members, it is the responsibility of the Prime Minister's office to facilitate the data and the required information. The data may pertain to issues like space, atomic energy, etc., which are under the charge of the Prime Minister usually. Besides, the Prime Minister's office prepares the drafts of the speeches to be delivered by the Prime Minister pertaining to issues of national interest.

It is the responsibility of the Prime Minister's office to prepare speeches of the Prime Minister to be delivered at international forums like the United Nations and Non-Aligned Movement. The speeches, notes and addresses are drafted in such a way by the Prime Minister's Office that they enhance the image of the country among the world leaders and also strongly put forward the points regarding Indian stance. In his recent address at the UN General Assembly, the Prime Minister emphasized three points:

- Failure of UN in solving crises.
- Membership of Security Council and its efficacy.
- Reforming Security Council voting pattern.

Besides, it is the responsibility of the Prime Minister's office to keep track of the commitments made by the Prime Minister at various international forums. The responsibility of the Prime Minister's office includes liaison with various ministries or departments regarding trade agreements if the Prime Minister visits any country to promote bilateral ties. It is the responsibility of the Prime Minister's Office to bring together various ministries and departments to discuss the issues that are to be highlighted during the Prime Minister's visit to that country.

Thus, the Prime Minister's office has occupied an important position in Indian administration since its inception. Although its role had waxed and waned depending on the nature of the individuals occupying it, it nevertheless maintained its independent identity as an office working exclusively for the secretarial assistance of the Prime Minister. To a larger extent, it proved its existence by objectively providing assistance to the Prime Minister. But there are some criticisms levelled against it. It has sometimes acted as an agent of the Prime Minister and often some important appointments have been made by the Prime Minister in connivance with the civil servants often by passing the council of ministers. Sometimes it transgressed it's authority and entered the legal jurisdiction of the cabinet and the central secretariat. The civil servants manning the Prime Minister's office are under the impression that it is to the Prime Minister to whom they owe their allegiance, not to any other external source leading to the dilution of civil service neutrality.

COUNCIL OF MINISTERS

A Parliamentary form of government can be described as a rule by the majority party under the able guidance of Prime Minister with the assistance from his colleagues with various portfolios. Each minister is responsible to the Parliament and also towards the people. It is an exaggeration if we call a Parliamentary government as Cabinet government owing to its popularity. Ramsay Muir described the Council of Ministers as 'the steering wheel of the ship of the State'. The Indian Cabinet system has certain specific features to it. Firstly, there exists a nominal head who acts as the head of the State and the entire administration is carried out in his name with the help of ministers who are accountable to the Parliament. The best example is the President of India. Secondly, the real executive is the Prime Minister, who is the chief spokesperson of the Government, leader of the House and kingpin in the cabinet arch. Thirdly, all the ministers belong to the same political party. In case of coalitions, two or more parties join together and form the government. Fourthly, the council of ministers are bound by the principle of collective and individual responsibility. This implies they remain in office as long as they enjoy the pleasure of the Parliament. They all swim and sink together. An attack on one minister is considered as an attack on all. They believe in the principle of one for all and all for one. Lastly, a cabinet system is not successful without a strong opposition. An opposition is a constant check on the government that prevents it from taking any action that is likely to disturb the democratic set-up of the country.

Powers and Functions of the Council of Ministers

The functions of the Council of ministers have been broadly classified into three:

- ***Legislative Powers:*** The Council of Ministers formulates policies, submit and also provides an explanation for the approval of the same. Most of the time the policies are approved because of the majority support in the legislature.
- ***Financial Powers:*** The Cabinet controls the finances of the entire country. It is the responsibility of the Finance Minister to prepare and submit the budget to

the Parliament. If majority of the members support the annual financial statement, also called the budget, then it is implemented.

- ***Executive Powers:*** The union executive comprises of the Council of Ministers who preside over various departments and carry on the differences or conflicts among them. The Cabinet also formulates five-year plans, defense and foreign policies for the entire country and executes them.

However, over a period of time, with the rise in population, the number of functions is also increasing. Its role in providing benefits to the people is extending to areas which were hitherto unknown. It is certainly impossible to cater to the needs of the people if the cabinet system is not strong. It is only a stable government with ministers, who are both responsible as well as responsive, that can take the country forward.

COMPTROLLER AND AUDITOR GENERAL OF INDIA (CAG)

The concept of accountability forms an important part in a Parliamentary form of government. The executive is always accountable to the legislature in terms of expenditure incurred. To ensure a safe financial administration this accountability is needed. For this purpose, the Constitution of India created an office of CAG which is an independent Constitutional authority. Dr. B.R. Ambedkar observed that "the Comptroller and Auditor General of India shall be the guardian of the public purse and it is his duty to see that not a farthing is spent out of the Consolidated Fund of India or of a State without the authority of the appropriate Legislature. In other words he is the impartial head of the audit and accounts system of India".

Appointment: Article 148 of the Constitution stated that the Comptroller and Auditor General of India is appointed by the President of India. C&AG, before joining office, has to take an oath of affirmation before the President of India or some person appointed on behalf of him. He is drawn from the Indian Audit and Accounts Services (IA&AS). C&AG, after retirement or having relinquishing his office or resigned, is not eligible for any appointment to any office, either under the Government of India or under the Government of any state. This provision is made to ensure that C&AG discharges his functions with independence and fearlessness.

Term of Office: The term of office of C&AG is six years or till the age of 65 years, whichever is earlier. He holds his office during the pleasure of the President. The salary and other conditions of service are determined by the laws of the Parliament. The salary of C&AG and his staff is charged from the Consolidated Fund of India (CFI). The service conditions shall not be liable to variation to his disadvantage during his term of office.

Removal from Office: The C&AG can be removed from office by an order of the President of India passed after an address by each House of Parliament supported by a majority of the total membership of that house and by a majority of no less than two thirds of the members of the House present and voting on the premise of proved misbehavior or incapacity.

Powers and Functions of CAG

The office of the CAG is of considerable autonomy and independence, and is shielded from executive and legislative interference. Since the CAG is the only institution in the Indian Parliamentary form of government, which acts a check against the frauds and misappropriations of the executive branch of the Government, the office is endowed with greater functional autonomy. This functional autonomy makes certain the discharge of functions without fear or favour. With the Constitutional protection of her/his tenure and removal, the main responsibility is to uphold the provisions of the constitution and the rules and regulations of financial administration. Any violation of the constitution and its provisions are brought to the notice of the Parliament for rectification. Her/his duty is to inform the legislature of any deviations of funds, frauds, extravagance, misappropriations, etc. of the executive branch of the Government. Her/his role is thus extended not only to financial certification but also administrative decisions of the executive organ. Thus, the Comptroller and Auditor General functions like a watch dog in the financial administration of a country by undertaking audit from various perspectives to ensure the accountability of the executive to the legislature. The powers and the functions of the Comptroller and Auditor General have been discussed in the constitution so as to ward off any ambiguity and ensure a clear role. Her/his powers and functions are as follows:

- The CAG is responsible for the compilation of accounts of the Union and State Government offices under his control. From time to time, the President may make additions to the list of offices/departments for which accounting has to be performed by the CAG. Besides, the accounting of some of the departments/services of the state may be included or excluded, if the Governor of the state, with the prior consultation of the President, requests the CAG. The CAG shows the receipts and expenditure of the Union government, State governments and the union territories to the respective heads. The CAG also prepare and submits accounts to the President, the Governors of states and the administrators of the Union Territories.
- The CAG is authorized to audit all the expenditure from the revenues of the Union Government in and out of India and to make sure that money shown in accounts and legally disbursed was utilized for the authorized service and the expenditure conforms to the authority.
- The CAG audits the transactions of the finances of the Union and State governments with regard to debt, deposits, sinking funds, advances and remittances, etc.
- CAG undertakes the audit of all trading, manufacturing, profit and loss accounts and balance sheets and also reporting on the expenditure and the accounts audited by her/him.

- The CAG is empowered to give suggestions with regard to the compilation and maintenance of accounts to the Union Government, the State Governments and the union territories from time to time, and render assistance in the preparation of the annual financial statements.
- It is the duty of the CAG to audit all the expenses from the Consolidated Fund of India, as well as that of the states and the union territories to ensure that the money shown in the accounts as disbursed was legally available to the services or for the purposes for which they have been allocated.
- In case of the bodies or the authorities which are financed by grants or loans from the Consolidated Fund of India or of any state or of union territory having a legislative assembly, the CAG is empowered to audit all their receipts and expenditure.
- It is the duty of the CAG to audit the receipts payable into the Consolidated Fund of India, and of the states and of the union territories having the legislative assemblies and to satisfy himself that the rules of procedure have been adhered to and are designed to secure efficient checking system with regard to the assessment, collection and the allocation of revenue.
- The CAG is empowered to inspect any office of accounts under the control of the Union or State governments.
- S/he is duly authorized to call for the papers, accounts, books and other documents relevant to the transactions of accounts and audit to any place for inspection. Besides, he is authorized to question the person in charge of the accounts and audit affairs and obtain necessary information. The person in charge of the office is under obligation to follow the instructions with regard to the preparation of accounts and render requisite information.
- Regarding the audit of the accounts of the companies, his duties are in accordance with the provisions of the Companies Act of 1956, and the reports of the companies are laid before the Government.
- With regard to the corporations, the CAG's powers of audit are in accordance with the provisions of the act made by the legislative body and the reports of the corporations are laid before the Government.
- In some specific cases, the CAG is authorized to dispense with the details of the audit.
- The CAG submits the audit reports on the Appropriation Accounts to the President, to be placed before the Parliament.
- The CAG is empowered to give suggestions to the President, or the Governor of a state, or the Administrator of the Union territory, to authorize him to undertake the audit of accounts of any authority which is not originally entrusted to him by law. This is an instance where the CAG feels that large public money has been invested in that authority or the body.

The role of CAG, as a crucial entity of Union executive, is not free from criticism. It was observed that the functions of the CAG are not clear in the aspects of economy and extravagance. Some consider that the CAG has a right to check matters relating to that of the economy as not only essential but also constitutional. The reason they give is that the CAG is an office of independence and autonomy for the work he does. So, he should use his prerogative to bring forth the cases of over-spending and wrong policies of the executive organ of the Government. But the administrative departments oppose the undefined powers of the CAG as they feel that it is a direct interference in the administrative affairs and their jurisdiction, which is not fair. Secondly, another problem is the extension of the audit of CAG to the public sector undertakings. Since the Government has invested large sums of money in these commercial undertakings, the money of the tax payer is at stake and it is incumbent upon the CAG to audit the financial transactions of these undertakings. The auditing process of these undertakings is governed by the Articles of Association and other statutory provisions in case of corporations. The CAG cannot intrude into the auditing process of these undertakings and the accounts of these undertakings do not form a part of the Public Accounts Committee report. This defect is partly rectified by the Act of 1971 and now the CAG is empowered to audit the expenditure of these undertakings which are substantially financed by the Government.

SUMMARY

- In India, the Union Executive consists of Nominal and Real Executives, namely the President, Prime Minister and the Council of Ministers. India adopted a Parliamentary form of Government, which means the Union Executive is answerable to the Parliament for all its acts and decisions. Some observe that the dominance of the Real Executive over the Nominal Executive is of Constitutional importance only. In fact, this is because, our forefathers visualized that the Head of the State, namely the President shall be nominal and shall not interfere in the day-to-day functioning of the government. It was expected that Real Executive as the Head of the Government shall march the nation towards political stability and uphold all the Parliamentary conventions too. In the end, the Union Executive is pivotal to the success of the Government since it has to administer various policies for the people of the nation.

QUESTIONS

1. "The Prime Minister is the keystone of the cabinet arch". Examine this statement in the context of the relationship of the Prime Minister with the Council of Ministers.
2. Write an analytical essay on changing role of Indian President in Indian polity.

3. 'President of Indian is the Nominal head of the Executive, who is always bound by the advice of the Council of Ministers'. In the light of this statement discuss the role and position of the President.
4. Controller and Auditor General of India is considered to be the guardian of the public purse. In other words, he is the impartial head of the audit and accounts system of India'. In the light of this statement, examine the powers of functions of the CAG.
5. Write short notes on the following:
   (a) Vice-President
   (b) Article 356
   (c) Council of Ministers
   (d) PMO

5

Parliament

After reading this chapter, you will be conversant with:

- Legislature – Election, Power and Functions
- Parliamentary Procedures
- Parliamentary Committees
- Decline of Parliament
- Speaker
- Relationship between Lok Sabha and Rajya Sabha

The word Parliament has its origin from French word, “Parler”, meaning ‘to talk’. Parliament refers to a House where the policy makers sit and discuss the national and international issues. Legislation making for the country is the most important function of the Parliament. The present Parliamentary System, being followed by several democratic countries, is based on the system of U.K. and U.S.A.

Our Constitution has adopted the best practices of the Parliament system of U.K. in giving the country a broad based Parliamentary System with two Houses – Lok Sabha and Rajya Sabha. Indian Parliament symbolizes the supreme power of people for governing the country.

Our Constitution has adopted the Parliamentary system of government which results in a harmonious blending of the legislative and executive organs of the State. The executive power is wielded by a group of members of the legislature party who command a majority in the popular chamber of the legislature and remain in power as long as they can retain that majority. Article 79 of the Indian Constitution provides that, “There shall be a Parliament for the union which shall consist of the President and two houses to be known respectively, as the Council of States and the House of the people”. These two Houses are called Rajya Sabha (Upper House - Council of States) and the Lok Sabha (Lower House - House of the people). In England, Parliament is constituted by the King, the House of Lords and the House of commons.

LEGISLATURE – ELECTIONS, POWERS AND FUNCTIONS

Lok Sabha – Composition (Article 81A)

The Lok Sabha (House of the peoples) is known as the Lower House of Parliament and it's members are chosen by direct election from the territorial constituencies in the states and not more than twenty members represent the Union Territories. In addition, two members of the Anglo-Indian community may be nominated by the President (Article 331).

The total elected strength of the Lok Sabha is distributed among the states in such a way that the ratio between the number of seats and the population of any state is the same for all the states.

DIRECT ELECTION

The election to the Lok Sabha is conducted on the basis of adult franchise and every man or woman who has completed the age of eighteen years is eligible to vote. The Constitution provides for a secret ballot. The candidate, who secures the largest number of votes, is declared elected.

Duration of the Lok Sabha

The term of Lok Sabha is five years. After the expiry of five years the House is dissolved but it can be dissolved before the expiration of its full term under certain circumstances. When a proclamation of emergency is in force, the term of Lok Sabha can be extended by the Parliament for a period not exceeding one year at a time and not exceeding, in any case, a period of six months after the proclamation has ceased to operate.

Qualifications for Membership

The member of Lok Sabha should be an Indian citizen and must have completed the age of twenty five years. A striking feature of the electoral law is that a candidate for election to the Lok Sabha may stand from any Parliamentary constituency from any of the states in India.

Disqualifications for Membership

The Constitution has laid down certain disqualifications for membership (Article 102). These are:

- If he holds any office of profit under the Government of India or the Government of any State.
- If he is of unsound mind and declared so by a competent court.
- If he is an undischarged insolvent.

- If he is not a citizen of India.
- If he is disqualified by or under any law made by Parliament.

Sessions

The Lok Sabha shall meet at least twice in a year and the interval between two consecutive sessions shall be less than six months. The President, who summons the House to meet, will decide the time and place of meeting. He also has the power to prorogue the House. The Lok Sabha can also be summoned in a special session for disapproving the proclamation under Article 352 (National emergency), if a notice in writing signed by not less than one tenth of the members of the Lok Sabha is given to the Speaker. When such a notice is given, the President must summon the session within fourteen days.

Rajya Sabha

The Rajya Sabha (Council of States) is the upper House of the Parliament and also called the House of Elders. It was the Government of India Act, 1919 which established the second chamber.

Composition

The maximum membership of the Rajya Sabha is limited to two hundred fifty. According to Article 80 of the Constitution, the Rajya Sabha shall consist of the following:

- Twelve members to be nominated by the President having special knowledge or practical experience in respect of literature, science, art and social service.
- Not more than two hundred and thirty eight representatives of the states and union territories.

Indirect Election

The members (except for a few nominated by the President for special knowledge) are indirectly elected on a proportional representation basis by the state legislature. For the purpose of election, each state is allotted a certain number of seats in the Rajya Sabha. The main basis of such allotment is the strength of the population in each state. According to Article 80 of the Constitution, "The representatives of each state in the Rajya sabha shall be elected by the elected members of the legislative assembly of the state in accordance with the system of proportional representation."

Term

Unlike Lok Sabha, which has a fixed term of five years, the Rajya Sabha enjoys continuity. As per the Constitution, the Rajya Sabha cannot be dissolved. There is also no provision in the Constitution for the abolition of the Rajya Sabha like that for a state legislative council. The term of the members of the Rajya Sabha is six years but one third of the members retire after every two years. In other words, at the end of every second year, one third of the members are elected afresh.

Chairperson and Deputy Chairman of the Rajya Sabha

The Vice President of India is the ex-officio chairperson of the Rajya sabha. An electoral college consisting of the elected members of both the Lok Sabha and the Rajya Sabha elects her/him. As the presiding officer of the Rajya Sabha, her/his functions and powers are the same as those of the Speaker. She/he is however not a member of the House. While the office of the chairman is vacant or during any period when the Vice-President acts as the President of India or discharges the functions of the President, the duties of the Chairperson of the Rajya Sabha are performed by the Deputy Chairperson.

The members of the Rajya Sabha elect the Deputy Chairman who presides over the sittings of the Rajya Sabha whenever the Chairperson does not do so. The Deputy Chairperson is a member of the House and when he ceases to be a member of the Rajya Sabha, he automatically vacates the office of the Deputy Chairperson. Deputy Chairperson can resign the office by writing to the Chairperson and may be removed from the office by a resolution passed by a majority of all the members of the Rajya Sabha.

The Rajya Sabha also has a panel of members called Vice Chairperson nominated by the Chairperson for the purpose of presiding over the Rajya Sabha in the absence of both the Chairperson and Deputy Chairperson.

The Drafting Committee consisted of the following members:

FORMER CHAIRMEN* OF THE RAJYA SABHA

NAME	TERMS
Dr. Sarvepalli Radhakrishnan	13.5.1952 to 12.5.1962
Dr. Zakir Husain	13.5.1962 to 12.5.1967
V.V. Giri	13.5.1967 to 3.5.1969
Gopal Swarup Pathak	31.8.1969 to 30.8.1974
B.D. Jatti	31.8.1974 to 30.8.1979
M. Hidayatullah	31.8.1979 to 30.8.1984
R.Venkataraman	31.8.1984 to 24.7.1987
Dr. Shanker Dayal Sharma	3.9.1987 to 24.7.1992
K.R. Narayanan	21.8.1992 to 24.7.1997
Krishan Kant	21.8.1197 to 27.7.2002
Bhairon Singh Shekhawat	19.8.2002 to 21.7.2007

* Vice-President in exofficio chairman of Rajya Sabha.
Source: rajyasabha.nic.in/rsnew/chairman/former_chairman.asp

Powers and Functions of the Parliament

Parliament today is not only a law-making body but it has become a multi-functional institution performing a variety of roles. The important powers of the Indian Parliament are:

Legislative Functions:

The Constitution has classified the subjects for legislation into three lists:

- The Union list.
- State list.
- Concurrent list.

The Union List includes those items over which Parliament has exclusive authority to make laws. The concurrent list enumerates those subjects over which Parliament as well as states have power to make laws. The Parliament is empowered to make laws in certain special circumstances on the subjects included in the state list as well. The Parliament can take steps in this direction, provided Rajya Sabha declares a resolution supported by a special majority that it is necessary or expedient in the national interest to do so.

When a proclamation of emergency is in operation, the legislative competence of the Parliament is widened so as to extend to any matter in the state list. Parliament also enjoys the power to legislate for implementing any treaty or agreement with any country. During emergency, Parliament can issue directions to the State Governments in the matters of exercising executive powers. In case a state government cannot be carried on in accordance with the provisions of the Constitution, the Assembly may be suspended or dissolved by the President and Parliament can make laws in respect of that state.

In addition to these three lists, Constitution mentions about the residuary powers of the Center in respect of any matter not enumerated in any of the three lists. The residuary powers, i.e. power to legislate on a matter not enumerated in any one of the three lists belong to Parliament.

Parliament enjoys the power to legislate for implementing any treaty, agreement or convention with any country or any decision made at an international conference, association or other body on any subject, even if it falls in the state list. Parliament may enter the state list by invitation also. If two or more state legislatures consider it desirable that any of the matters within their exclusive legislation competence should be regulated by Parliamentary legislation and pass resolutions to that effect, then Parliament can undertake the necessary legislation. However, the legislation so passed has effect only in the states which requested for it and others which may adopt it afterwards by resolutions passed in that behalf.

The Constitution empowers Parliament to make changes in the boundaries of the states and effect changes in the names of existing states. It can create new states by unifying two or more states and also by dividing existing states. It can regulate the citizenship. The Constitution empowers the Parliament to amend the Constitution itself.

- *Control of executive*: Parliament exercises control over the executive through questions, calling attention notices and other procedures like votes of censure, adjournment motions and numerous other procedures. It can also prevent executive from taking a course of action by refusing to pass legislation required by the government or by its refusal to give its consent. More particularly, the Estimates Committee, the Public Accounts Committee and the Committee on Public Undertakings also exercise control through the various committees of the Parliament. The Executive is not a separate body. It is a part of the Parliament.
- *Financial power*: The Parliament also controls the finances of the Union. It sanctions money to the government to enable it to run the administration. It may pass, reduce or reject the demands for grants presented to it by the government, but it cannot increase them. No taxes can be charged and no money can be spent without the authority of the Parliament. The two Houses of Parliament enjoy equal power and status in all spheres except in financial matters. The following limitations have been placed on the power of Rajya Sabha:
    - A money Bill cannot be introduced in Rajya Sabha.
    - Rajya Sabha has no power either to reject or amend a Money Bill. It can only make recommendations on the Money Bill. If such a Bill is not returned to Lok Sabha within a period of fourteen days, the Bill shall be deemed to have been passed by both the Houses at the expiration of the said period in the form in which the Lok Sabha passed it.
    - Whether a particular Bill is Money Bill or not is to be decided by the Speaker of the Lok Sabha.
    - Rajya Sabha may discuss the Annual Financial statement. It has no power to vote on the demands for grants.

Parliament's Control over the Financial System

- **Consolidated Fund of India:** All money received by or on behalf of the Government of India will be credited to either of the two funds: the Consolidated Fund of India or the Public Accounts of India. Thus, subject to the assignment of certain taxes to the states, all revenues received by the Government of India, all loans raised by the government and all money: received by that government in repayment of loans shall form one consolidated fund to be called 'the Consolidated Fund of India' [Article 266(1)].

- **Contingency Fund of India:** Article 267 of the Constitution empowers Parliament and the legislature of a state to create a Contingency Fund for India or for a state, as the case may be. The Contingency Fund of India Act, 1950 constitutes the Contingency Fund of India. The fund will be at the disposal of the executive to enable advances to be made from time to time for purpose of meeting unforeseen expenditure, pending authorization of such expenditure by the legislature by supplementary, additional or excess grants. The amount of the Fund is subject to be regulated by the appropriate legislature.
- **Parliament regulates the following:** The custody of the Consolidated Fund of India and the Contingency Fund of India, the payment of money into such funds, withdrawal of money, custody of public money other than those credited to such funds, their payments into the public accounts of India and the withdrawal of money from such accounts and other matters.

Judicial Powers

Parliament has power to make laws regulating the constitution, organization, jurisdiction and powers of the courts. The President can remove a judge from his office, if a joint resolution passed by both Houses of Parliament with a special majority is presented to him. Parliament may, by law provide for the establishment of an administrative tribunal for the Union and a separate administrative tribunal for each state or for two or more states. In brief, the Parliament of India has rather extensive powers and performs a variety of important functions It is considered as the chief law-making body. Its functions in this respect are limited legally by the federal nature of the Indian Republic and by the power of the Supreme Court. Supreme Court can declare those legislations as unconstitutional which violate the Constitutional provisions. In such circumstances, the Parliament has to exercise its option to amend the forbidding provisions of the Constitution.

Criticism of the Cabinet and of Individual Ministers

The cabinet initiates both the executive and the legislative policies. However, the critical function of Parliament continues to be that of ensuring the accountability of the Cabinet on the implementation of policy decisions. While the cabinet is left to formulate the policy, the function of Parliament is to bring about a discussion and criticism of that policy on the floor of the House, so that not only the cabinet can get advice of the deliberative body and learn about its own errors and deficiencies but the nation also as a whole can be appraised of an alternative point of view. Parliament thus, reflects the voice of the people and in turn educates the people on the implementation of policies by Union Government.

An organ of information

Parliament is more powerful than the press or any other private agency as it secures the information authoritatively. The information is collected and disseminated not only through debates but also through specific medium of putting questions to ministers.

PARLIAMENTARY PROCEDURES

The different stages in the legislative procedure in Parliament relating to Bills other than Money Bills are as follows:

Law making Procedure

One of the important functions of Parliament is to make laws for the country. This function forms the bulk of Parliament's time. The Constitution provides that Money bills must be introduced in the Lok Sabha. The Rajya Sabha, within fourteen days make recommendations with respect to a Money Bill transmitted to it but Lok Sabha may reject them and the bill may yet be considered to have been passed. Bills, other than Money Bills can be introduced in either house of the Parliament, though, in fact a vast majority of them are introduced in the Lok Sabha. To become a law, both Houses must pass a non-Money Bill disagreement between the two, if any, which is resolved by means of a joint sitting.

Ministers present most legislative proposals even of the non-financial type to Parliament. As soon as a legislative proposal has been conceived, the ministry concerned works out its political, administrative, financial and other implications, and where necessary, takes the advice of experts. If the proposed legislation concerns other ministries or state governments, they are also consulted.

The Ministry of Law and Attorney General of India are consulted in respect of the legal and constitutional aspects of the proposed legislation. When the proposal has been examined in this manner, the ministry, which has initiated the bill, prepares a memorandum for the cabinet. The cabinet may give its approval after briefly considering the broad aspects of policy underlying the proposed legislation or, if it is of an important or controversial character, refer it to one of its standing committees or to an ad hoc committee so that the bill may receive a more detailed consideration. In some cases, the cabinet may, after approving the underlying principle of a proposed legislation, require that the bill, when it has been drafted be submitted again for closer scrutiny. After a legislative proposal has received a clearance from the cabinet, the relevant papers are sent to an official draftsman who puts the proposal into the form of a bill. Drafting a bill is a highly technical job calling for a great deal of expert knowledge and experience. The ministry concerned examines the draft prepared by the draftsman, and quite often several drafts have to be prepared before a bill is finally put into shape.

Introduction and First Reading

A Bill is the draft of a legislative proposal. It has to pass through various stages before it becomes an Act of Parliament.

FIRST READING

The legislative process starts with the introduction of a Bill in either House of the Parliament—Lok Sabha or Rajya Sabha. A Bill can be introduced either by a minister or by a private member. In the former case, it is known as a Government Bill and in the later case, it is known as a Private Member's Bill.

It is necessary for a member-in-charge of the Bill to ask for leave to introduce the Bill. If leave is granted by the House, the Bill is introduced. This stage is known as the First reading of the Bill. If the motion for leave to introduce a Bill is opposed, the Speaker may, in his discretion, allow brief explanatory statements to be made by the member who opposes the motion and the member-in-charge who moved the motion. Where a motion for leave to introduce a Bill is opposed on the ground that the Bill initiates legislation outside the legislative competence of the House, the Speaker may permit a full discussion thereon. Thereafter, the question is put to vote of the House. However, the motion for leave to introduce a Finance Bill or an Appropriation Bill is forthwith put to the vote of the House.

Publication in Gazette

After a Bill has been introduced, it is published in the Official Gazette. Even before introduction, a Bill might, with the permission of the Speaker, be published in the Gazette. In such cases, leave to introduce the Bill in the House is not asked for and the Bill is straightaway introduced.

Reference of Bill to Standing Committee/Select Committee/JPC

After a Bill has been introduced, Presiding Officer of the concerned house can refer the Bill to concerned Standing Committee for examination and make report thereon. The bill may also be referred to the select committee of the concerned house or to the Joint Parliamentary Committee. The bill may directly go for the consideration.

If a Bill is referred to department related standing committee, the committee shall consider the general principles and clauses of the bill referred to them and make report thereon. The committee can also take expert opinion or the public opinion from those who are interested in the measure. After the Bill has thus been considered, the Committee submits its report to the House. The report of the Committee being persuasive shall be treated as an advice given by the committee.

Committee Stage

After the motion for reference of the bill to a select committee is carried, the House appoints a select committee to consider the bill. The date by which the committee's report should be presented to the House is also indicated in the motion. Each select committee is separately constituted and there is a nucleus of members who generally participate in the work of select committees. The chairman is appointed by the Speaker from among the members of a committee and is normally a member of the majority party. The chairman conducts the work of the select committee concerned, subject to the rules of the House and directions issued to him by the Speaker. As the general principles, if a bill referred to a select committee has already been discussed on the floor of the House, the committee concentrates its attention on details. A select committee may appoint one or more sub-committees to examine particular points connected with the bill under its consideration. A sub-committee submits its reports to the parent select committee.

Procedure in a select committee is informal and confidential. Meetings are held in private. No verbatim record of the proceedings is kept but a summary of decisions taken is kept by the secretary to the committee and is circulated to the members at the end of each meeting.

The committee stage is a vital step in the career of a bill because it is at this stage that it receives detailed minute examination. Amendment to the bill can be proposed during the committee stage subject to the provision that these amendments must conform to the general principles of the bill. If the committee decides to propose substantial amendments, it may advise that the bill be circulated, or re-circulated if it has already been circulated.

When the select committee has heard the experts, examined the witnesses and has completed the clause-by-clause consideration of the bill, it prepares its report embodying the recommendations including such amendments as it proposes. Committee reports are published as soon as they have been presented to the House.

Report Stage

The committee's report is signed by its chairman and presented to the House by him or in his absence by another member of the committee. The report and the bill as amended by the committee are then printed and copies are made available for the use of members of the House. After the presentation of the committee's report, the member-in-charge of the bill may move:

- That the bill as reported by the select committee, may now be taken into consideration.
- That the bill as reported be taken to the select committee with or without instruction.
- The bill, as reported, be circulated or re-circulated for eliciting opinion or further opinion thereupon.

If the motion that the bill as reported by the select committee is taken into consideration is carried, the bill is taken up for clause-by-clause consideration. Each clause is placed before the House for discussion and amendments may be moved. The Speaker determines the admissibility of the amendments and is empowered to select amendments to be discussed. In practice, however, the Speaker does not exercise this power of selection.

SECOND READING

The Second Reading consists of consideration of the Bill which is in two stages.

First Stage

The first stage consists of general discussions on the Bill as a whole when the principle underlying the Bill is discussed. At this stage, it is open to the House to refer the Bill to a Select Committee of the House or a Joint committee of the two Houses or to circulate it for the purpose of eliciting opinion thereon or to straight away take it into consideration.

If a bill is referred to a select/joint committee, the committee considers the Bill clause-by-clause just as the House does. Amendments can be moved to various clauses by the members of the Committee. The committee can also take evidence of associations, public bodies or experts who are interested in the measure. After the Bill has thus been considered, the Committee submits its report to the House which considers the Bill again as reported by the Committee.

If a Bill is circulated for the purpose of eliciting public opinion thereon, such opinions are obtained through the Governments of States and Union Territories. Opinions so received are laid on the table of the House and the next motion in regard to the Bill must be for its reference to a select/joint committee. It is not permissible at this stage to move motion for consideration of the Bill.

Second Stage

The second stage of the Second Reading consists of clause-by-clause consideration of the Bill as introduced or as reported by Select/Joint committee. Discussions take place on each clause of the Bill and amendments to clauses can be moved at this stage. Amendments to a clause that has been moved but not withdrawn are put to the vote of the House before the relevant clause is disposed of by the House. The amendments become a part of the Bill if they are accepted by a majority of the members present and voting. After the clauses, the schedules, if any, the Enacting Formula and the Long Title of the Bill have been adopted by the House, the Second Reading is deemed to be over.

Third Reading

Thereafter, the member-in-charge can declare that the Bill be passed. This stage is known as the Third Reading of the Bill. At this stage, debate is confined to the arguments either in support or rejection of the Bill without referring to the details. Only formal, verbal or consequential amendments are allowed to be move at this stage.

In passing an ordinary Bill, a simple majority of members present and voting is necessary. But in the case of a Bill to amend the constitution, a majority of the total membership of the House and a majority of not less than two-thirds of the members present and voting is required in each House of the Parliament.

The Bill in the other House

When the bill has passed through all these stages in the originating House, the presiding officer authenticates it and transmits it to the other house for its concurrence. Here, it again goes through all the stages described above. If the second House passes the bill as transmitted by the first, a message to that effect is sent to the presiding officer of the originating House. The bill then goes to the President for his assent. If, on the contrary, the other House proposes amendment to the bill, it is returned to the originating House. There the amended bill is laid on the table of the House. After two days notice, any Minister or any member may move that the amendment or amendments proposed by the other House be taken into consideration. If the originating house agrees to the amendments proposed by the other House, the bill is deemed to have been passed by both. If the originating House is unable to agree to these amendments, the bill is sent back to the other House with a message to that effect. If this House continues to insist on its amendments, the result is a deadlock, which can be resolved by means of a joint sitting of the two Houses, the decision being taken by a majority of votes.

The President's Assent

Finally, when all necessary stages in the two Houses have been completed, the bill, as passed by both Houses, is presented to the President for his assent. The President may either give his assent to the bill or withhold his assent or return the bill to the originating House with the message that the bill or any specified provision thereof should be reconsidered. If the bill is passed a second time with or without amendments and presented to the President for his assent, the latter cannot withhold his assent from it.

PARLIAMENTARY COMMITTEES

The Indian Parliament has functioned as a sovereign body, resulting in the remarkable developments in Parliamentary practices and procedure. A noteworthy part of these developments has been in the direction of Parliamentary committees. Parliament discusses policies, but unless there are committees which can discuss the matters, and where matters can be thoroughly examined, Parliament's control tends to be feeble. In the committees, the members can meet in an informal and peaceful atmosphere and concentrate in a truly business like fashion on the problems entrusted to them. It is here that the greatest advantage of the committee system lies.

Parliamentary committees are of two types: a. Ad hoc committees, and b. Standing committees. An Ad hoc committee is appointed for a specific purpose and when it has finished its assigned work and has submitted its report, it ceases to exist. The best known and most regular examples of Ad hoc committees are the Select and Joint committees on the Bills.

Each House has a number of standing committees. The Rajya Sabha and the Lok Sabha have a Business Advisory Committee, a committee on petitions, privileges and rules. The Lok Sabha has, in addition, a number of other committees. Of special importance is yet another class of committees given below:

The Committee on Subordinate Legislation, the Committee on Government Assurances, the Estimates Committee, the Public Accounts Committee, Committee on Public Undertaking. The Committee on Public Undertakings plays an important role in exercising check on governmental expenditure.

The functions and composition of the important committees of Parliament are discussed below:

Public Accounts Committee

This committee consists of twenty two members. Out of these, fifteen members are elected by Lok Sabha and seven members from Rajya Sabha. The main duty of the committee is to ascertain whether Government within the scope of the demand has spent the money granted by Parliament. If any money spent under any account for any service during a financial year is in excess of the amount granted by the House for that purpose, the committee examines the circumstances leading to such excesses and makes such recommendation as it may deem fit. Such excesses are required to be brought up before the House by government for ratification. The appropriation accounts of the Government of India and the audit report presented by the Comptroller and Auditor General mainly forms the basis for examination by the committee. Cases involving losses, nugatory expenditure and financial irregularities come in for severe criticism from the committee. The committee is concerned with the execution of the policy laid down by Parliament and its results. The life of the committee is one year.

Estimates Committee

This committee consists of thirty members who are elected by the Lok Sabha for one year from among its members. A minister is not eligible for this committee. The life of the committee is one year. The committee examines estimates of the various ministries, departments and projects of the Government of India and suggests economic improvements in organizational efficiency or administrative reforms which can be effected in consistence with the policy underlying the estimates. It makes a detailed examination of the annual budget estimates in order to:

- Report what economics, improvements in organization, efficiency or administrative reform, consistent with the policy underlying the estimates, may be affected.
- Suggest alternative policies in order to bring about efficiency and economy in administration.
- Examine whether the money is well laid out within the limits of the policy implied in the estimates.
- Suggest the form in which the estimates shall be presented to the Parliament.

If it is found that a particular policy is not going in the desired direction and will lead to waste, it is considered the duty of the Estimates Committee to point out the defects and bring to the notice of the Parliament the need for change in policy.

Committees on Public Undertakings

The Committee on Public Undertakings consists of twenty two members - fifteen elected by the Lok Sabha and seven from the Rajya Sabha. The members of the committee hold office for a term of one year. The Committee for the first time, was constituted with effect from May 1, 1964.

The functions of the Committee on Public Undertakings are:

- To examine the reports, and accounts of the Public Undertakings.
- To examine the reports, if any, of Comptroller and Auditor-General on the Public Undertakings.
- To examine in the context of the autonomy and efficiency of public undertakings, whether the affairs of the public undertakings are being managed in accordance with some sound business principles and prudent commercial practices.
- To exercise such other functions vested in the Public Accounts committees and the Estimates Committee in relation to the Public Undertakings, as are not covered by clause (a), (b) and (c) above and as may be allotted to the committee by the Speaker from time to time.

Business Advisory Committee

The Business Advisory committee of Lok Sabha consists of fifteen members, including the Speaker who is the ex-officio chairman. The Speaker nominates the members. Almost all sections of the House are represented on the committee. In the Rajya Sabha, this committee consists of eleven members including the chairman of the committee. The function of the committee is to recommend the time that should be allotted for discussion of legislative and other business issues which the speaker/chairman, in consultation with the leader of the House, may refer to it. This committee, on its own initiative, may also recommend to the Government to bring forward particular subjects for discussion in the House and recommend allocation of time for such discussion. The decisions reached by the committee are always unanimous in character and represent the view of the House. The committee generally meets at the beginning of each session and thereafter as and when necessary.

Evaluating Committee System

The Committee reports instill fear and respect in the administration. Administration misdeeds of negligence, nepotism and waste are not prevented for the simple reason that they may be looked into and exposed to public gaze by a committee of Parliament. Reports of committees have been of great educative value for members as well as the general public. By their constant vigilance, fair and constructive appraisals of the functioning of Government departments, the committees have made a distinct contribution to the effective working of the Parliament and have played a significant role in generally strengthening Parliamentary institutions in the country. An integrated system of committees could provide a powerful mechanism for a meaningful multilateral dialogue between the government and the members of the Parliament enabling a proper appreciation of each other's views, reasonable accommodation of varying viewpoints and harmonization of conflicting interests. The committees are an additional supervisory or overseeing authority, along with the minister and on behalf of Parliament like the minister himself.

DECLINE OF PARLIAMENT

The pivotal position of Parliament in the Indian political system, in recent years, has suffered decline in its role. The reasons for the decline of Parliament are:

- The cabinet has usurped the area of authority originally belonging to the Parliament. It is the cabinet which decides about many things like summoning and proroguing the session of the Parliament, writing the text of the inaugural address to be delivered by the head of the state, preparing a daily time table of the session of the House or Houses, effective initiation of the debate on the bills and resolutions moved by it, and doing a host of other things that constitute the stock of Parliamentary business. The role of the members of the Parliament has also not been praiseworthy. The sense of responsibility of members to Parliament, has been gradually going down. In the absence of competence and commitment, it has become difficult for them to perform the job of closely scrutinizing the work of the ministries.

- The standard of debates in Parliament has been considerably falling. Debates in Parliament were once characterized by sharp irony, wit and humour. Today, they have been reduced to character assassination, abuse and violent protest in the House.
- The financial accountability of cabinet to Parliament is not properly monitored.
- Freedom to obtain vital information by members is curtailed by the privileges of official secrets enjoyed by the Government.
- The reach and influence of media, especially electronic media is also considered to be a factor for downfall in importance of Parliament.

SPEAKER

The Lok Sabha is presided over by the Speaker who is elected by the House from among its own members.

Election and Removal of the Speaker

Under the present Constitution, both the Speaker and the Deputy Speaker of the Lok Sabha are elected in accordance with the procedure laid down under Article 93 of the Constitution. The election to the office of Speaker is to be held on the very first sitting of the House. Both the Speaker and the Deputy Speaker are elected separately on motions moved and seconded by the respective party leaders.

Once elected, the Speaker holds office from the date of his election and shall be deemed to be a Speaker until a new one is chosen by the new Lok Sabha. If a person holding the office of the Speaker ceases to be a member of the House, he shall also cease to be the Speaker as well. He can, however, be removed only by a resolution of the House for which a fourteen days notice is given (Article 94 c), which shall be effective only if passed by a majority of the House. When a resolution for the removal of the Speaker is under consideration, he cannot preside over the meetings, even though present in the House, till the fate of the motion has been decided.

POWERS AND FUNCTIONS OF THE SPEAKER

The Speaker of the Lok Sabha enjoys extensive powers. Some of his powers and functions are as follows:

- Her/His foremost duty is to see that there is decorum and discipline in the House and that the business of the House is conducted in an orderly manner and in accordance with the wishes of the House.
- The Speaker is the only authority to decide who shall hold the floor and speak.

- The Speaker decides about the time which should be allotted to each item on the agenda.
- Her/His authority in the precincts of the House and over the galleries is final.
- As presiding officer of the House, the Speaker decides what should appear in the proceedings. She/he has the right to expunge objectionable words, phrases and expressions from the proceedings.
- She/he is the custodian of the rights and privileges of members of the Lok Sabha.
- She/he Certifies whether a particular Bill is a Money Bill or not.
- Whenever there is a joint meeting of both the Houses of Parliament, the Speaker presides over such meetings.
- All members are supposed to address the Speaker only while participating in the debates. He decides all points of order raised during the course of discussion and his decision is binding.
- His role during question hour is important. The Speaker decides which questions should not be admitted. It is the Speaker who allows half an hour discussion and admits adjournment motions. He also admits a vote of no confidence against the government.
- The Speaker admits all the resolutions for discussion and decides when a discussion on a bill should be adjourned.
- He puts the motion to vote and announces the result of voting, in case, there is a tie.
- He is the head of the Lok Sabha secretariate. Without his permission no officer or employee of the Lok Sabha can appear as a witness in any court of law.
- He can instruct the government to place a document on the table of the House.
- No arrest or any other type of warrant can be issued by any executive authority against any member of the Lok Sabha within the four walls of the House without his prior permission.
- He accepts all resignations sent to him by members of the House.
- The Speaker authenticates all the bills passed by the House. It is the responsibility of the chair to protect the House from unnecessary executive intrusion.
- The Speaker may ask a member to withdraw from the House for a day or part of a day for disorderly behavior, or may even suspend a member from the service of the House on a proper motion for gross disorderly behaviour.
- All the Parliamentary Committees of the Lok Sabha are constituted by him or by the House. They function under his control and direction.

Thus, the Speaker has vast powers to ensure the smooth and orderly conduct of the business of the House. He is the channel through which all communications between the House and the President must pass.

Joint Sessions

In Parliament, any Bill, other than a Money Bill, can become a law only if both the Houses, with or without amendments, agree for it. A machinery should then exist for resolving a deadlock between the two Houses, if they fail to agree either to the provisions of the Bill as introduced by the amendments that may have been proposed by either House.

As regards all other Bills (including Financial Bills), the machinery provided by the Constitution for resolving a disagreement between the two Houses of Parliament is a joint sitting of the two Houses. The President may notify to the Houses her/his intention to summon them for a joint sitting in case of disagreement arising between the two Houses in any of the following ways:

If, after a bill has been passed by one House and transmitted to the other House, it may so happen that:

- the bill is rejected by the other House.
- the houses have finally disagreed to the amendments to be made in the Bill.
- more than six months have elapsed from the date of the reception of the Bill by the other House without being passed by it.

The Speaker presides at the joint sitting. In the absence of the Speaker, such person as is determined by the Rules of Procedure made by the President (in Consultation with the Chairman of Council of States and the Speaker of the House of people) shall preside [Article 118 [4]].

RELATION BETWEEN LOK SABHA AND RAJYA SABHA

Rajya Sabha in India can not be described as a secondary chamber as its assertiveness has been gradually increasing with growing federalisation of the polity and advent of the coalition government at the centre. The relationship between the Lok Sabha and the Rajya Sabha are as follows:

Financial Powers

In the legislative sphere, the Rajya Sabha enjoys an equal status with the Lok sabha in all respects except in certain financial matters. A Money Bill or a Financial Bill cannot be introduced in the Rajya Sabha. It is to be introduced in the Lok Sabha. A Money Bill when passed by the Lok Sabha has to be transmitted to the Rajya Sabha for its recommendations. The Lok Sabha then can either accept or reject its recommendations, if any, made by the Rajya Sabha. Under the procedure established by the Constitution, however, the Rajya Sabha is not altogether prevented from scrutinizing Money Bills. But its power is only of an advisory character. Every Money Bill passed by the Lok Sabha will go to the Rajya Sabha for its consideration and within fourteen days after the receipt of the Bill, the Rajya Sabha must take whatever action it deems necessary. It may pass it, in which case the Bill goes to the President for his assent. If the Bill is amended or rejected by the Rajya Sabha it goes back to the Lok Sabha where it is reconsidered and voted by a simple majority and sent to the President. Thus, in financial matters, the Rajya Sabha plays an advisory role and the Lok Sabha has the final say. The Rajya Sabha can, at the most delay a Money Bill by fourteen days only.

Mere perusal of the financial provisions in the Constitution cannot give an adequate idea of the impact of the discussions in the Rajya Sabha on the financial affairs of the country. The lengthy debates on budget and financial bills in the Rajya Sabha provide valuable suggestions to the Government. By discussing the budgetary proposals, the Rajya Sabha examines the government's whole economic policy.

Legislative Powers

The Rajya Sabha enjoys equal powers with the Lok Sabha in the field of ordinary legislation. An ordinary bill or a non-Money Bill can be introduced in the Rajya Sabha and it has to be approved in both the Houses of Parliament before it becomes an Act. The Lok Sabha has no power to overrule Rajya Sabha. In case of disagreement between the two Houses on any such bill, it has to be resolved in a joint sitting in which each member of each House has to vote. This gives an advantage to the Lok Sabha which is more than twice the size of the Rajya Sabha. It is possible to contemplate a situation in which the decision of the Lok Sabha may be out-voted in a joint sitting of the two Houses.

Constitutional Amendments

With regard to the amendment of the Constitution, both the Rajya Sabha and Lok Sabha have been placed at par. Though it is true that most of the Bills to amend the Constitution had been introduced in the Lok Sabha, both Houses have got equal powers with regard to the amending process, and in order to amend the Constitution, both the Houses of Parliament must pass a Bill.

Control Over the Executive

The executive is responsible to the Lok Sabha alone. A vote of no confidence against the government, if passed by the Rajya Sabha would be a mere expression of opinion. The Lok Sabha alone can pass a vote of censure and no confidence against the cabinet. The Rajya Sabha can simply discuss the government policy and exercise some influence through questions, adjournment motions and critical speeches.

Electoral Powers

The electoral powers of the Rajya Sabha are the same as the Lok Sabha for the election of President. Its elected members along with the elected members of the Lok Sabha participate in the election of the President. Even the Vice President is elected by the members of an electoral college consisting of the members of both the Houses of Parliament. Rajya Sabha members also elect one of its members as Deputy Chairman.

Impeachment of the President

The Rajya Sabha along with the Lok Sabha also plays an important role in the impeachment of the President. According to Article 61 of the Constitution, the resolution for the removal of the President must be passed by each House by a majority of not less than two thirds of the total membership of each House separately, which means that the President cannot be impeached without the concurrence of the Rajya Sabha.

Approval of Emergency Proclamation

The power of the Rajya Sabha is equal to that of the Lok Sabha so far as the approval of the emergency proclamations under Article 352, 356, and 360 is concerned. .

The Constitution has assigned some special powers to the Rajya Sabha in this context. It is provided that if a proclamation of emergency is issued, when the Lok Sabha remains dissolved or its dissolution takes place during the period of one month there from and a resolution approving the proclamation is passed by the Rajya Sabha, the proclamation would be legally effective up to a maximum of thirty days from the date on which the Lok Sabha sits after the reconstitution. The Constitution by this provision assigns a special role to the Rajya Sabha when the Lok Sabha stands dissolved.

Special Powers

There are two other provisions which confer upon the Rajya Sabha, a status of the sole representative of the states. Under Article 249, the Rajya Sabha may by a resolution supported by not less than two-thirds of the members present and voting declare that it is necessary or expedient in the national interest that Parliament should make law with respect to any matter enumerated in the state list specified in the resolution. After such a declaration, it is lawful for the Parliament to make laws for the whole or any part of the territory of India with respect to that matter while the resolution remains in force. Such a resolution will remain in force for a period not exceeding one year, as may be specified therein, but its period can be extended by one year at a time by passing a further resolution. This Constitutional provision specifically recognizes the Rajya Sabha as the representative of the states, and on the authority of the Rajya Sabha. In that capacity, the Parliament becomes competent to legislate on a subject exclusively reserved for the state legislatures.

The second exclusive power of the Rajya Sabha is connected with the setting up of All India Services. All India Services is common to the Union and the states.

As such the setting up of such a service affects the powers of the states. Hence, the council is given the power to decide, by a resolution supported by a two-thirds majority, the question of setting up of an All India Service. Hence, any laws connected with such a service can be initiated only if the Rajya Sabha passes such a resolution.

In both these cases, the Lok Sabha comes into the picture only after the Rajya Sabha has acted and the Lok Sabha does not share the power of the Rajya Sabha in deciding as to what action is necessary under both the contingencies mentioned above.

Our Parliament is a law making body like the legislature of other countries including Britain. The written provisions of the Constitution have circumscribed the powers of the Parliament by the norms of a federal polity and by the provisions of judicial review. Parliament occupies a pre-eminent and central position in Indian polity. It embodies and epitomizes the sovereign will of the people. It is the mirror and voice of the nation.

To quote Jawaharlal Nehru, who said; "Parliament today has become the supreme temple of democracy and freedom, an institution of great importance in our national life, the only guarantee against tyranny and bad administration. It should, therefore, be treated with reverence and deference".

SUMMARY

- Indian Constitution adopted the Parliamentary system of Government. This Parliamentary system of Government leads to harmonious blending of the legislative and executive organs of the State. The election to the Lok Sabha is conducted on the basis of adult franchise. The members of the Rajya Sabha are indirectly elected on a proportional representation basis by the state legislatures.
- The Parliament has right to make and unmake any law as and when required, that is required to satisfy the needs of the people. Such law is considered to be the highest law of the country within the jurisdiction of the Constitution.
- Parliament functions as a sovereign body of the state. It appoints several committees to look in to the various issues that arise in the country and to check the administrative policies of the government departments.
- Speaker is the leader of the House. He is the channel through which all communication between the House and the president must pass. He controls the House by exercising his powers. He is the only authority to decide who shall hold the floor and speak.
- Joint session is a feature of Parliamentary procedure. Speaker takes the advantage of arranging joint sessions whenever there is a deadlock between the two Houses in case of passing the bill.

- Lok Sabha is considered to represent the popular will, whereas Rajya Sabha is supposed to be federal chamber. The relation between these two houses depends upon constitutional provisions and the political context of the country.

QUESTIONS

1. Compare the power and functions of Lok Sabha and Rajya Sabha.
2. Discuss the process of legislation in India Parliament.
3. Do you agree with the 'decline of parliament' arguments? Give reasons.
4. Write a critical essay on the speaker of the Lok Sabha.
5. What are the powers and functions of Indian Parliament? What is its significance in Indian Political system?

6

Judiciary

After reading this chapter, you will be conversant with:

- Organization of Judiciary
- Supreme Court - Composition, Powers and Functions
- High Court - Composition, Powers and Functions
- Subordinate Courts
- Independence of Judiciary
- Judicial Review
- Public Interest Litigation (PIL)
- Judicial Activism
- Judicial Accountability
- Judicial Reforms

INTRODUCTION

One of the unique features of the Indian Constitution is a single integrated system of Courts to administer both Central and State laws—civil and criminal. The Constitution of India, Part-V provides for a union judiciary. India is said to have one of the most powerful and independent judiciaries in the world. Unlike many countries with federal Constitution, India has a single, integrated, and hierarchical judicial system. The Supreme Court is at the apex of this judicial hierarchy. Then comes the High Courts with similar powers and the subordinate courts at the bottom of judicial pyramid.

Origin

Indian Judiciary owes its origin to the judicial system exiting in the British India. There were three High Courts of the Judicature established in 1861 at Calcutta, Bombay and Madras under which there existed a large number of subordinate courts. Then in 1937, the Federal Court came into existence under the Government of India Act of

1935 enacted by the British Parliament. The origin of the Supreme Court of India can be traced back to the Federal Court, though it was not the ultimate judicial authority in British India as appeals could go to Judicial Committee of the Privy Council in London.

ORGANIZATION OF JUDICIARY

- The Supreme Court of India.
- High Courts in each state or group of states.
- Hierarchy of Subordinate Courts.
- Panchayat courts also function in some states under various names like Nyaya Panchayat, Panchayat Adalat, and Gram Kachehari to decide civil and criminal disputes of petty and local nature.
- State laws provide for different kinds of jurisdiction of courts. Each state is divided into judicial districts presided over by a District and Sessions Judge, which is the principal civil court of original jurisdiction and can try all offences including those punishable with death. The Sessions Judge is the highest judicial authority in a district. Further below are courts of civil jurisdiction, known in different states as Munsifs, Sub-Judges or Civil Judges.
- Similarly, the criminal judiciary comprises of the Chief Judicial Magistrates and Judicial Magistrates of First and Second Class.

One of the unique features of the Indian Constitution is that despite adopting a federal system, it has provided for a single integrated system of courts to administer both Union and State laws.

SUPREME COURT

Composition

The Supreme Court in India is the final interpreter of the Constitution and the laws of the land. It has appellate jurisdiction over all civil and criminal proceedings involving issues concerning the interpretation of the Constitution. The court has the original and exclusive jurisdiction to resolve disputes between the central government and one or more states and union territories, as well as between different states and union territories. The Supreme Court also has the right to issue advisory rulings on issues referred to it by the President. The Supreme Court has wide discretionary powers to hear special appeals or any matter from any court except those of the armed services. It also functions as a court of record and supervises the functioning of every High Court. As regards the strength of the Supreme Court judges, it has been raised from time to time.

Appointment

The Constitution provides that a judge of the Supreme Court will be appointed by the President in consultation with other judges of the Supreme Court and of the High Courts in the state, as the President may deem necessary. In case of appointment of a judge other than the Chief Justice, the Home Ministry recommends the Chief Justice of India as well as other judges of the Supreme Court.

Qualifications

A person to be appointed as a the judge of the Supreme Court must be:

- A citizen of India.
- Has been serving as a judge for five years in a High Court or two or more such courts in succession.
- Should be an advocate of a High Court or *of* two or more such courts in succession for at least ten years.
- Is a distinguished jurist in the opinion of the President.

TENURE

No minimum age is prescribed for appointment as a judge of the Supreme Court. Once appointed, a judge of the Supreme Court under following conditions may cease to be so, if:

- He has attained the age of sixty five years.
- He resigns his office by giving his resignation to the President.
- If he has been removed by the President upon an address to that effect being passed by a special majority of each House of Parliament.

PROHIBITION OF PRACTICE AFTER RETIREMENT

No person who has held office as a judge of the Supreme Court can plead or act in any court or before any authority within the territory of India. But, there is no constitutional prohibition against a retired judge being appointed for a specialized form of work by the government.

REMOVAL

The constitution ensures the independence of Supreme Court judges in various ways. It has laid down the procedures for the removal of a judge of the Supreme Court. A judge of the Supreme Court is removed from his position/office only on the ground of proved misbehaviour or incapacity. He can be removed from his office by an order of the President passed after an address from each House (Lok Sabha and Rajya Sabha) of the Parliament, supported by a majority of the total membership of that House and by a majority of not less than two by three of the members present and voting.

POWERS AND FUNCTIONS OF THE SUPREME COURT

The Supreme Court of India is an extremely powerful body equipped with wider powers. As regards the powers and functions, the Supreme Court has original jurisdiction, appellate jurisdiction and the advisory jurisdiction.

Original Jurisdiction

Under Article 131, its original jurisdiction covers all disputes:

- Between the government of India and one or more states.
- Between the Government of India and any state or states on one side and one or more other states on the other.
- Between two or more states, if the dispute involves any question on which the existence or extent of a legal right depends. However, disputes arising out of the provisions of the treaties with the former Indian states or to which any such state is a party, are excluded from the original jurisdiction of the Supreme Court.

Appellate Jurisdiction

The Supreme Court is the highest court of appeal in India. The appellate jurisdiction of the Supreme Court has been divided into three heads:

- **Constitutional:** With regard to the constitutional cases, an appeal lies to the Supreme Court from the High Court, and if the High court certifies that the case involves a substantial question of law so as to the interpretation of the Constitution.
- **Civil:** With regard to the appeals in the civil cases, an appeal lies to the Supreme Court from any judgment or order in civil proceedings of a High Court, if the High Court certifies that the case involves a substantial question of law of general importance and the question needs to be decided by the Supreme Court.
- **Criminal:** An appeal shall lie to the Supreme Court from any judgment, order or sentence in a criminal proceeding of a High Court, if the High Court, on appeal, has reversed an order of acquittal of any accused person and sentenced him to death or in case it has withdrawn for trial before itself any case from any

court which is subordinate to it and has sentenced the accused to death or has certified that the case is fit for an appeal to Supreme Court.

Article 134 of the constitution for the first time provided for an appeal to the Supreme Court from any judgment, final order or sentence in a criminal proceeding of a High Court in two specified cases:

- Where the High court has, on an appeal reversed an order of acquittal of an accused person and sentenced him to death.
- Where the High Court has withdrawn for trial before itself any case from any court subordinate to its authority, and has in such trial connected the accused, and sentenced him to death. In these two classes of cases relating to a sentence of death by the High Court, appeal lies to the Supreme Court.
- Besides the above two cases, an appeal may lie to the Supreme Court in any criminal case, if the High Court certifies that the case is fit for an appeal to the Supreme Court.

Appeal by Special Leave

The constitution provides for regular appeals to the Supreme Court from decisions of the High Courts in Article 132 to 134, but there may still remain some cases where justice might require the interference of the Supreme Court with decisions not only of the High Courts, outside the purview of the article 132-134 but also of any other court or tribunal within the territory of India. Article 133 confers upon such residuary power outside the ordinary law relating to appeal to the Supreme Court by Article 136. According to this article, "the Supreme Court may, in its discretion, grant a special appeal from any judgment, decree, determination, sentence or order in any cause or matter passed or made by any court or tribunal in the territory of India".

The court has used this special appellate power to review the decisions of Election, Labour and Industrial Tribunals.

Advisory Jurisdiction

The Advisory jurisdiction of the Supreme Court is provided in Article 143 of the constitution. According to this jurisdiction, if at any time, the President feels that a question of law has emerged or is likely to emerge which is of some public importance, that it is useful to obtain the opinion of the Supreme Court, he may seek the advice of the Supreme Court. Up to 1981, there were seven cases of reference of this class made by the President. The most important among these were: the Kerala Education Bill; the Indo-Pak agreement on the Bera-Bari; Delhi Laws Act, 1912; and the President's Election 1974.

Court of Record

The Supreme Court shall be a Court of Record whose judicial proceedings are stored as records for future purposes involving cases and shall have all the powers of such a court including the power to punish for contempt of itself.

Writ Jurisdiction

The Supreme Court safeguards the liberties and Fundamental Rights of the Citizens of India. The court can declare a law, passed by any legislature, null and void if it encroaches upon the Fundamental Rights guaranteed to the people by the Constitution. The Supreme Court can issue writs in the form of Habeas Corpus for enforcement of Fundamental Rights.

Guardian of the Constitution

The Supreme Court of India has been vested with power to review laws passed by the legislature as in case of the USA. It declares them *ultra vires* or unconstitutional, if they disregard any provision of the Constitution. It is for the Supreme Court to interpret the provisions of the Constitution. In other words, the Supreme Court is the custodian of the Constitution.

THE SUPREME COURT'S PROCEDURE

In the matter of procedures, the Supreme Court has powers to make rules. A bench of not less than five judges decides cases involving interpretation of the Constitution and single judges may hear other cases. All judgments are made by a majority vote and differing judges can give dissenting opinions.

The law declared by the Supreme Court is binding upon all the other courts in India, and the decrees and orders of the court are enforceable throughout the country.

Appointments of officers and servants of the Supreme Court are made by the Chief Justice of India or such other judge or officer of the court as he may direct. The condition of service of officers and servants of the Supreme Court is prescribed by rules made by the Chief Justice, as per the President's approval.

The administrative expenses of the Supreme Court, including all salaries, allowances and pensions of the officers and servants of the courts are charged upon the Consolidated Fund of India.

HIGH COURTS

The Indian Constitution provides for an integrated judicial system. At the apex is the Supreme Court of India whose decisions are applicable all over the country. Each state has a High Court exercising power within the territorial jurisdiction of the state concerned.

The position of the High Courts under a Federal Constitution, like that of India is to a large extent different from that of the states of America. In the latter, the High Courts in the constituent stages are constituted under the state constitutions. As such, they do not in any way link themselves with the federal judicial system. The method of appointment and conditions of service of the judges of the state courts and their respective jurisdictions vary from state to state. On the contrary, in India there is uniformity in all these matters and the Constitution lays down detailed provisions for dealing with them. Neither the state executive nor the State Legislature has any power to control the High court or for that matter to alter the constitution or organization of the High Court.

Composition of the High Courts

High courts comprise of a chief justice and such other judges as determined by the President of India from time to time. The number of the judges of the State High Courts has not been fixed by the Constitution, hence it varies from court to court.

Appointments

The President has the power to make appointments of the judges of the High Court. The President consults the Chief Justice of India, the Governor of the State and the Chief Justice of the High Court concerned in appointing the judges of High Court. In case of the appointment of the Chief Justice of High Court, the President consults the Chief Justice of India and the Governor of the State concerned.

Qualifications of the Judges

A person to be appointed as a judge of the High court must have the following qualifications:

- He must be a citizen of India, and has held a judicial office in the territory of India for at least ten years.
- Has for at least ten years been an advocate of a High Court in any state.

TENURE AND REMOVAL

A judge shall hold office till he attains the age of sixty-two years. In other words, a High Court Judge retires at the age of sixty-two. He may resign his office by writing to the President. He can be removed from the office by the President in the manner provided for the removal of a judge of the Supreme Court. A judge can be removed from the office before the expiry of his term on the grounds of proved misbehaviour or incapacity. However, the President can take such an action only if both the Houses of Parliament pass a resolution by a two-thirds majority of the members present in each House which should also be the total majority of the total membership of the house on levelling charges of proved misbehaviour or incapacity. A person who has held office as a permanent judge of the High Court shall not plead or act in any authority in India except the Supreme Court and other High Courts (Article 220).

TRANSFER OF A JUDGE

The President is empowered to transfer a judge from one high court to any other High Court after consultation with the Chief Justice of India. When a judge has been or is to be transferred, he shall, during the period he serves, after the commencement of the Constitution Act of 1963 as a judge of the other High Court, be determined by parliament by law and until so determined some compensatory allowance as the President may by order, fix.

Apart from the monthly salaries, the judge of a High Court is entitled to certain allowances and other rights.

POWERS AND FUNCTIONS OF HIGH COURTS

The jurisdiction of the High Court has not changed ever since the commencement of the Constitution. Hence, the High Courts retain their existing jurisdiction. Their civil and criminal jurisdictions are primarily governed by the two codes of civil and criminal procedure. At present, the High Court of a state enjoys the following powers:

Original Jurisdiction

The High Courts at the three presidency towns of Calcutta, Bombay and Madras had original jurisdiction, both civil and criminal, over cases arising within the respective presidency towns. The original criminal jurisdiction of the High Courts has been completely taken away by the criminal procedure court of 1973. The original jurisdiction of the High Courts is related to the settlement of disputes with regard to the election of the Union and State Legislatures, enforcement of Fundamental Rights, and revenue matters.

Appellate Jurisdiction

The Appellate jurisdiction of the High Court is both civil and criminal. On the civil side, an appeal to the High Court is either a First Appeal or a Second Appeal. Appeals from the decisions of the District Judges and from those of subordinate judges come under this jurisdiction. On the question of fact, as well as law when any court, which is subordinate to the High Court, decides an appeal from the decision of an inferior court, a second appeal lies to the High Court from the decisions of the lower appellate court but only on question of law and procedure.

The criminal appellate jurisdiction of the High Court extends to appeals from the decisions of a sessions judge or an additional sessions judge where the sentence of the imprisonment exceeds seven years, and from the decisions of an assistant sessions judge, metropolitan magistrate or other judicial magistrates in certain specified cases other than petty cases.

Power of Superintendence

According to Article 277, every High Court has the power of superintendence over all courts and tribunals, except the armed forces/military. This power includes the jurisdiction to intervene in cases of injustice or non-exercise or abuse of jurisdiction.

The Supreme Court stated that all types of tribunals including the election tribunals operating within a state are subject to the superintendence of the High Courts.

Control Over Subordinate Courts

The High Court, being the head of judiciary in the state, has got an administrative control over the subordinate judiciary in the state in certain matters. Article 288 empowers the High Courts to transfer constitutional cases from lower courts. Thus, if the court is satisfied that a case pending in one of its subordinate courts involves a substantial question of law, as to the interpretation of the Constitution, the determination of which is necessary for the disposal of the case, it shall then withdraw the case and may either dispose of the case or send the case back to the court from where it was withdrawn.

The Writ Jurisdiction of the High Court

The High Courts are conferred with the power of issuing writs. Every High Court has the right to exercise jurisdiction to issue to any person or authority, including the government in those territories, orders or writs including writs, such as Habeas corpus, Mandamus, Prohibition, Quo warranto and Certiorari. Comparatively, the High Courts enjoy more powers than the Supreme Court when it comes to issuing the writs, as Supreme Court can issue writs only when Fundamental Rights are encroached. Thus, according to Article 32[2] of the Constitution, both Supreme Court and the High Courts have concurrent powers to issue such orders.

Power of Appointment

According to article 229, the Chief Justice of the High Court is empowered to appoint officers of the court. The governor may consult Public Commission of the state in this regard. He also consults the High Court in the appointment, posting and promotion of district judges and along with the state Public Service Commission in appointing persons to the judicial service of the state. The Chief Justice regulates the conditions of the service of the staff subject to any law made by the State Legislature in this respect. The Chief Justice also enjoys the power to dismiss any such member from the service of the court. The powers of posting and promoting and grant of leave to persons belonging to the judicial service is also vested in the High Court.

As per the Constitution, all the administrative expenses of the High Court are charged on the Consolidated Fund of the state.

Position of High Courts

High courts of India have complete freedom and independence in imparting justice to the people and ensure that executive and legislature shall, in no way, interfere in the day-to-day life of the citizens. As a court of record, the High court has the power to punish those who are found guilty of contempt of court.

SUBORDINATE COURTS

Under the High courts, there is a hierarchy of courts which is referred to in the Constitution as Subordinate Courts. They have come into existence because of the state enactments. The nomenclature and designation of these subordinate courts differs from state to state, but there is uniformity in terms of organizational structure.

The state is divided into districts and each district has a district court which has an appellate jurisdiction in that district. The principle function of a district court is to hear appeals from the subordinate courts. The court of the Sessions Judge is the highest court for criminal cases in a district. Below this court, there is Metropolition Magistrate. There are three kinds of Magistrates: First, Second and Third class magistrates. A First class magistrate can award punishment up to three years of imprisonment and a fine up to five thousand rupees or both. A Second class magistrate can award imprisonment up to one year and fine up to one thousand rupees or both; and a Third class magistrate can give imprisonment up to one month and impose a fine up to one hundred rupees. All these courts are called Criminal courts. Small cases at the village level fall under the jurisdiction of the *Nyaya Panchayats*.

Criminal cases, like murder, are sent to the court of the Session Judge which can award even death sentence. But, no person is actually hanged to death till the death sentence is confirmed by the High Court of the state concerned.

Revenue Courts deal with the cases of land revenue in the district. The highest revenue court in the district is the Board of Revenue and all the Courts of Commissioner, Collector, Tehsildar and Assistant Tehsildar come under it. The Board of Revenue hears the final appeals against all the lower revenue courts under it.

Independence of the Subordinate Judiciary

The Constitution ensures independence of subordinate judiciary. The Governor in consultation with the High Court makes appointments, postings and promotions of district judges in a state.

Panchayat Courts

The Panchayat courts (Nyaya Panchayat, Gram Panchayat) are at the bottom of the hierarchy of the subordinate courts. However, under the purview of the criminal courts jurisdiction these are not considered as courts. During the pre-British days, Nyaya courts provided a viable and strong base for dispensing indigenous system of justice.

INDEPENDENCE OF JUDICIARY

The judiciary occupies a unique position in a democratic society. It decides disputes that cannot or should not be left to the political branches or private individuals. It upholds the law for all, and in doing so, it also safeguards the rights of individuals and minority groups of all types against the excesses of majoritarianism. This sometimes requires judges to confront the interests of the political branches or powerful individuals, but as the judges are not democratically elected, they must derive their authority and legitimacy from different sources. One of the most important sources of legitimacy and authority of the judges is their independence.

Meaningful independence (and public perception of that independence) is essential to the judiciary's legitimacy as a guarantor of rights and freedom. If the judiciary is not independent of the executive and legislature, it will not have a proper control over those branches. If courts are not seen as independent (and impartial), citizens will not turn to them to resolve their problems, but may seek recourse through political or extra legal means. The legislature and the executive themselves have a direct interest in judicial independence; they often need the judiciary to resolve problems which do not have easy political solutions, but the judiciary can do this only if all parties see it as a neutral arbiter, independent of the branches and parties which have turned to it in the first place.

The importance of judicial independence is essential. Economists have noted the importance of an independent and impartial judiciary to a stable and prosperous economy. Individuals and institutions must be able to rely on justice - free of the vagaries of political interference or economic influence by either party - in the adjudication of their claims. In societies struggling to reform their economies, judicial independence contributes to the confidence, security and predictability of economic transactions.

Independence serves important social needs; it is not an end in itself but rather a means to achieve the goals of a just and prosperous society. For this reason, independence needs to be complemented with means to ensure that judges and the judiciary as a whole comport with society's democratic principles and legitimate interests, even as they are independent. In other words, judges need to be accountable to society.

Independence of judiciary is of great importance in a democratic political system. It implies three conditions as:

- The judiciary must be free from the encroachments of other departments of the government.

- The judgments and decrees of the judiciary must be free from the onslaughts of executive and legislative interference.
- The judges must be free to do justice without fear or any favour.

In this context following provisions are important:

- In simple words, the independence of judiciary requires that the judges must be independent in their allotted sphere and give judgment over the cases referred to them without falling prey to the charms of material temptations or physical fears. In a representative form of government, it is required that the judges remain aloof from the influence of party politics that has its full and unrestricted influence in the spheres of executive and legislative departments.
- A study of the provisions of the Indian Constitution shows that adequate arrangements have been made to maintain the independence of judiciary. For instance, the President can appoint only such a person as a judge of the Supreme Court or of a High Court who is well versed in the sphere of law. Once appointed, the tenure of the judge is fixed until he/she completes the age of retirement, i.e. sixty five years. He cannot be removed unless each House of Parliament passes a special resolution.
- The salary and allowances of the judges are charged on the consolidated fund and they are not subjected to the vote of the legislatures.
- It is provided that the actions and decisions of the judges in their official capacity are immune from criticism in the sense that no motives can be imputed to them. Even, the Parliament cannot discuss the conduct of a judge unless a substantive motion of impeachment is moved in the House.
- It is also provided that a judge of a High Court, after his retirement cannot plead in a court other than a High Court or a Supreme Court and that a judge after retirement from the Supreme Court cannot work as a private practitioner of law in any court of the country.

The above discussion evidently points out the independence of judiciary

JUDICIAL REVIEW

The power of judiciary to review and determine validity of a law or an order may be described as the power of Judicial Review. It means that the Constitution is the supreme law of the land and any law which is against the provisions of the Constitution is void. The term Judicial review refers to "the power of a court to inquire whether a law, executive order or other official action conflicts with the written Constitution, and if the court concludes that it does, to declare it unconstitutional and void". In other words, judicial review is "the power exerted by the courts of a country to examine the actions of the legislative, executive and administrative arms of government and to ensure that such actions conform to the provisions of the Constitution of the country".

Judicial review has two prime functions;

- To legitimize government action.
- To protect the Constitution against any undue encroachment by the government.

As guardian of the Constitution, the Supreme Court has to review the laws and executive orders to ensure that they do not violate the constitution of the country and the laws passed by the Parliament. We borrowed the feature of Judicial review from the constitution of the U.S.A. Judicial review was practiced by the court in the United States, early in the 19th century and has since then been adopted by several countries.

The power of judicial review is pronounced by certain principles. The following is the description of each principle:

- **Principle of Severability:** While interpreting the impugned law, the court sees, if some parts of the law are constitutional or the entire law itself. If the entire law is defective, then is it declared *ultra vires;* it can declare so even in the case of a part of the law and allow the rest as operative. The court will decide such a matter on the construction of the provisions of the law in question.
- **Principle of Progressive Interpretation:** The provisions of the Constitution, if understood in the light of the changing times and changing socio-economic conditions of the country or be fixed at the time of framing the Constitution, leads to some amount of confusion. Fortunately, the judiciary in India is provided with the power of progressive interpretation, wherein changes can be incorporated as per the changing times that suit the conditions.
- **Principle of Dynamism:** The courts in India are not bound by the earlier affirmation. They may change their views or precedents from time to time while making a dynamic interpretation of the provisions of the constitution. The Supreme Court reiterated that interpretation of law should be done in a dynamic way, so that it may reconsider its earlier rulings and also depart from them, if necessary.
- **Principle of the Spirit of the Constitution:** It has been clearly mentioned in the Constitution that any law that jeopardizes Fundamental Rights shall be declared void. However, Fundamental Rights are not absolute and are subject to certain restrictions, in the interests of morality, order, public health, and national security, etc., and it is the function of the courts to examine whether the restrictions imposed by the law are in consistence with the tenor of the provisions of part III or not. It is in the light of this special arrangement that Supreme Court has invalidated several important laws made by the union as well as the state government.
- **Principle of Empirical Adjudication**: Courts, while exercising the power of judicial review, do not entertain hypothetical cases. It is essential that a matter brought before the court must be specific and not ambiguous. Moreover, the court must confine itself in giving a practical decision within narrow limits of the controversy between the concerned parties in a particular case.

- **Principle of Indirect Judicial Review:** Sometimes, it so happens, that an impugned law can be understood in both positive and negative aspects or that it has two interpretations. At this juncture, the court will consider the positive aspect of the law and tries to interpret it.

Judicial Review in India

The Constitution of India is more similar to the U.S. Constitution than the British as regards judicial review. There is division of powers between the union and the states. Parliament is competent to pass the laws only with respect to those subjects, which are guaranteed to the citizens against every form of legislative encroachment. Being the guardian of the Fundamental Rights, the Supreme Court stands in a unique position, where from, it is competent to exercise the power of reviewing legislative enactments, both of Parliament and the State Legislatures. This is what makes the court a powerful instrument of judicial review under the Constitution. In India, it is the Constitution that is supreme law of the land and that a statute law to be valid must be in conformity with the constitutional requirements. It is for the judiciary to decide whether any enactment is constitutional or not, and if a legislature transgresses any constitutional limits, the court has to declare the law unconstitutional, for the court is bound by its oath to uphold the Constitution. Therefore, the courts in India cannot be accused of usurping the function of Constitutional adjudication. It is a function which has been imposed on them by the Constitution.

The constitutional validity of a law can be challenged in India on the ground that the subject matter of the legislation,

- Is not within the competence of the legislature which has passed it.
- Is repugnant to the provisions of the constitution.
- It infringes upon the fundamental rights.

Although, it is said that the Indian Constitution does not afford the same scope of judicial creativity to the courts as does the U.S. Constitution. In spite of all this, the Supreme Court does play a significant role in the constitutional process. The Supreme Court rendered hundreds of decisions expounding various provisions of the Constitutions and thus a distinct Constitutional Jurisprudence has come into existence. In many cases, the Supreme Court displayed judicial creativity of a higher order. The high water mark of such judicial creativity has reached in such landmark cases as Golak Nath, Kesavananda Bhatari and Menka Gandhi.

PUBLIC INTEREST LITIGATION (PIL)

In Black's Law dictionary states that, "Public Interest Litigation means a legal action initiated in a court of law for the enforcement of public interest or general interest in which the public or class of the community have pecuniary interest or some interest by which their legal rights or liabilities are affected".

In simple words, public interest litigation may be defined as a litigation undertaken for the purpose of redressing public injury, enforcing public duty, protecting social, collective and diffused rights and interests or vindicating public interest.

Public Interest Litigation's purpose is to alienate the suffering of all those who have been subjected to insensitive treatment. The increase in violation of legal rights can be checked by transparency in public life and fair judicial action. Traditional rule was that the rights to move the Supreme Court is only available to those whose Fundamental Rights are encroached.

The High Courts started following the practice in their jurisdiction under Article 226 and the Supreme Court approved this practice, observing that where public interest is undermined by an arbitrary and perverse executive action, it would be the duty of the High Court to issue a writ.

In the beginning, it was confined to a few cases like those of combating inhuman conditions inside the jails or horrible exploitation of the bonded labour. But now, its scope has become wider so as to include any situation calling for speedy trial, the right to legal aid, the right to livelihood, right to protection of life from pollution of air and water or any environmental hazards, and right to lead a life of dignity or fulfillment of basic needs. Willingness has been shown by the judiciary in altering the rules of procedure whenever necessary, so much so that now actions may be commenced not only by way of a formal petition but also by way of letters addressed to the court or to a judge who may choose to treat it as a writ petition.

- Supreme Court has now realized its proper role in a welfare state and it is using its new strategy for the development of a whole new corpus of law for effective and purposeful implementation of Public Interest Litigation. An individual can simply approach the court for the enforcement of Fundamental Rights by writing a letter or post card to any judge. That particular letter, based on true facts and concept will be converted to writ petition. When court welcomes Public Interest Litigation, its attempt is to endure observance of social and economic programmes framed for the benefits of have-nots and the handicapped. Public Interest Litigation has proved a boon for the common individual. Public Interest Litigation has set right a number of wrongs committed by an individual or by society. By relaxing the scope of Public Interest Litigation, Court has brought legal aid to the doorsteps of the teeming millions of Indians which the executive has not been able to do despite a lot of money being spent on new legal aid schemes operating at the central and state level. Supreme Court's pivotal role in expanding the scope of Public Interest Litigation as a counter balance to the lethargy and inefficiency of the executive is commendable.

In the words of former Chief Justice P. N. Bhagwati, "Public interest litigation is essentially a co-operative or collaborative effort on the part of the petitioner, the state or public authority and the courts to secure observance of the constitutional or legal rights, benefits and privileges conferred upon the vulnerable sections of the community and to reach social justice to them".

When can a Public Interest Litigation be Filed

Public interest litigation can be filed in a case where public interest at large is affected. Some of the possible areas where public interest litigation can be filed are:

- Air pollution caused by a factory/industry by which people are getting affected.
- Inconvenience caused to commuters in an area where there are no streetlights.
- Where noise pollution is caused due to playing of loud music.
- Where construction companies cause environmental pollution due to the cutting down of trees.
- Where poor people are affected due to imposition of heavy tax by the state government.
- For directing the police and jail authorities to take decisions in regard to jail reforms, such as segregation of convicts, delay in trial, and production of undertrial before the court.
- For abolition of child and bonded labour.
- To safeguard the rights of working women and curb sexual harassment.
- For keeping a watch on corruption and crime by political officers.
- For maintaining roads, sewer, etc. in good conditions.
- To avoid traffic problems by removal of big hoarding and signboard from the busy roads.

WHO CAN FILE A PUBLIC INTEREST LITIGATION

Earlier, a person, whose interest or fundamental right was directly affected filed a public interest litigation but now on behalf of a group of persons, whose rights are affected, any public spirited person can file a case (Public Interest Litigation). It is not necessary that a person who is filing a case should have a direct interest in this Public Interest Litigation.

AGAINST WHOM A PUBLIC INTEREST LITIGATION CAN BE FILED

Public Interest Litigation can be filed only against a state/central government, Municipal Authorities and not any private party. Private party can be included in the Public Interest Litigation as 'respondent' after making concerned state authority a party.

JUDICIAL ACTIVISM

During the last few years, Judicial Activism has brought about a new facet for the judicial process and has given a new hope to the millions. There is no reason why the court should not adopt activist approach similar to court in America, so as to provide remedial amplitude to the citizens of India.

"Judicial Activism in India is an examination of judicial reviews. It traces the evolution of the Supreme Court of India from a passive, positivist court into an activist one, articulating counter-majoritarian checks on democracy."

Judicial activism has not been a spontaneous development. It is the result of a situation which necessitated it. In 1985, the then Chief Justice of India, Justice P. N. Bhagavati converted a letter written to him on a post card by an aggrieved citizen into public interest litigation. That was the beginning of judicial activism. The court's role in sensitizing the central intelligence agencies to discharge their constitutional obligations in the 'Hawala case' in which top leaders both in the Government and in the opposition were involved was pivotal. Its various judgments have attached both praise and criticism ranging from the need to have a uniform Civil Code, pollution control, preservation of historical monuments, cleaning and keeping the metropolis more hygienic, directing the eviction of unauthorized occupation of government buildings, trial of rape victims and award of compensation to them, punishing senior civil servants for contempt and many others. Following the examples set by the Supreme Court, the High Courts also followed the suit. Some welcomed the infusion of new blood in judicial activity hailing it as a check on the misuse of power by the executive, others expressed apprehension about the executive and activist role of the judiciary.

JUDICIAL ACCOUNTABILITY

Whether judges are appointed or elected, it is their performance on the bench and their accountability for improper activities that is crucial. While there is a great debate as regards their performance, the public dissatisfaction with the so-called independence of the judiciary and with the inadequacy of the judicial disciplinary machinery is disregarded by the Bench and Bar.

The judges and lawyers maintain their stronghold on the legal system on the myth that they are the guardians of the constitutional rights of the people and that the lawyers champion these rights in a court of law that is just and fair. However, the legal profession has become big business where justice is not the objective. Although judges and lawyers hypothetically take an oath to uphold the laws and the constitution of the land, in many cases that oath might have been taken to prepare litigation to use the legal system for an assembly line conversion of the victim's assets into fees or to confiscate it outright.

Even if, there are some judges and lawyers dedicated to the proper administration of justice, unfortunately there are many who are not. Lawyers can litigate frivolous, false claims or defenses endlessly and can drag on a simple case for years together. To stop the litigation, the attorneys can demand payment, a so-called settlement that in many cases is nothing more than a form of extortion. These practices not only harm the individual litigants but also, are a waste of the taxpayers' money and block the court system.

Many judges acting in conjunction with attorneys abuse the judicial independence given to them in trust and confidence of the people. The myth is dispelled when we are confronted by judges who disregard the rules; allow the distortion of facts sometimes to the point of false swearing; exclude evidence; rely on laws which have no relevance to the legal and factual issues; issue decisions which fabricate facts and are contrary to the record; deliberately omit critical facts from the record; fail to follow the controlling law and precedent or issue decisions without any stated facts or law; and approve unreasonable fees for attorneys. It is not unusual that property and money are taken from the victims without the required due process and the victims are left with nothing.

Government accountability is critical for the rule of law. The judiciary has traditionally been the primary accountability mechanism through its legal review of government actions. Accountability, or the means of holding government entities answerable for possible misuses, abuses and misapplications of power, is increasingly important. Limited enforcement powers, a necessary selectivity in cases received and an ultimate recourse by the government to change laws or amend constitutions may undercut the courts' role. Additional mechanisms to hold governments accountable include an expanded use of quasi-judicial bodies to review administrative cases.

Maintaining an appropriate balance between judicial accountability and independence is vital to ensure that the judiciary maintains its role to hold governments accountable. Judicial accountability also includes external pressure and controls to ensure that internal institutional control mechanisms are in place. Civil society is playing an integral role by monitoring judicial performance. In addition, Bar associations, as well as, the media, anti-corruption agencies, think tanks, universities and civil society organizations can be effective resources to avoid corruption.

JUDICIAL REFORM

There is an extreme need for urgent and comprehensive reforms in our judiciary. By consistently enforcing clear rules, an independent and impartial judicial system supports legal reform and promotes economic and social development. An effective judiciary applies and enforces laws and regulations impartially, predictably and efficiently. Economic growth and social development cannot be sustained and promoted in countries where the justice system fails.

The government is assisted to develop and implement judicial reform programs to achieve sustainable economic growth and social development based on empowerment, opportunity, and security for all citizens. For about two decades after independence, most people reposed their faith in the political class to govern wisely and to ensure freedom and justice to all. Over the next two decades, as the politicians have become the objects of scorn and ridicule, the public relied heavily upon the civil services for ensuring probity, efficiency and impartiality in administration. As the bureaucracy has also lost the trust of the general public in a large, in recent years the people have come to recognize the judiciary as the last bulwark against the abuse of executive authority and for providing justice. However, the judiciary is collapsing under the weight of the caseload and speedy justice. Also, there are serious questions about the efficacy, impartiality and integrity of judiciary at certain levels. There is an increasing unease and disquiet about the functioning of the judiciary and the character, competence and commitment to public service of several judges, particularly in the subordinate judiciary.

There is an increase in litigants because of faulty legislations. Cumbersome procedures and forbidding cost of justice is another weakness of the judicial system.

If these challenges are not taken notice of immediately and if far reaching judicial reforms are not initiated with a great sense of urgency and devotion, the judiciary may also fall in public esteem endangering the whole civil society and adversely affecting the public welfare. The judiciary should recognize that it is an organ of state with the sole objective of serving the public in a fair, efficient and accountable manner. Its loyalty should only be for public welfare and not to the convenience of advocates or politicians or bureaucrats. Concerted efforts should be made to make judiciary efficient and effective without usurping the functions of the organs of the state.

The Tenth Law Commission had invited suggestions to create a constitutional court which will replace the Supreme Court. The idea of having such a court was to deal exclusively with constitutional matters. Legal experts also suggested to the law commission the idea of creating zonal courts of appeal in the country. This would help in reducing the workload of the Supreme Court.

SUMMARY

- After having a thorough understanding of judiciary, we come to know that among the noble aims and objectives of the Constitution, the founding fathers accorded the highest place to 'Justice'. The Preamble speaks of "We, the people of India", resolving to secure inter alia "Justice - social, economic and political, to all its citizens'. The juxtaposition of words and concepts in the Preamble is important. Most significantly, 'Justice' is placed higher than the other principles of 'Liberty', 'Equality' and 'Fraternity'. Again, the Preamble clearly enjoins precedence to social and economic justice over political justice. People turn to the judiciary in the quest of justice. There is need to review the working of the judiciary during the last half-a-century and more, to assess how far our justice delivery system has been able to ensure equal economic and political justice to all the people as ordained by the Constitution and its Preamble.
- Indian constitution provides integrated and independent judiciary.

- At the apex, the Supreme Court commands immense power and prestige. Its jurisdiction includes original jurisdiction, appellete jurisdiction and advisory jurisdiction.
- Indian constitution also provides for the High Courts at the state level, which also supervises the subordinate courts at the sub-state level.

QUESTIONS

- Discuss the power of Judicial Review of the Supreme Court of India, citing important cases.
- In the light of Judicial Review, discuss the powers and functions of the Supreme Court of India.
- What is PIL? When can a PIL be filed?
- What are the major issues in judicial reforms? Analyze.
- What do you mean by judicial activism? Do you think that it is affecting judicial accountability?
- Write a short note on the following:

  (a) Subordinate Courts

  (b) Independence of judiciary

  (c) Impeachment

7

State Government

After reading this chapter, you will be conversant with:

- Governor – Appointment, Power and Functions
- Chief Minister - Council of Ministers
- State Legislatures - Composistion, Powers and Functions
- The Advocate-General of the State

As we have pointed out earlier, Indian costitution is federal in nature and provides exclusive jurisdictions for the union and the state governments. The system of government in states is organized on the similar pattern to that of the Central government. Part VI of the Constitution lays down a uniform structure for the state governments and stipulates a parliamentary form of government similar to that of the Centre (except Jammu & Kashmir). In accordance with the parliamentary framework of the Union government, the state governments also have two forms of Executive, the constitutional head and the real executive. The state executive consists of Governor and Council of Ministers with Chief Minister as its head. The Governor, is appointed by the President of India. Though the nominal executive authority is vested in the Governor, the Chief Minister and the Council of Ministers exercise the real executive authority. They are collectively responsible to the State Legislature. The States Legislature consists of Legislative Assembly and Legislative Council, though many states have only one House (unicameral legislature). The State Legislatures make laws for the concerned states on the subjects mentioned in the State List.

OFFICE OF GOVERNOR

Governor is the executive head of the state and all the executive actions of the state are taken in his name. The Governor holds a Constitutional position, much like that of the President of India. Under Article 153 of the Indian Constitution, each state has a Governor. According to the Constitution the same individual can be appointed as the Governor of two or more States.

Appointment & Tenure

The Governor, unlike the President is not elected but is appointed by the President. According to Article 155 of the Constitution, the President of India appoints the Governor for a term of five years. He may be appointed as the Governor for one or more states. Though, the tenure of the Governor is five years, according to Article 156(1) of the Constitution, the Governor holds the office during the pleasure of the President, i.e. he can be recalled or dismissed or transferred to another state before expiry of the term.

Qualifications

According to Articles 157 & 158 the following are the terms and conditions for the appointment of the Governor:

- He should be a citizen of India and have completed thirty-five years of age (Article 157).
- At the time of assuming the office, the Governor should not be a Member of Parliament or State legislatures.
- The Governor should not hold any other office of profit during his tenure.

Emoluments

With regard to the emoluments, allowances and privileges of the Governor, Parliament has the right to make laws. As determined by the Parliament from time to time, Governor is entitled to a free official residence, a regular monthly salary and other emoluments. The Governor gets a monthly salary of Rs. 36,000 (w.e.f. 1 January 1996) plus allowances. His salary and allowances cannot be reduced during his term of office. These are charged on the Consolidated Fund of the state. In case, the same person is appointed as Governor of two or more states, the emoluments and allowances payable to the Governor shall be allocated among the states in such proportion as the President may, by order, determine.

Immunities and Privileges

According to Article 361 of the Constitution, the Governor enjoys the following immunities and privileges: a) The Governor shall not be answerable to any court for the exercise and performance of the powers and duties of his office or any act done or purporting to be done by him in the exercise and performance of the powers and duties; b) No criminal proceedings, whatsoever, shall be instituted or continued against the Governor of State in any court during his term of office; c) No process for the arrest or imprisonment of the Governor of State shall be issued from any court during his term of office; and . d) No civil proceedings, in which relief is claimed against the Governor of a State, shall be instituted during his term of office in any court in respect of any act done or purporting to be done by him in his personal capacity, whether before or after he entered his office as Governor of such State, until the expiration of two months, after notice in writing has been delivered to the Governor.

Powers and Functions of the Governor

The Constitution vests all the executive powers in the Governor. According to Article 163 of the Constitution, the Governor, while discharging his duties is to be guided by the aid and advice of the Council of Ministers. The Governor has executive, legislative, financial and judicial powers.

Executive Powers

Executive power of the State is vested in Governor. The administration of the state is carried in the name of the Governor by the Council of Ministers. Under Article 164, the Governor appoints the leader of the majority party in the Legislative Assembly as the Chief Minister. The Governor, on the advice of the Chief Minister appoints other ministers. He can remove any minister on the Chief Minister's advice. It becomes the duty of the Chief Minister of the state to inform the Governor all the Government decisions pertaining to the administration of the affairs of the state and proposals of the legislation. Further, the Chief Minister must furnish the information relating to administration or proposals for legislation, if the Governor demands. The Governor has the power to appoint the Advocate General of the state, and the Chairman and members of the State Public Service Commission. The Governor is consulted by the President with regard to the appointment of the Judges for the High Court of the State. He nominates one-sixth of the members to the Legislative Council in the state (if such a council exists in that particular State). He can also nominate a representative of the Anglo-Indian community to the Legislative Assembly, if he is satisfied that this community is not sufficiently represented in the House.

Discretionary Powers

The Governor of a State can exercise discretionary powers under certain circumstances. He acts independently without the aid and advice of his Council of Ministers, while exercising such powers. The discretional powers of the Governor are: dismissal of the ministry, imposition of President's rule, and withholding of a bill. The Governor can make recommendations and can send reports to the President periodically with regard to the breakdown of the Constitutional machinery. According to Article 356, the Governor may also recommend to the President for the imposition of President's rule in the state if there is complete breakdown in the Constitutional machinery of the state and the State cannot be carried on in accordance with the Constitutional provisions. The

Governor may also dismiss a state government and dissolve the legislative assembly. During the President's rule, the Governor becomes the actual ruler and he exercises all the powers.

The Governor exercises his discretionary powers if any bill passed by the State Legislature is in question which affects the powers of the union or contravene with the provisions of the Constitution or may not be in the national interest. In such a case, the Governor may differ with the ministry and reserve that particular bill for the consideration of the President. For instance, the then Governor of Kerala differed with the Communist government led by E. M. S. Namboodiripad and withheld the bill for the consideration of the President, as he felt that it affected the rights of the minorities protected by the constitution.

In the dismissal of the Ministry also, the governor can exercise his discretionary powers, if he is convinced that the Ministry is engaged in the activities, which may jeopardize national security or solidarity. Apart from the above mentioned discretionary powers, the Governor can exercise his own judgment while discharging his constitutional functions, such as, decision on a question of disqualification of a legislator [Article 192 (1)] or discharging his statutory non-governmental functions, such as functions entrusted to him as Chancellor of Universities.

Moreover, the Governor also has the right to be kept informed of all the Cabinet decisions. He may also call for any information from the Chief Minister.

Legislative Powers

Apart from the executive powers, the Governor also exercises the following legislative powers. According to Article 168 of the Constitution, the Governor is part of the State legislature. As the administrative head of the State, the Governor has power to summon, prorogue and dissolve the Legislative Assembly of the state (Article 174). He has to summon sessions of the legislature so that a gap of six months does not intervene between its last sitting in one session and the date appointed for its first sitting in the next session.

He addresses the Legislature at the beginning of its first session every year. The Governor promulgates/issues ordinances when the Legislature is not in session (Article 213). The ordinance issued by the Governor has the same force and effect as an act of the State Legislature. But all such ordinances cease to operate after the expiration of six weeks. The Governor can also withdraw the ordinance at any time.

Every bill passed by the State Legislative Assembly cannot become a law until and unless the Governor gives his consent. When the Governor receives a bill passed by the State Legislature, there are four options before the Governor: a. He can send the bills for the consideration of the President; b. Withhold his assent; c. Give his assent to the bill; d. The Governor can return any bill to the Assembly for its reconsideration, except the Money Bills. The Governor of a state may reserve any bill for the consideration of the

President. However, when a bill is returned by him to the Legislature for reconsideration, and if it is again passed by the Legislature in its original or amended form, the Governor is bound to give his assent to it.

Governor also has the power to nominate members of the Anglo-Indian community to the Legislative Assembly. The Governor can also nominate one by six of the total members of the Legislative Council from among persons having specialized knowledge or practical experience in respect of literature, science, art, and social service (If there is a *Vidhan Parishad* /Legislative Council) in a state.

Some of the other legislative powers of the Governor are: he can give decisions on the matters relating to the disqualification of a member of the legislature, if a voter challenges the member's election. Similarly, the annual reports submitted by the State Public Service Commission and Auditor General to him are placed before the Legislature for its consideration.

Financial Powers

All demands for grants are placed before the Assembly on the recommendations of the Governor. The State Finance Minister presents the annual budget showing the estimated receipts and expenditure for the next financial year in the name of the Governor. All bills that the State Legislature passes, must receive the assent of the Governor. The Governor can reserve a non-Money Bill for consideration to the President and has the power to promulgate ordinances. The Governor is not authorized to refuse his assent in case of money and financial bills. The Governor can also make advances from the Contingency Fund of the State to meet the unforeseen expenditure with the approval of the legislature.

Judicial Powers

According to Article 161 of the Constitution, "The Governor of a State can grant pardon and reprieve, and suspend, remit or commute the sentence of any person convicted of any offence against any law relating to a matter to which the executive power of the State extends". But this power has to be exercised by the Governor on the advice of the Council of Ministers. Governor is consulted by the President in the appointment of the judges of the State High Court (Article 217). He appoints and transfers judges of the subordinate courts. He also inspects the working of the courts in the state. He has the power to carry out the administration of Scheduled Areas with Scheduled Tribes therein.

Miscellaneous Powers

Apart from the above mentioned powers, the Governor also performs certain miscellaneous powers. The Governor, after receiving the annual report of the State Public Service Commission passes it to the State Council of Ministers for its comments. Once the comments of the Council of Ministers are available, he passes the same to the Speaker of the Assembly for the purpose of placing it before the House.

COUNCIL OF MINISTERS

Every state has a Council of Ministers, with the Chief Minister as its head, which aids and advises the Governor in the conduct of the affairs of the State(Article 163). The Chief Minister of a state occupies a position equivalent to that of the Prime Minister at the Centre. The Council of Ministers is headed by the Chief Minister. The Governor appoints the leader of the majority party in the State Legislative Assembly as the Chief Minister. On the advice of the Chief Minister, the Governor appoints ministers and allocates the portfolios. The Council of Ministers is collectively responsible to legislative Assembly (Article 164). Even though the Governor is considered as chief executive of the state, in practice, Council of Ministers of the state exercise the real executive powers. The Council of Ministers formulates various policies, initiates legislation and co-ordinates the work of the different agencies of the Government. They implement policies of the Government with the assistance of the bureaucracy. A minister has to be a member of any of the Houses of State Legislature within six months from the date of his appointment otherwise he ceases to be a minister. The salaries and allowances of ministers are such as the State Legislature from time to time prescribes by the law. There are three different categories of ministers in the state. These are: Cabinet Ministers, Ministers of State, and Deputy Ministers.

Collective Responsibility

The Council of Ministers is collectively and individually responsible to Legislative Assembly of the State, i.e. the ministry comes into office and relinquishes it collectively as a team. They are collectively responsible to the assembly for various acts of omission and commission. They remain in office as long as they enjoy the confidence of the House. They can be removed by a vote of no confidence. All the ministers must abide by the cabinet decision and support them in the Legislature as well as outside. In simple terms, the ministry sails or sinks together. Even if a Cabinet Minister wants to oppose any particular decision, he must go by the decision of the Cabinet and support it's decision, otherwise he must quit the ministry.

CHIEF MINISTER

The position of the Chief Minister in the Council of Ministers as the real executive in the state is equivalent to that of the Prime Minister. The Chief Minister is the leader of the majority party in the Legislative Assembly and is the head of the State Council of Ministers. He is the real administrator of the state. He is the chief spokesperson of the government. The Chief Minister remains in office as long as he enjoys the support of the majority members in the Legislative Assembly.

Powers and Functions

Some of the powers and functions of the Chief Minister are as follows:

- The Chief Minister is the real head of the state government. Based on the advice of the Chief Minister, the Governor appoints Cabinet Ministers, Ministers of State, and Deputy Ministers.
- The Chief Minister selects the ministers, and also allocates the portfolios to the Council of Ministers. He can reorganize or reshuffle his ministry as and when he deems necessary.
- He presides over the cabinet meetings and co-ordinates the activities of different departments. He can seek the resignation of any or all the ministers, and in case of defiance by any minister, he can advise the Governor to dismiss the minister.
- The Chief Minister can recommend the dissolution of the Legislative Assembly even before the expiry of its term. The Governor can dissolve the *Vidhan Sabha* on the advice of the Chief Minister.
- The sessions of the Legislative Assembly are summoned and prorogued by the Governor on the advice of the Chief Minister. Appointments of high officials are made on his recommendation by the Governor.
- He communicates all decisions of the Council of Ministers relating to the administration of the affairs of the state and proposals for the legislation to the Governor (Article 167).
- He also furnishes to the Governor such informations relating to the administration of the affairs of the state and proposals for legislation as the Governor may call for (Article 167).
- He acts as a link between the Council of Ministers and the Governor. Similarly, he also acts as a link between the legislature and his ministers.
- Being leader of the majority party, the Chief Minister ensures that Legislature passes all the bills moved by the government. All the bills, resolutions, etc. must have his prior approval before being placed in the Legislature.
- He appoints the whips and sees that his orders are carried out in order to maintain the decorum in the State Legislature.

LEGISLATURE

The Constitution provides for a legislature in each state and Union territory. The State Legislature consists of one house or two houses, as the case may be (Article 168). The lower house, known as the *Vidhan Sabha* or legislative assembly is the real seat of legislative power. The upper house is known as the *Vidhan Parishad* or Legislative Council. Governor is an integral part of the State Legislature. Council functions are advisory, and any objections expressed to a bill may be overruled if the assembly passes the bill for the second time. In the composition of State Legislature, there is no uniform pattern.

In some states, Legislature is bicameral (two houses) and in some states, it is unicameral (single house). In states where there are two houses, there is Legislative Council along with Legislative Assembly. For instance, in Bihar, Jammu and Kashmir, Karnataka, Maharashtra and Uttar Pradesh, there are two Houses, known as Legislative Council and Legislative Assembly. The remaining states have unicameral legislatures (Legislative Assembly). Parliament may, by law, provide for abolition of an existing Legislative Council or for creation of one where it does not exist, if proposal is supported by a resolution of the Legislative Assembly.

LEGISLATIVE ASSEMBLY (VIDHAN SABHA)

According to Article 168 of the Constitution, there should be a Legislative Assembly for each state. Legislative Assembly is the actual seat of legislative power. It is a popularly elected house. The members of the Legislative Assembly are elected on the basis of adult franchise and the Council of Ministers is responsible to Legislative Assembly. The Legislative Assembly consists of a Speaker and a Deputy speaker

Composition

The number of seats of the Legislative Assembly varies from state to state. The biggest and the most populous state Uttar Pradesh has four hundred twenty five members in its Assembly. States, such as Pondicherry, Mizoram and Arunachal Pradesh which have small population and are small in size, have only thirty members each. Sikkim has thirty two members. The state is divided into equal, single-member constituencies in such a manner that the ratio between the population of each constituency and the number of seats allotted to it shall be the same throughout the state. Certain seats are reserved for the Scheduled Castes and Scheduled Tribes in the Legislative Assembly. The reservation of seats varies from state to state and it is done on the strength of the population. Just as the President has the power to nominate two Anglo-Indians to the Lok Sabha, similarly, the Governor has the power to nominate a certain number of members of the Anglo-Indian community, as he deems fit, if in his opinion they are not adequately represented in the Assembly. The total number of seats in each state and the division of seats into territorial constituencies is readjusted from time to time after each census.

Qualifications and Term

The members of the Legislative Assembly are elected through direct election on the basis of universal adult franchise. The term of the Legislative Assembly is five years. But the Governor, on the request of Chief Minister, may dissolve it even earlier than five years. Further, the Governor, under Article 356 has the power to dissolve the Legislative Assembly before the completion of its duration of five years. The term of the *Vidhan*

Sabha can be extended by an act of Parliament in the event of national emergency, under Article 352. Though it can be extended for any length of time, it cannot exceed the duration of six months.

Some of the essential qualifications to become a member of the Legislative Assembly of the state are as follows:

- He must be a citizen of India.
- Must take an oath to the Constitution.
- The member must be at least twenty five years old. The Constitution also lays down, that:
  - No person can be a member of both the Houses of Legislature.
  - No person can be a member of the Legislatures of two or more States.
  - No person can be a member of both the Parliament and a House of the Legislature of a State.
  - No person can become a member of the Legislative Assembly or the Legislative Council of any state, unless he himself is a voter from any constituency of the state.

Disqualifications: The Constitution mentions the following disqualifications which bar an individual from becoming a member of the legislature: No person can be a member of the legislature if:

- He holds any office of profit under the Government of India or the Government of the State.
- He is of unsound mind.
- He is disqualified by any law made by the Parliament.

Quorum

Even though the period for which the house should meet is not mentioned in the Constitution, but as per the Constitution, the State Assembly must sit at least twice a year, and the gap between the two sessions of the legislature must not be more than six months. For the transaction of the business in the Assembly, a quorum of at least one-tenth of the total membership of the House should be present

Privileges of the Members

According to the Constitution, "No member of the Legislature is liable for any proceeding in any court in respect of anything said, or any vote given by him in the Legislature of any committee thereof". Members are also entitled to receive salaries and allowances as may, from time to time, be determined by the legislature of the state by law.

Powers and Functions

- The most important function of the Legislature is law making. State Legislature has exclusive powers over subjects mentioned in the State List. For instance, it can make legislation on the items mentioned in the State List like police, prisons, irrigation, agriculture, local governments, public health, and pilgrimages. It can also make a law on a subject mentioned in the Concurrent List, provided it does not come into conflict with a law already made by the Parliament.
- Money Bills can originate in Legislative Assembly only. The Legislative Council can only make certain recommendations. The Legislative Assembly can either accept or reject the Legislative Council's recommendations on the Money Bill. Further, the financial powers of legislature include authorization of all expenditure, taxation and borrowings.
- With regard to the sanction of grants, the legislature is the final authority. It also ensures that grants sanctioned by legislature are properly utilized. Further, the Government cannot draw Money Bill from the Consolidated fund, until and unless the Appropriation Act is passed.
- State Legislatures, apart from exercising the usual power of financial control, keeps vigil over day-to-day work of the executive through following ways: asking questions and putting supplements, short-notice discussions, seeking assurances from the ministers, adjournments, no-confidence motions, resolutions and criticism of government policies in the implementation of its policies and programmes.
- The Council of Ministers (Cabinet) is responsible to the Legislative Assembly. Further, if a no confidence motion is passed by a majority of the members present and voting (in the House), the Chief Minister and Council of Ministers must resign.
- The Legislative Assembly considers the reports submitted by the State Public Service Commission, Auditor General and others.
- Members of the Legislative Assembly elect the Speaker and the Deputy Speaker. The Legislative Assembly can remove the speaker and deputy speaker from their offices by means of a resolution passed by the majority vote.
- In the election of the President of India, the elected members of the Legislative Assembly also take part along with the elected members of Parliament.

Speaker and Deputy Speaker

The Legislative Assembly and the Legislative Council have Presiding Officers. The Legislative Assembly consists of a Speaker and a Deputy Speaker. They are elected from among the members of the Legislative Assembly. Similarly, the Legislative Council has a

Chairman and a Deputy Chairman. The Speaker and Deputy Speaker hold their offices as long as they enjoy the support of the house. They can also be removed from the offices by means of a resolution passed by a majority of the members present in the House, preceded by a fourteen days' notice. According to the law of the State Legislature, the salaries and emoluments of the speaker and the deputy speaker are fixed.

The functions performed by the Speaker and Deputy Speaker of the State Legislative Assembly are similar to that of the Speaker and Deputy Speaker of the Lok Sabha. The Speaker of the Assembly can decide whether a bill is a Money Bill or not. Presiding Officers of both the Houses have the right to exercise casting vote in case of tie. If the office of the Speaker becomes vacant, then the duties of the office of the Speaker are performed by the Deputy Speaker. The Deputy Speaker also presides over the sessions of the Legislative Assembly in the absence of the Speaker. In the absence of both the Speaker and Deputy Speaker, person as may be determined by the rules of procedure of the Assembly or a member of the panel of presiding officers, acts as the Speaker. The Speaker cannot preside over such session, while any resolution for the removal of the Speaker is under consideration in the Assembly, but he has the right to speak and take part in the proceedings.

LEGISLATIVE COUNCIL (VIDHAN PARISHAD)

The position of the Legislative Council in a State resembles to that of the upper chamber, the Rajya Sabha. It is also known as *Vidhan Parishad.* The Legislative Council consists of the Chairman and Deputy Chairman. The Constitution of India provides for both the abolition as well as the creation of the Legislative Council of a State (Article 169). For the abolition of the Legislative Council, the Legislative Assembly of the concerned State should pass a resolution to that effect by a majority of not less than two by three of the members of the Assembly present and voting. When the Parliament enacts a law following the resolution of the State Legislative Assembly, the abolition of the Legislative Council takes effect. Similarly, the same procedure is followed for the creation of the Council.

Composition

The Constitution fixes the size of the Legislative Council and prescribes the composition (Article 171). With regard to the composition of the Legislative Council, it is not permanent and the Parliament has the final say in determining its structure. The size of the Legislative Council is in proportion to the size of the Assembly. The Legislative Council consists of not more than one by three of the total strength of the Legislative Assembly of the state and not less than forty. The strength of the Legislative Council varies with the strength of the Legislative Assembly. For instance, the bigger and more populous states like Uttar Pradesh and Bihar, have larger Council membership than the less populous states like Karnataka.

Members of the council are elected, as well as nominated through the following means:

- About one-third members of the council are elected by the Assembly members from among the persons who are not members of the Assembly.
- One-third members are elected by electorates consisting of members of the local bodies, such as corporations, municipalities and zilla parishads.
- One-twelfth of the members are elected from the graduates engaged in teaching within the state, for not less than three years in the state universities and other higher educational institutions (i.e. not lower than the secondary schools).
- One-twelfth of the total members are elected from the graduates of at least three year's standing, residing in that state.
- The Governor nominates the remaining one-sixth members from persons having knowledge or practical experience in fields, such as legislature, science, arts, co-operative movement and social service.

Qualifications

According to the Constitution, to be a member of the Legislative Council he should have the following qualifications:

- He must be a citizen of India.
- He must be above thirty years of age.
- He must have all other qualifications as laid down by a law of the Parliament.
- He cannot be a member of both the Houses of State Legislature nor a member of Parliament Legislatures, or one or two Houses of the State at the same time.

Term

The Legislative Council is the Upper House in the State. The term of a member of the Legislative Council is six years. However, the members can be re-elected. One-third of its members retire after every second year (Article 171).

Powers and Functions

Unlike Rajya Sabha, the State Legislative Council's functions are advisory, and any objections expressed to a bill may be overridden, if the assembly passes the bill for the second time. It can, at the most, delay the passage of a bill. It has no powers with regard to Money Bills. No Money Bill can be introduced in the Council. The Council has no say on non-Money Bills. Legislative Council can only make recommendations. Legislative

Assembly can accept or reject these recommendations. The Legislative Council has no real control over the Executive. The State Council of Ministers is responsible to the Assembly and not the Council.

The Advocate-General.

Article 177 provides for the office of the Advocate-General in the state, which is similar to that of Attorney-General of India in the Union. The Advocate-General is appointed by the State Governor and holds office during the pleasure of the Governor. A person qualified as the judge of the High Court is appointed as an Advocate-General. He receives remuneration as decided by the Governor. The function of the Advocate-General is to advice the Government on legal matters, and to perform such other duties of a legal character, as may from time to time be referred or assigned to him by the Governor. He must discharge the functions conferred on him by the Constitution or any other law for the time being in force. The Advocate-General of a State has the right to speak and take part in the proceedings of the Legislative Assembly of the state or the Legislative Council. He has the right of audience in all the courts of the state and he can also take part in the proceedings of any committee of the Legislature of which he may be named a member, but he is not entitled to vote on any issue, as he is not a regular member of the Legislature.

SUMMARY

- The Constitution of India provides for a two-tier Government, one at the Union-level and the other at the states-level. The State Executive consists of the Governor and Council of Ministers with Chief Minister as its head.
- The Constitution vests all executive powers in the Governor. According to the Article 163 of the Constitution, the Governor, while discharging his duties, is to be guided by the aid and advice of the Council of Ministers. The Governor has executive, discretionary, legislative, financial and judicial powers.
- Though the Governor is vested with nominal executive powers, the Chief Minister and the Council of Ministers exercise the real executive authority. The Council of Ministers is collectively responsible to the State Legislature.
- The Governor appoints the leader of the majority party in the State Legislative Assembly as the Chief Minister. The Governor appoints ministers and allocates the portfolios on advice of the Chief Minister.
- Chief Minister is the leader of the majority party in the Legislative Assembly and is the head of the state Council of Ministers.
- The Constitution provides for a Legislature in each state and Union territory. The state Legislature consists of one House or two Houses, as the case may be

(Article 168). The Lower House, known as the *Vidhan Sabha,* or legislative assembly, is the real seat of legislative power. The upper house is known as the *Vidhan Parishad* or Legislative Council. Legislative Council functions are of advisory nature.

- State Legislature has exclusive powers over subjects mentioned in the State List and Concurrent List. Apart from exercising the usual power of financial control, financial powers of the legislature include authorization of all expenditure, taxation and borrowings.
- The State Legislature keeps watch on the day-to-day work of the executive through parliamentary devices like questions, discussions, debates, adjournments, and no-confidence motions and resolutions.
- The functions of the Advocate-General is to advice the Government on legal matters, and to perform such other duties of a legal character, as may, from time to time, be referred or assigned to him by the Governor.

QUESTIONS

1. Examine the power and role of the Governor in the Indian political system.
2. What are the powers and functions of the Chief Minister? Discuss.
3. Discuss the composition and function of Legislature in the states in India.
4. Write the short note on the Advocate-General.

8

Union-State Relations

After reading this chapter, you will be conversant with:

- Meaning of Federalism
- Nature of Indian Federalism
- Division of Powers
- Union-State Relation and Tension areas
- Recommendations of Rajamannar Committee and Sarkaria Commission on Union-State Relations
- Emerging Trends in Union-State Relation Post 1990s

MEANING OF FEDERALISM

The word Federation is derived from the Latin word 'foedus', meaning contract, pact, agreement, treaty or convention. In Federalism, constitutional division of authority between a central government and several provincial or State governments can be seen. The responsibility for governance is shared between a central authority and component state authorities. The distribution of powers between the federal and State governments is usually accomplished by means of a written constitution. Another important feature of federalism is that it provides for an independent judiciary. It settles the disputes between the Union and the constituent units. Germany, Russia, Mexico, Canada and India are examples of federal governments.

A federation differs from a unitary system. In the unitary system, the concentration of power is in one single sovereign authority. The supremacy of the Union government and the absence of subsidiary sovereign polities are some of the other features of unitary system. On the contrary, in the federal system, there is a division of sovereignty between national and several regional governments. It also permits autonomy to its constituent units. Generally, in a federal system, there is a central authority for the whole state which controls the external affairs of that state together with such internal matters, which are agreed to be of common interest to the constituent parts of the whole state.

DEFINITIONS

K.C. Wheare defined the federal principle as "The method of dividing powers so that the general and regional governments are each within a sphere, co-ordinate and are independent".

A.V Dicey defines the federal system as, "A means of distribution of powers of the state among a number of co-ordinate bodies, each originating in and controlled by the constitution".

According to Garner, "Federal Government, as distinguished from Unitary government, is a system in which the totality of the government power is divided and distributed by the national constitution or the organic act of Parliament, creating it between the central governments and the governments of the individual states or other territorial sub-division of which the federation is composed of".

Nature of Indian Federalism

Article 1 of the Constitution describes India as a Union of States. Although the term federation nowhere appears, the founding fathers of the Indian Constitution provide for a Constitution that was federal in character and unitary in spirit. The framers of the Constitution intended to make the Central Government strong enough to tide over the difficulties created by the fissiparous tendencies. According to Bipan Chandra, "The constitutional structure established in 1950's encompassed the demands of diversity as well as the requirements of unity. The reason for a federal structure with a strong Centre was kept in mind by the makers of the Constitution in view of the difference between decentralization and disintegration and between unity and centralization".

In the Constituent Assembly, the Drafting Committee decided in favour of India as a Union, although its Constitution might be federal in structure. The reason for avoiding the term "Federation" in the draft Constitution, as explained by Ambedkar was to "make it clear that though India was to be a federation, the federation was not the result of an agreement by the states to join in a federation, and that the federation not being the result of an agreement, no state has the right to secede from it". Further, he said, "... What is important is that the use of the word 'Union' is deliberate . . . Though the country and the people may be divided into different States for the convenience of administration, the country is one integral whole, its people a single people living under a single imperium derived from a single source." Finally, when the Constitution was adopted on 26 November 1949, it provided for India being a Union of States.

Federal Structure with Unitary Features

The Drafting Committee described the Constitution as federal in structure but preferred to call it 'Union of States' to indicate three essential features of federalism, namely:

- Indian federalism is not the result of an agreement by the units.
- The component units have no freedom to secede from it.

- The country and the people are divided into different states for convenience of administration and the state's boundaries can be altered. The country is one integral whole, its people a single people, living under a single rule derived from a single source, the Constitution.

Unitary Trends

The Indian Constitution contains many unique unitary features and it has been variously described as 'Quasi-Federal', 'unitary with subsidiary federal features', and a 'federation with a strong centralizing tendency'. The predominant position of the Union is emphasized by the power of the Parliament to create new states, to alter the boundaries of existing States, to abolish a state by ordinary legislative procedure. Under article 249, the Rajya Sabha may, by a two-thirds vote make laws for a temporary period with respect to any matter on the State List. During the proclamation of emergency, Parliament is empowered "to make laws for the whole or any part of the territory of India with respect to any of the matters enumerated in the State List" (Article 250).

The Constitution empowers the Union Parliament to alter the boundaries and name of any state, and does not give the states the right to secede from the Union. In the distribution of revenue resources, the Union's tax resources are greater than those of the states. Revenues collected by the Union are allocated to the states, on the basis of recommendations by the Finance Commission. The states are dependent on the Centre for grants in-aid. Some of the other unitary characteristics of the Indian Constitution are the amending process, the single judicial system, the All-India Services, the independent Election Commission, and the provision for reservation of certain state bills for presidential assent.

Some of the federal features of the Indian Constitution are - Written Constitution, Supremacy of the Constitution, Division of Powers, Independent Judiciary, and Bicameral Legislature.

UNION-STATE RELATIONS: DIVISION OF POWERS

The Constitution of India clearly demarcated the division of powers between the Union and the states. The Constitution prescribed separate areas of operation and interaction for both the Union and states, in order to maintain relationship and preserve the identity. Basically, there are three broad areas of Centre-State relations. These are: legislative, administrative and financial relations. According to the Indian Constitution, Part XI specifies legislative and administrative relations; Part XII deals with financial relations between the Centre and the States.

Legislative Relations

Articles 245 to 254 of the Indian Constitution deal with the legislative relations between the Union and the states. The Constitution makes a clear division of legislative subjects between the Union and the states. The legislative powers between the Union and the states are enumerated into three lists namely the Union List, the State List, and the Concurrent List. The Seventh Schedule of the Constitution specifies the exclusive powers of the Centre in the Union List, exclusive powers of the States in the State List and those falling under the joint jurisdiction of both the Union and the State are placed in the Concurrent List. Residual powers are vested in the Union.

Union List

List I is referred to as the Union List and it includes ninety nine subjects. This list includes defense, external affairs, armed forces, railways, national highways, major ports, airways, communications, currency and coinage, shipping and navigation, post and telegraphs, inter-state trade and commerce, insurance, banking and customs. The subjects enumerated in this list are of national importance. The Parliament has an exclusive right to legislate in respect of items appearing in this list. In the beginning, the Union List consisted of ninety seven subjects, but later by the 42nd amendment of the Constitution, one more subject was added to this list.

State List

The State List includes sixty one subjects. The items included in the State List are police, law and order, agriculture, prisons, public health and sanitation, education, taxes on lands and buildings, libraries, fisheries, markets, pilgrimage and local government. The State Legislatures have exclusive powers to make law in the subject matters appearing in this list. Moreover, the laws made by a particular State Legislature over the subjects in the State List are applicable only to individual institutions within that state. Initially, there were sixty six subjects in the State List, but this number was reduced by the 42nd amendment in Constitution. Some of the item like weights and measures, forests, protection of wild animals and birds were transferred from the State List to the Concurrent List by this amendment.

Concurrent List

Intially, there were forty seven subjects under the Concurrent List but through the 42nd amendment, the number of subjects in this list were decreased to forty two items. Both the Union and states have the powers to make laws over the subjects mentioned in this list. This list includes economic and social planning, population control, family planning, trade and industry, protection of wild animals, trusts and trutees, marriage and divorce, social security and price control. On the Concurrent List, the Union government exercises overriding powers. In the event of conflict between Union law and State law on any subject enumerated in the Concurrent List, Union law will prevail. Further, the residual powers lie with the Union, i.e. the Parliament has the exclusive powers to make any law with regard to any matter not listed in the Concurrent List of the State List (Article 248). The criticism against the Concurrent List is the unilateral approach of the Union in regard to the exercise of the legislative powers.

Under the Constitution, Parliament has the power to make laws for the whole or any part of the territory of India. The Constitution empowers the Parliament to legislate with respect to a matter in the State subjects under the following circumstances:

- Under Article 249, Parliament has the power to make legislation with respect to any matter in the State List, in the national interest. The Rajya Sabha passes a resolution with two-third majority of the members present and voting, and requests the Union Parliament to make a law on the subjects of the State List.
- According to Article 250, Parliament is vested with the powers to legislate in respect to the subjects in the State List, in case of emergencies arising out of war, external aggression or internal disturbance and the constitutional breakdown in the states.
- According to Article 252, Parliament can also legislate for two or more states, if the concerned states request through written resolution.
- According to Article 253 of the Constitution, the Parliament has the power to make any law for the whole or any part of India for implementing any treaty, agreement or convention with any other country or countries or any decision made at any international conference.
- Under Article 356 A, during the period of President's rule, the Parliament can make laws over the subjects included in the State List.
- The Parliament can also make laws with regard to the state subjects during the proclamation of the financial emergency under Article 360 of the Constitution.

It is clear that in the sphere of the legislative relations, the Centre plays a predominant role. This distribution formula was meant to accommodate diversity within the framework of a strong Central government.

Administrative Relations

Articles 256 to 265 deal with the administrative relations between the Union and the states. According to the Constitution of India, Union government is vested with the powers to issue directions to the State governments to remove any obstacles or difficulties for any Union agency to function in the states. The Union government can also issue directives to the State governments in the construction and maintenance of communication of national and military importance and the protection of the railways. The Constitution, further vested in the Union government, powers to deal with inter-state river water disputes. Provisions were made in the Constitution, by virtue of which the President could declare emergency in the states and take over the government of the states, if the states failed to comply with or give effect to any direction given by the Union government.

Some of the Articles dealing with the Union-State Administrative relations are enumerated below:

- According to Article 256, the executive power of every state shall be so exercised as to ensure compliance with the laws made by the Parliament and the existing laws.
- Article 257 states that the executive power of the Union shall also extend to the giving of such directions to the states, as they may appear to the Government of India to be necessary for that purpose.
- Article 258 says that the President may, with the consent of the government of the State, entrust either conditionally or unconditionally, to it or to its officer's functions in respect of any matter to which the executive power of the Union extends.
- According to article 261, full faith and credit shall be given to Public Acts, records and judicial proceedings of the Union and the states in all parts of the Indian territory.
- Article 262 states that the Parliament may, by law, provide for the adjudication of any dispute or complaint with respect to the use, distribution and control of the waters in any Inter-State river valley.
- Article 263 empowers the President to establish Inter-State Council to inquire into and advice upon Inter-State disputes and matters of common interest between states or between the Union and the states and make recommendations for better co-ordination of policy.

ZONAL COUNCILS

The first Prime Minister of India, Pandit Jawahar Lal Nehru mooted the idea of creation of Zonal Councils in order to overcome the centrifugal forces that emerged in the wake of the linguistic re-organization of the states in India. Five Zonal Councils were set up vide Part-III of the States Re-organization Act, 1956. This Act sought to divide entire country into five zones, each having its own council. The five zones are: the Northern zone, the Southern zone, the Central zone, the Eastern zone and the Western zone. Several factors, such as natural divisions of the country, requirements of economic development, cultural and linguistic affinities, means of communication and requirements of security, and law and order were taken into account while forming these zones.

The main idea behind the formation of these Zonal Councils is to provide in each zone a council of states in the region, which could become a forum where the states could discuss and resolve their inter-state disputes. Creating a healthy inter-state environment, providing a common meeting ground in each zone, fostering balanced regional development and building harmonious Centre-state relations are some of the other main objectives of the Zonal Councils. However, Zonal Councils are purely deliberative and advisory bodies.

Composition of Zonal Councils

The present composition of each of these Zonal Councils is as follows:

- The Northern Zonal Council, comprising the states of Haryana, Himachal Pradesh, Jammu and Kashmir, Punjab, Rajasthan, NCT of Delhi and Union Territory of Chandigarh.
- The Central Zonal Council, comprising the states of Chhattisgarh, Uttaranchal, Uttar Pradesh and Madhya Pradesh.
- The Eastern Zonal Council, comprising the states of Bihar, Jharkhand, Orissa, Sikkim and West Bengal.
- The Western Zonal Council, comprising the states of Goa, Gujarat, Maharashtra and the Union Territories of Daman and Diu, and Dadra and Nagar Haveli.
- The Southern Zonal Council, comprising the states of Andhra Pradesh, Karnataka, Kerala, Tamil Nadu and the Union Territory of Pondicherry.

The seven North-Eastern states, i.e. (i) Assam, (ii) Arunachal Pradesh, (iii) Manipur, (iv) Tripura, (v) Mizoram, (vi) Meghalaya, and (vii) Nagaland are not included in the Zonal Councils and their special problems are looked after by the North-Eastern Council, set up under the North-Eastern Council Act, 1972.

Organizational Structure of Zonal Councils

The Zonal Council for each zone consists of the following members:

- The Union Home Minister as the Chairman for each of these councils.
- The Chief Minister of each of the states included in the zone and two other ministers of each such state nominated by the Governor.
- Two members from each such territory nominated by the President where any Union Territory is included in the zone.

Further, the Zonal Council for each zone has the following persons as advisers to assist the Council in the performance of its duties:

- One person nominated by the Planning Commission;
- Chief Secretaries in the states of the respective zones;
- Another officer holding the office of the Development Commissioner, as nominated by the states.

Role and objectives of the Zonal Council

The then Union Home Minister, Pandit G.B. Pant, in the first meeting of the Northern Zonal Council held on 23rd April 1957, stated that the main objectives behind setting up of these Zonal Councils are:

- Achieving an emotional integration of the country.
- Arresting the growth of acute state consciousness, regionalism, linguism and particularistic tendencies.
- Enabling the Centre and the states to co-operate and exchange ideas and experiences.
- Establishing a climate of co-operation amongst the states for successful and speedy execution of major development projects.
- Securing some kind of political equilibrium between different regions of the country.

Financial Relations

The division of financial powers underlined by the Constitution envisaged two distinct schemes: the division of powers to levy taxes and the distribution of revenues. The Union and the states were empowered to levy taxes, but the division of revenues was subject to the principle of their needs and requirements. Thus, certain taxes included in the Union List were wholly or in part intended for the states and in certain cases their collection was entrusted to the states. A constitutional body, the Finance Commission oversees the division of financial resources between the centre and the states. State finances are supervised by the Central government through the Comptroller and Auditor General.

In the allocation of the financial sources between the Union and the states, the Constitution of India classified the exclusive Union sources, the exclusive State sources, the duties levied by the Union but assigned to the states, the duties levied by the Union but collected and appropriated by the states, and the duties levied by the Union and distributed between the Union and the States. The provisions concerning the distribution of the sources of revenue between the Centre and the states may be classified into following sub-divisions:

- Article 268 states about duties to belevied by the Union but collected and appropriated by the states. For instance, it includes duties on medicinal and toilet preparations, corporation tax, customs and import duties.
- Article 269 states about the taxes to belevied and collected by the Union but assigned to the states. For example, it includes terminal taxes on goods and passengers carried by rail, sea or air, taxes on railway fares and freights.
- Article 270 deals with the taxes to belevied and collected by the Union and distributed between the Union and the states. It includes taxes on income other than agricultural income.

- Article 271 deals with the surcharge on certain duties and taxes for purposes of the Union. Parliament may increase any of the duties or taxes by a surcharge for purposes of the Union. And the whole proceeds of any such surcharge shall form part of the Consolidated Fund of India.
- Article 272 states about the taxes to belevied and collected by the Union and which may be distributed between the Union and states. It includes many items given in the Union list, such as railways, post and telegraph, telephones, foreign exchange, customs and exports duties.
- Article 275 deals with the grants-in-aid given by the Union to the states for implementing its plan programmes, and for the development of Scheduled Castes and Scheduled Tribes and other weaker sections of the community.

Finance Commission

Article 280 pertains to the setting up of a Finance Commission. The President constitutes the Finance Commission for every five years. Finance Commission is a quasi-judicial body. The Finance Commission oversees the division of financial resources between the Centre and the states. State finances are supervised by the Central government through the Comptroller and Auditor General. So far, the Government of India constituted twelve Finance Commissions. The chairman of the present Finance Commission is C. Ranga Raj, a well-known economist and ex-Governor of Andhra Pradesh.

The Finance Commission does the transfer of resources from the Union to the states. Its function is to ensure orderly and judicious devolution of resources from the Union to the states. The Planning Commission advises the Union government regarding the desirable formula for the transfer of resources to the states over and above those recommended by the Finance Commission. Bulk of the transfer of revenue and capital resources from the Union to the states is determined largely on the advice of these two Commissions.

Composition of Finance Commission

The qualification of the Chairman and the members of the Finance commission are laid down in the Finance Commission Act, 1951. The composition of the Finance Commission is as follows:

- There shall be a Chairman, and four members in the Council.

Appointment of the Chairman and Members

The chairman of the commission will be selected from among the persons who have experience in public affairs. The members are selected from among the persons who:

- have been or are qualified to be appointed as judges of a High Court.
- have specialized knowledge of the finance and accounts of the government.

- have wide experience in financial matters and in administration.
- have special knowledge of economics.

It is interesting to observe that there are certain qualifications/specializations laid down for persons to be appointed as members of the commission but there is nothing of that sort mentioned with regard to the appointment of the Chairman of the Commission. Mostly, persons with rich experience and who are noted economists, administrators, and experts in public affairs adorned the positions of all the Finance Commissions. Further, the composition of members indicates a bias towards administrators. But it shall have to be noted that some of the chairmen were drawn from ruling political party who never possessed the required background and skill in the specialized field.

Disqualifications

Article 280, Clause (4) of the Constitution of India requires that the President of India, before appointment of members, has to satisfy himself, that:

- the person does not have any personal, financial or other interest which are prejudicial to his function as a member of the Commission.
- the President of India has to satisfy himself about the interests mentioned above from time-to-time during the tenure of the member.
- the members have to furnish the President, whenever required, any such information which is necessary while performing the functions.
- a person holding the position of a member of the Commission shall cease to be the member of the Commission if he is found to be:
  - of unsound mind.
  - an undischarged insolvent.
  - convicted of an offence involving moral turpitude.

Term of Office

The members of the Commission shall remain in office for a period specified in the orders issued by the President of India. A member is eligible for re-appointment. He ceases to be the member of the Commission if he resigns and the resignation is accepted by the President of India. The member has to address his resignation letter to the President stating the reasons for his resignation.

Conditions of Service

The following are the conditions of service which are notified in the Official Gazette issued by the Union government of India. The President of India may appoint a member as stated below:

- A member may be appointed to the Commission for a whole-time or part-time service.
- The members will be paid such salaries, fees and allowances as determined by the Union government.
- Further rules made in this regard have to be laid down before each house of Parliament while it is in session and that session shall be for thirty days. Such a session shall comprise one or two or more successive sessions. If the session is to expire the immediate successive sessions must have to endorse the said rules. The Parliament may agree to the total rules made or modified.
- Any modification or annulment made shall have to be without prejudice to the validity of anything previously done under that rule.

Terms of Reference

It is the Ministry of Finance of the Union government that drafts the specific terms of reference of each Finance Commission. The President of India does not have any role in determining an independent appraisal of suggested terms of reference. The paradox in the process is that the State governments are never consulted about the terms of reference. This practice is perhaps adopted keeping in the apprehension that several states may not come to a consensus amongst themselves because of diverse situations and viewpoints. Each Finance Commission has a landmark in terms of reference. It is pertinent for them to understand how the finance commissions were asked to proceed with the important subjects. They are shown as under:

In the first Finance Commission, it was asked *inter alia* grant in lieu of export duty on jute and jute products apart from revenue gap grants for 'B' states.

The second Finance Commission was requested to make recommendations on the principle of distribution of net revenue levied under the Article 269 of the Indian Constitution. For instance, estate duty and tax on railway fares levied and collected by the Union government, but such proceeds are given to states.

The third Finance Commission, under any other item, was requested to examine any additional matter.

The concern of fourth Finance Commission was the use of states' share of Estate duty towards payment of union loans to states; and extra burden of debt servicing expenditure devolving states; combined incidence of sales tax and also union excise on production and consumption;

Fifth Finance Commission was asked to suggest ways and means discouraging the states going in for unauthorized overdraft; scope for exploiting revenue sources given according to Article 269; and the states' own revenue resources.

Sixth Finance Commission was asked to look into:

- States debt status vis-a-vis their non-plan needs.
- The technique of consolidating the union loans to the states.

- Constitution of National Relief Fund (NRF) to which union and state governments contribute a part of their revenues.
- To examine the issue of augmenting revenues from taxes and duties.

Ninth Finance Commission was asked to:

- establish a norm or standard assuring the receipts and expenditures on revenue account of each state and also of the union pertaining to special problems of each state and union government.
- estimate the status of surplus on revenue account of union and state for capital investment.
- examine both the plan and non-plan revenue expenditure.

Tenth Finance Commission was concerned with:

- the requirements of the states to improve the administration and important social services.
- reviewing the schemes of central assistance to states towards natural calamities.

The Commission is empowered to make recommendations on the following issues:

- Distribution between the union and the states of the net proceeds of taxes which are to be divided between them and allocation between the states of the respective shares of such proceeds.
- It has to recommend and lay down the principles which should govern the payments of grants-in-aid of the revenues of the Consolidated Fund of India to the states.
- Any other matter referred to the Commission by the President with regard to financial relations between union and states.

Working Procedure of Finance Commission

Generally, the Finance Commission takes more than a year to complete its work and forward the recommendation to the President a few months ahead of the presentation of budget by the government in Parliament. The work of the Finance Commission commences immediately after the government's announcement of its composition and terms of reference. The first function that the Finance Commission takes up is to address letters to the State governments to submit the following.

- The estimates of the normal expenditure.
- Estimates of amounts of revenue over next five years.
- In the next phase, the Commission scrutinizes the reliability of the estimates received by it. The third phase of activity pertains to reduction of estimates of

different states on comparable basis, eliminating abnormal and unusual items in their estimates.

The Commission, thereafter, undertakes visits or tours of all the states and prepares the report. The final report is, thereafter submitted to the President of India. The President in turn recommends to the Union government for consideration and implementation.

Some of the major criticisms against the Finance Commission are the scope of the Finance Commissions, and the terms of referring through the President have to be restricted. The methodology for the transfer scheme employed by the Commission has not led to optimal equity and incentive consequences.

In spite of the criticism against Finance Commission, according to Subhash C. Kashyap, "The provision for the appointment of a Finance Commission every five years to examine the distribution of tax proceeds between the union and states and to determine the principles which should govern the grants-in-aid is an innovation of the Indian Constitution and has contributed to the generally smooth financial relationship between the union and the states".

Role of Extra-Constitutional Devices

The Planning Commission and National Development Councils were constituted to promote uniform national policy and programmes, and bring about an all round growth of the nation as a whole. The structural growth of these agencies is that they have mostly developed outside the framework of the Constitution

PLANNING COMMISSION

The Planning Commission was established in March 1950, not by an Act of Parliament or by a constitutional provision but by a cabinet resolution. It is an extra-constitutional agency and its role is of an advisory body in planning. The main idea of constituting Planning Commission is to suggest various measures for augmenting the resources of the country and the effective and balanced utilization of resources, determining the priorities, and progress of planning in the country. To promote a rapid rise in the standard of living of the people through exploitation of the resources, increasing production and providing opportunities for employment to all are some of the other major objectives of the Planning Commission. One of the major tasks of the Planning Commission is to make recommendations to the Cabinet. Another important job of the Planning Commission is to work in close tandem with the ministers of both the Central and State governments. It is one of the major sources of allocator of funds to the states. The Planning Commission works out five-year plan investments for each sector of the economy and each state. Based on the report of the Planning Commission, the states work out their respective annual plans for each year, based on the estimated resource availability which includes the balance from the current revenue, contributions of public enterprises, additional resource mobilization, plan grants and loans, market borrowings, and other miscellaneous capital receipts. The Planning Commission approves the state plans. The plans finalized by the Commission are discussed and finally approved by the National Development Council (NDC). If necessary, the NDC also has the provision to make necessary modifications to the draft plan and approve it. Finally, after approval of the NDC, it goes to the Parliament for its final approval. Thus, the distribution of the funds is done on the basis of a consensus formula evolved by the National Development Council (NDC).

The Planning Commission launched its first five-year plan in 1951. The second five-year plan was started in 1956 and third-five year plan in 1961. In 1965, there was a break in the launching of the fourth five-year plan due to the Indo-Pakistan Conflict. Two successive years of drought, devaluation of the currency, rise in prices disrupted the planning process. During this period, plan holiday was declared and three annual plans between 1966 and 1969 were made. The fourth five-year plan was started in 1969. Fifth five-year plan was started in 1974, but the Janata government, in 1977 terminated this plan. Sixth- and seventh-plans were launched in 1980 and 1985 respectively. The eighth-Plan could not take off in 1990 due to the fast changes in party in power at the Centre. As a result, the years 1990-91 and 1991-92 were treated as Annual Plans. The Eighth Plan was finally launched in 1992 after the initiation of structural adjustment policies.

During the first eight plans, more emphasis was given to public sector with massive investments in basic and heavy industries. The ninth-plan was launched in 1997, and the emphasis on the public sector has become less pronounced from this plan onwards. The tenth five year plan was formulated in 2002.

The main objectives of the planning, as enunciated in various plan documents are: to achieve planned development, to ensure rapid progress and equitable distribution of the resources, to expand and improve agricultural production, to build the necessary industrial infrastructure, to increase and distribute national wealth, to make the country self-sufficient and self-reliant, to promote trade and commerce, to remove illiteracy, poverty and unemployment, and to make the Indian economy modern, efficient and competitive.

ORGANIZATION

The Planning Commission consists of the Chairman and Deputy Chairman. The Prime Minister is the Chairman of the Planning Commission. The other members of the Commission include Union Ministers for Finance, Planning and other ministers holding key portfolios and a few non-official members who are experts in various fields relating to planning, namely, economics, finance and industry, etc. The Deputy Chairman looks after day to day work of the Planning Commission. The Deputy Chairman and the full time members of the Commission, as a composite body, provide advice and guidance to the subject divisions for the formulation of Five Year Plans, Annual

Plans, State Plans, Monitoring Plan Programmes, Projects and Schemes. The Planning Commission functions through several divisions, each headed by a senior officer, Secretary and Grievance Officers who are normally . drawn from amongst the experts in the respective field

Some of the divisions through which the planning commission functions are mentioned below:

- Divisions dealing with a group of activities, like agriculture and rural development, education, employment, manpower, health and family planning, industry and minerals, village and small scale industries, housing and urban development, water supply and sanitation, irrigation and command area development, energy including non-conventional sources of energy, roads and communications, and welfare of backward classes.
- Divisions dealing with special aspects, like economic affairs and finance, information and monitoring, perspective planning, multi-level planning, plan co-ordination, scientific and technological research, social planning and socio-economic research, statistics and surveys, programme evaluation, and the twenty-point programme.
- State Plans Division, dealing with a group of states and co-ordination between the central and state plans.

Functions

Some of the functions outlined in the 1950-resolution, setting up the Planning Commission are as follows:

- To make an assessment of the capital, material and human resources of the country; and to investigate the possibilities of augmenting such of these resources as are found to be deficient in relation to the nation's requirement.
- To formulate a plan for the most effective and balanced utilization of the country's resources.
- To determine national priorities of development and define the stages in which the plan should be carried out, and propose and suggest allocation of resources for the due completion at each stage.
- To indicate factors tending to retard economic development and determine the conditions necessary for the successful execution of the plan.
- To determine the nature of machinery required for successful implementation of each stage of the plan in all its aspects.
- To apprise from time-to-time the progress achieved in execution of the plan, implementation and to recommend necessary adjustments of policy and measures.

- Make recommendations for its own effective working and regarding necessary changes in the prevailing economic conditions, current policies, measures and development programmes, or on an examination of such specific problems referred to it for advice by the central or state governments.

NATIONAL DEVELOPMENT COUNCIL (NDC)

The National Development Council (NDC) is considered to be the apex body in the planning process at the national level. On the advice of the Planning Commission, the National Development Council (NDC) was constituted in 1952. It was established under Article 263 of the Constitution and was set up by a Cabinet resolution. It provides a forum where policies, priorities and programmes are discussed and a close co-ordination between centre and the state is brought about. According to the government resolution, the council should meet as often as may be necessary and at least twice in each year. It lacks constitutional status. It is directly under the control of the Prime Minister. He is ex-officio Chairman of the NDC. It also includes the Chief Ministers of all states, Lt. Governors of the Union Territories, the members of the Planning Commission and all Union Cabinet ministers as its members. It was set up in order to make more amenable for the union to manage inter-governmental affairs and for the approval of the five-year plans. It symbolizes the federal approach to planning and is the instrument for ensuring that the planning system adopts a truly national perspective.

The National Development Council is one of the key organizations of the planning system in India, and is considered as the highest policy making body at the national level. The main responsibility of NDC is the approval of Five-Year Plans and to look after the issues related to economic development in the country. It is entrusted with the responsibility of laying down guidelines for formulation of the national plans, review their implementation, take appropriate decision on the adjustments warranted from time to time, and guide the states and Union Territories in regard to the plan development. It is a unique forum, as it brings together the executive heads of the two orders of government. One of the major tasks of the NDC is to bring about co-operation between the central, state and local governments and ensure all round development. It also provides understanding and consultation between the centre and the states on planning and economic policies. The decisions at the meeting of the NDC are arrived at through method of consensus.

The criticisms against the NDC are: It has been convened irregularly; and the procedures adopted for its deliberations have been most perfunctory. The council has hardly met more than once a year on an average since its establishment in August 1952. Further, its meetings have been reduced to a mere ritual. Of late, its importance has been reduced with the formation of minority/coalition governments in the post-1989 phase as the regional parties have direct access in the cabinet coalition, so the need for a separate forum was not necessarily felt.

The functions of the NDC, as revised in 1967, following the adoption of the recommendations of the Administrative Reforms Commission, are as follows:

- To prescribe guidelines for the formulation of the national plan.
- To consider the national plan as formulated by the Planning Commission.
- To assess resources required for implementing the plan and to suggest ways and means for raising them.
- To consider important questions of social and economic policy affecting development.
- To review the working of the plan from time-to-time and to recommend such measures as are necessary for achieving the aims and targets articulated in the national plan.

Inter-State Council

The Constitution under Article 263 provides for the provision of an Inter-State Council for harmonizing Union-State and for policy co-ordination. However, it was only in 1990 that this constitutional provision was implemented. The Inter-State Council established in 1990 is a forum for effective co-ordination and co-operation between the units in the federal system. It was established to provide a platform for both the Union and the states to discuss and deliberate on matters of common interest.

The composition of the Inter-State Council includes the Prime Minister, all Chief Ministers, Administrators of Union territories, Governors of states under President's Rule, six Union ministers of cabinet rank in the Union Council of ministers, nominated by the Prime Minister and two ministers of Cabinet rank in the Union Council of ministers to be nominated by the Prime Minister as permanent invitees.

The Inter-State Council, under the Constitution, is entrusted with the duty of:

- Inquiring into and advising upon disputes which may arise between the states.
- Investigating and discussing subjects in which Union or some or all of the states or one or more of the states have a common interest.
- Making recommendations on any such subject and, in particular, recommendations for the better co-ordination of policy and action with reference to that subject.

The Council, in its first meeting held on October 10, 1990 considered the recommendations made by the Sarkaria Commission on Centre-State relations. Some of the major recommendations made by the Council at its meetings are: a. An alternative plan for devolution of share in central taxes to states; b. Proposal to the Union Home ministry to take steps to initiate appropriate amendments in the Constitution for the disposal of bills pending before Governor and the President; c. Residuary powers of legislation may be transferred from the Union List to the Concurrent List; d) Active consultation between the Centre and the states on legislation on the matters in Concurrent List; e) Need for comprehensive legislation with regard to imposition of taxes by local bodies on the properties of the Union government, which are of industrial and commercial nature ; f) Initiate a Constitutional amendment to make it mandatory for the Centre to consult the Chief Minister concerned before appointing the Governor; and g) Governors could be eligible for a second term but are not expected to return to active politics.

Since its formation in 1990, eight Inter-State Council meetings were held. In the eighth Inter-State Council (ISC) meeting held in Srinagar on 27 and 28 August, 2003, a general consensus was reached on safeguards to prevent the misuse of Article 356 of the Constitution. The Inter-State Council also accepted most of the recommendations of the Sarkaria Commission. Prime Minister Atal Bihari Vajpayee, in the recently held Inter-State Council meeting said that, "The Inter-State Council strengthens the bond of partnership between the Union and the states which is the mainstay of our democratic polity and also the main requirement for achieving India's speedy all-round development".

Both the National Development Council and the Inter-State Council have proved to be necessary and integral parts of the federal structure. Their utility is established beyond doubt. According to Sandeep Shastri, "In context of the emerging trends in Indian politics in general, revitalizing and strengthening the Inter-State Council appears imperative as it provides the right institutional platform for ensuring Centre-state and inter-state cordiality, besides securing for the states their legitimate role in federal politics".

Union-State Relations: Conflict Areas

The structure of India's federal system not only created a strong Central government but has also lead to the concentration of power in the Union government. Centralization of power has been the reason for many controversies and political tensions in Union-State relations.

Some of the unitary trends in the working of India's federal policy, which led to the major source of confrontations are as follows: Firstly, the Congress dominance in the national and state politics. Secondly, Indira Gandhi's 'personalized politics' further resulted in centralization of decision-making at various levels of governance. Thirdly, the centralized nature of institutions like Planning Commission, All India Civil Services, the arbitrary dismissal of State governments, and imposition of President's Rule (misuse of Article 356). Fourthly, the partisan role of the Governor in acting as an agent of the Central government during hung Parliament. Finally, constitutional provisions relating to the division of the subjects (which privileged the Centre) and sharing of taxation and revenue distribution between the Centre and the states.

The popular demands for the re-organization of the states on a common linguistic basis in the 1950s were a major irritant in the Union-State relations. It was considered to be the most divisive issue in the first twenty years of Independent India. This problem led to the dispute over official language and linguistic re-organization of the states.

With the growing demand for the linguistic re-organization of the states in different parts of the country, Nehru appointed the State Reorganization Commission. It recommended that the political divisions of the Union be redrawn generally in accordance with the linguistic demands. On the basis of its report, the States Reorganization Commission Act was passed by the Parliament in November 1956. Accordingly, the Telengana area of Hyderabad state was transferred to Andhra Pradesh and two new states Kerala and Karnataka were created. In 1960, following widespread agitation and violence, the state of Bombay was bifurcated into Maharashtra and Gujarat. Finally, Punjab was the last state to be divided in 1966. Punjab was split into two states, Punjab and Hindi-speaking Haryana. Thus, the re-organization of the states on the linguistic basis has strengthened the Indian states and federation.

The rise and growth of the Dravidian parties in Tamil Nadu contributed to the movement against imposition of Hindi by the Centre. Due to mounting pressure from Southern States, especially Tamil Nadu, an Official Languages Act was passed in 1963, which resulted in adoption of three-language formula by the Parliament in 1963. This Act provided for continuation of English as an official language in addition to Hindi. The Parliament decided to use English as a link language in addition to Hindi for the official work at the Centre, i.e. it adopted a bilingual policy as far as its official language was concerned.

Centralization of Power and Decision-Making

The increase in the powers of the Centre at the expense of the powers of the state governments led to the emergence of the centralizing tendencies in the federal system especially during Indira Gandhi's regime. The one-party dominance of the Congress party during the first four decades after Independence led to over centralization. Unlike the Nehru era, Indira Gandhi's era is not identified with the spirit of accommodation and compromise with the states. During Indira Gandhi's tenure as Prime minister (1966-77 and 1980-84), centralization of power increased dramatically and the principles of federalism were flouted. The keystone of her political strategy was an unprecedented centralization of power, within the ruling party, as well as in the Prime Minister's Office. She bypassed Parliament and Cabinet from decision-making. The specific measures taken by Indira Gandhi to centralize political authority involved the delinking of Parliamentary and Legislative Assembly elections, selection of Chief Ministers by her coterie in New Delhi rather than by the state legislative parties, and frequent impositions of President's rule in various states to influence state politics. The predominant pattern was one of Central intervention in state politics. For instance, the Central rule was imposed forty-four times upon the non-Congress ruled states during her tenure. With the over centralization of power, the states began to demand for greater devolution and decentralization of powers.

Apart from the centralizing tendencies of the Union, the partisan role of the Governors, misuse of Article 356 for dismissing popularly elected governments, deployment of paramilitary forces without the consent of the states, discrimination in matters of allocation of discretionary grants, conflict over All India Services and several other factors created resentment and generated a spirit of revolt. All these factors became major contentious issues in the Centre-State relations.

Office of the Governor

Under Article 154 (1) of the Constitution, the executive powers of the state are vested in the Governor. The Constitution provides for the appointment of the Governor of each state by the President on the advice of the Union Council of Ministers. The role of Governor is vital in the smooth conduct of the relations between the Centre and the States. In actual practice, however, the Governor is appointed by the Central Government to act as its representative at the state capital. In normal times, the Governor is the nominal head of the state. However, in exceptional conditions, he can exercise his discretionary authority and even recommend to the President the dismissal of the government. The power to declare a state of Emergency is the most effective tool in the hands of the Governor. During the President's rule, the Governor is vested with executive authority to carry out the functions of the state government.

The Central Government's control over states through Governors became one of the controversial issues in Centre-state relations. One of the major criticisms against the Governors was that 'they were acting as Centre's agents and were accused of their partisan role'. They repeatedly acted against the State governments and the legislature, setting aside all democratic norms. The recommendation to impose the President's rule by the Governors, particularly in a politically conflicting context without exploring all possibilities of having an alternative government raised questions on the integrity of the Governor as representative of the Centre.

Governors frequently acted as agents of the ruling party in New Delhi. The politicization of the institution of Governors and their appointments became a wide spread practice especially during Indira Gandhi's tenure as Prime Minister (1966-77 and 1980-84). President's rule was invoked forty one times to dismiss State governments. Also during 1989, shortly after the National Front government replaced the Congress (I) government, Prime Minister V.P. Singh (1989-90) asked eighteen Governors to resign so that he could replace them with his own men.

The interventionist character of the Governor's power to return bills passed by the State government on matters other than Money Bills became another major area of controversy. Governor, under Article 200 of the Constitution, can reserve certain bills passed by State Legislatures for consideration of the President. Under Article 201, the President may give his assent to such bills at his will, without a time-limit, or exercise his veto power kept pending. The Union government misused the provision extensively. This has undermined the legislative autonomy of the states. From 1977 to 1985, some 1,130 state bills were reserved for the President's consideration.

This has also made the role of Governor critical and controversial. The Centre-appointed Governor played an unfortunate role, bringing the status and integrity of the governorship into considerable disrepute. The Governor often tended to use his/her discretionary powers and interfered in matters relating to administration and legislation which go beyond the provisions of the Constitution. With the institution of Governor increasingly embroiled in controversy, the State governments demanded for a greater say in the appointments and the dismissal of the Governors, apart from seriously reviewing the nature and extent of their discretionary powers. In order to prevent the misuse of the discretionary powers of the Governor, many recommendations were made by different committees and commissions. Some of them are as follows:

The Sarkaria Commission Report made following recommendations with regard to the appointment of the Governor:

- He should be an eminent person.
- He should be a person from outside the state.
- Must not have participated in active politics at least for sometime before his appointment.
- He should be a detached person and not too actively connected with the local politics of the state
- He should be appointed in consultation with the Chief Minister of the state, Vice-President of India and the Speaker of the Lok Sabha.
- His tenure of office must be guaranteed and should not be disturbed, except for extremely compelling reasons
- After demitting his office, the person appointed as Governor should not be eligible for any other appointment or office of profit under the Union or a State government except for a second term as Governor or election as Vice-President or President of India, as the case may be.
- At the end of his tenure, reasonable post-retirement benefits should be provided.
- In case, none of the political parties secure absolute majority to form the government or even if the ruling party loses its mandate on the floor of the house, they should be given a chance to prove the same.
- If the President's rule shall be imposed, it should be publicized in the media.

The National Commission to Review the Working of the Constitution (NCRWC) in its consultation paper on 'The institution of the Governor under the Constitution' gave the following recommendations: It recommended a fixed term of five years for the Governor and deletion of the provision about the pleasure of the President. It also recommended impeachment of the Governor by the State legislature on the same lines as of the President by the Parliament. NCRWC also opposed the recall of a Governor and considered it as a disregard of the Constitution.

Article 356

The breakdown of constitutional machinery in the states is dealt with, in Article 356 of the Constitution. The Constitutional provision, which has the greatest impact on the federal principle, is Article 356 which has been frequently misused and abused. Article 356, enumerated in Chapter XVIII of the Constitution provides that the President, on receipt of a report from the governor of a state or otherwise, is satisfied that a situation has arisen in which the government of the state cannot be carried on in accordance with the provisions of the Constitution, the President may proclaim President's rule. Accordingly, the President may dismiss State government or dissolve a State Assembly or keep it under suspended animation. It gives Centre the overriding powers to take over the functions of State government.

Misuse of Article 356

Invoking of Article 356 has been the subject of considerable controversy and debate. Article 356 was first invoked in July 1959 against the Communist government, led by EMS Namboodiripad in Kerala. Since then, the Article has been abused several times to dismiss politically inconvenient governments. From 1950 till date, various political parties ruling at the Centre enforced/misused Article 356 on more than 111 occasions. In many cases, State governments, which enjoyed majority in the Assembly were dismissed. And in other cases, State governments were dismissed without being given an opportunity to prove their strength on the floor of the House.

Article 356 was misused to dismiss the State government of an opposition party or to manipulate political advantages to favour a particular political party or individual. The Centre used this provision to serve its own political interests. It has rarely taken into account the Article 355 before making proclamation under Article 356. Political misuse of this provision has been extensive, particularly by the Congress-ruled Centre. From 1967 onwards, when the non-Congress State governments were voted to power at the state-level, the Congress invoked Article 356 to dismiss the duly elected State governments.

By the mid-1980s, the emergence of the BJP and a number of regional political parties not only challenged the one-party dominance of Congress party but also questioned the arbitrary use of Article 356 and the partisan role of the Governor. In response to the demand by several opposition leaders, Indira Gandhi, on 24 March, 1983 appointed a commission headed by Justice R. S. Sarkaria to go into the Centre-State relationship.

The Sarkaria Commission made 12 recommendations relating to Article 356. The Commission recommended that the article should be resorted to "very sparingly, in extreme cases as a measure of last resort, when all available alternatives fail to prevent or rectify a breakdown of the constitutional machinery in the state". The Commission had said that the alternatives to Article 356 might be dispensed with only in cases of extreme urgency where failure on the part of the Union to take immediate action under Article 356 would lead to disastrous consequences. The alternatives suggested by the Sarkaria

Commission include issue of a warning to the errant state in specific terms, that it is not carrying on the government of the state in accordance with the Constitution. It had also suggested that before taking action under Article 356, any explanation received from the state should be taken into account. Prior to invoking Article 356, the commission recommended that it should be a 'speaking document' containing a precise and clear statement of all material facts and grounds.

The National Commission to Review the Working of the Constitution (NCRWC) has recommended that the Centre should first consider taking action against an errant state under Article 256 (regarding obligation of the states and the Union), Article 257 (regarding control of the Union over states in certain cases) and Article 365 (on the effect of a state's failure to comply with, or to give effect to directions given by the Union) instead of rushing to invoke Article 356.

Article 356 - Current Position

The Supreme Court's historic judgment in the Bommai case in 1994 on the misuse of Article 356 has discoursed its misuse. The Supreme Court's ruling that, "the Centre cannot dissolve State legislatures under Article 356, unless and until both the Houses of Parliament ratify it", has served as an effective deterrent against the misuse of the Article 356. The Court also held that any such proclamation is open to judicial review to the extent of examining whether it was issued on the basis of relevant material or whether it was a *mala fide* exercise of power. This pronouncement deterred the use of this Article for narrow political ends. Moreover, from mid-1990 onwards, due to the fractured mandate at the Centre and the emergence of the coalition governments, successive central administrations resisted the misuse of this article.

ALL INDIA SERVICES

To maintain harmonious relations between the Union and the State governments on a day-to-day basis, the Constitution provides for the continuation of the three All-India Services, i.e. the Indian Administrative Service (IAS), the Indian Police Service (IPS) and the Indian Foreign Service (IFS). The concept of the All-India Services was to foster national integration by recruitment of personnel through nationwide competitive exams. An eminent scholar, Maheshwari identifies three grounds/reasons for the creation of the All-India Services. "Firstly, an All-India Service is considered to be a bulwark of national integration as its members possess an all-India outlook. Secondly, based on all-India recruitment, it attracts the best talent in the country as necessity for the accomplishment of national tasks. Thirdly, it reinforces the sense of independence and impartiality of its members by affording protection against local pressures and influences." Under Article 312, the Union has the power to establish one or more All-India Services by means of parliamentary legislation upon the Rajya Sabha passing a resolution with the support of not less than two-thirds of its members present and voting.

One of the other major contentious issues between the Union and the states is over the All-India Services. The Union government recruits officers to these three services but their services are placed at the disposal of the State governments based on cadres constituted for each state. These officers can either serve the State government to whom they are allotted or the Government of India on a short-term deputation

Another area of conflict between the Union and the states is over the appointment, posting and control of the personnel of the IAS and IPS officials. One of the major criticisms of these services is that members are recruited and appointed by the Centre and posted in the states but they remain under the supervision and disciplinary control of the Central government. Further, under Article 311 of the Constitution, no member of an All-India Service shall be dismissed or removed by an authority subordinate to that by which he was appointed. Though they are permanently allotted to states after recruitment, their service conditions are controlled by the Union. In effect, the state's administrative authority over its own employees is severely undermined by the All-India Services.

In case of disagreement between the Union and states over Indian Police Service (IPS), the Union has the overriding power. The State governments, without the prior permission of the Union, initiate no disciplinary action against them. Moreover, the Centre can create an additional All-India Service, if the Rajya Sabha passes a resolution to this effect by two-thirds majority. Further, the members of the central services (IAS and IPS) are put on a different footing than the members of the state police forces, that is, those directly recruited by the State governments, even though IPS officers are assigned to a particular states. Under the Rules, for the deputation of an officer, the Centre needs the concurrence of the state government concerned and concurrence presupposes consultation. But in practice, the Centre has flouted all the rules and took a major role in the maintenance of law and order.

Opposition with regard to the appointment, posting and control of the personnel of all-Indian services came from different states. The staunch opposition to the All-India Services can be seen in the words of late Tamil Nadu Chief Minister M. G. Ramachandran, "It is not necessary to have All-India Services including IAS and IPS. There should be two services, namely, (1) State Civil Services for the purpose of the State government, and (2) Central Services for the purpose of the federal government".

The Rajamannar Committee appointed by the Tamil Nadu Government made following recommendation with regard to the All-India Services. The committee observed that, the "Recruitment through the Union Public Service Commission may be discontinued." The committee recommended that recruitment to the All-India Services be made by holding an examination confined to each state. It said that 'there appeared to be no justification for the constitution of any All-India Service which relates to the subjects that fall within the exclusive field of the state'.

In no other federal Constitution is there a provision for a service that is common to the federal government and the regional governments. The Study Team of the Administrative Reforms Commission on Centre-State Relations in its Report (September 1967) observed: "In a federal set-up, to have an All-India Service that serves the needs of the states but is controlled ultimately by the Union, is an unusual feature." It also recommended for the creation of new All-India Services.

Deployment of CRPF

In the sphere of administrative relations during 1967-1971, the deployment of the Central Reserve Police Force (CRPF) was a source of irritation and tension between the Centre and the states. Sending the CRPF without the prior consultation with the State government became another major controversy in Union-State relations. Generally, the Central armed and police forces are to be used at the State governments' request. But in practice, the Central Reserve forces were sent to the states, much against the wishes of the State governments, without consulting the concerned State governments for safeguarding the central offices. For instance, during E. M. S. Namboodiripad's tenure as the Chief Minister of Kerala, the CRPF was sent under the pretext of protecting the 'central government property', but in reality it was sent to 'punish' the striking government employees.

One of the major arguments put forth by the State governments against the deployment of the Para-military forces was that the 'Public Order' is exclusively a state subject. "Neither the Centre's legislative nor its exclusive power can transgress into the sphere of the state authority. Only if 'public order' is flouted on such a large-scale in a state as to constitute 'internal disturbance', does the Centre's duty as defined in Article 356 gets activated."

Deployment of any of the Centre's force 'in aid of the civil power' is being treated exclusively as a Union subject. The 42 amendment (1976) empowered the Union to deploy a central force at its own initiative, without consulting the State government for dealing with any grave situation of law and order in any State. But this provision was deleted in 1979 (during Janata rule) by the 44th Amendment. Off late, at the Inter-State Council discussions, most states have taken the view that the two subjects of Police and Public Order were included in the State List.

Fiscal Matters

The distribution of financial resources is another area of conflict between the Union and the states. The states demanded for a greater fiscal autonomy. In the division of the financial powers between the Union and the states, the Union gets precedence over the states. The Union government was entrusted with wide powers to tax the sources. For instance, the Union is vested with more taxation powers. The Constitution authorizes the Union to collect surcharges on taxes to raise additional funds in the times of emergency. In practice, surcharge has become a permanent feature of Income Tax structure. Another loophole in taxation system, on account of which states suffer, is the tax, which keeps on expanding and is under the exclusive purview of the Centre. Further, vast resources generated through deficit financing, loans from organized money market in the country, as well as huge funds of foreign aid are under the control of the Union. Moreover, the Centre is also vested with the residuary powers of taxation. As a result of all these, the states have to be dependent on Central assistance.

Grants-in-Aid

The Centre fixes the grants to the states in accordance with the recommendation of a Finance Commission. It is given to the states for undertaking schemes, meet natural calamities, for removal of disparities, etc. The grants-in-aid to states is given solely at the discretion of the Centre. One of the major criticisms against the provision of grants-in-aid is that no well-considered norms were followed in this regard and further the Centre discriminates between the states being ruled by different political parties.

One of the major irritants in the Centre-state relations has been the allocation of economic resources by the Union to the states. Allocation is carried out by the Planning Commission in the area of developmental expenditure, and this has led the states to complain that the resources allocated are inadequate. The states also have power to raise revenue. The role of the Planning Commission has been criticized because of its encroachments upon a "field which some regard as the sole preserve of the Finance Commission".

Working of both the Finance and the Planning Commissions, their design of the transfer system and the approach and methodology adopted by them has come under sharp criticism from various states. The Finance Commission was envisaged in the Constitution as the key institution responsible for dealing with fiscal imbalances between the Centre, as well as among the states. Instead, it's role has been circumscribed by the working of the Planning Commission, which has typically been put outside the Finance Commission's terms of reference.

The Centre-state relation over the distribution of resources has been another major area of controversy. The states demanded for the larger devolution of funds from the Union. The states were unanimous in their demand for a larger share in the Central revenues. The states have consistently argued that "the distribution of net proceeds of divisible taxes lay down the principles of grants-in-aid and any other matter referred to the Commission by the President in the interest of sound finance", has not been effectively implemented or enforced in the interest of resolving the issue of finances.

Apart from the role of Planning Commission in distribution/allocation of resources, the centralized planning machinery, the Central government's increasing hold over the finances of the states, imposition of a surcharge on Income Tax, considerable preponderance in legislative powers for the Union, the supremacy of Parliament in many legislative and other matters, the financial dependency of the states on the Centre's mercy further strained the Union-state relations in the fiscal front.

The initiation of economic reforms in the early 1990s, the increasing role of the regional parties, and the emergence of the coalition government has greatly altered the balance in favour of the states and led to the further devolution of resources from the Centre to the states.

Demand for Autonomy

The Centralizing tendencies of the Union, the failure of the Centre to respect the integrity of the state assembly elections and the frequent dismissal of the elected government led to the demand for more autonomy. The issue of Centre-State relations assumed prominence with the rise and growth of the regional parties like DMK, AIADMK, SAD, NC, AGP, and TDP in the 1970s and '80s. The emergence of new opposition-led governments in Andhra Pradesh and Karnataka in the early 1980's resulted in an intensification of the demands of states for greater autonomy. They accentuated the demands for decentralization in the form of an increased sharing of sovereignty. They dubbed the Constitution as 'essentially unitary in character' as it empowered the federal government 'with some powers at the expense of the autonomy of the states'. These parties emphasized for greater devolution of funds by Union to the states and demanded for greater decentralization. Further, they demanded for restructuring the relations between the Centre and the states with a view to impart a true federal character to the Constitution.

The increasing imbalances in the relationship between the Centre and the states and growing demands for autonomy can be seen from the following instances: a. In Tamil Nadu, for example, public outcry on the imposition of Hindi as the national language; b. In Punjab, Akali Dal pushed the demand for a greater state autonomy, and Sikh militants launched a campaign of terrorism for an independent nation of Khalistan; and c. Apart from this, the demand for separate states also came from the North-Eastern states of Assam, Mizoram, Manipur, Tripura, and Nagaland.

In order to address the concerns on growing centralizing tendencies in the political process, various Commissions and Committees were appointed since Independence, to look into the controversial issues of Union-state relations. Some of them are the JVP Committee, the Dar Commission, the States Reorganization Commission (SRC), the Administrative Reforms Commission, the Rajamannar Committee (1971), and the Sarkaria Commission (1983).

ADMINISTRATIVE REFORMS COMMISSION (ARC)

With the increasing centralizing tendencies of the Union government, especially immediately after 1967, Congress lost power in eight states and office of the Governor became controversial. In view of the widespread criticism, the Union government set up the Administrative Reforms Commission (1967) under the chairmanship of Sri K. Hanumanthayya to look into the Centre-State administrative relations. The commission submitted its report in 1969. Some of the important recommendations of the commission are:

- The commission expressed the view that centralized planning resulted in excessive interference in the freedom of the states to work out their policies and programmes. It also called for the establishment of new All-India Services.

- It also made recommendations with regard to the office of the Governor. A person appointed as Governor should have long experience in public life and administration. Further, it also suggested that proper guidelines should be formulated with regard to exercise of the discretionary powers of the Governor and he should act on his own judgment and discretion in matters relating to submission, as well as reservation of bills for the President's consideration.
- The commission recommended for the settlement of the Inter-state or Centre-state differences through mutual discussion and also suggested the need to establish Inter-State Council under Article 263 of the Constitution.
- On the Union government's role in matters relating to law and order, the committee recommended that the Army, Navy, Air Force or any other armed force might be deployed by the Union in any state, *suo motto*, either at the instance of the State government or the Centre.
- The Commission also recommended that powers should be delegated to the maximum extent to the states with regard to their work on projects in which the Centre is directly interested or which are carried out by them as agents of the Central government.
- It also recommended that the participation of the Union ministers in the Planning Commission be discontinued and the Commission be re-constituted as a non-ministerial expert advisory body, bereft of its entire functions executive in character. The recommendations of the Commission, however, remained on paper and process of centralization continued.

The Rajamarmar Committee and Sarkaria Commission made a number of proposals for restructuring the Union-states relations with a view to according greater autonomy to the states.

Rajamannar Committee

Not satisfied with the position of the State government in relation to the Central government, in 1969, the ruling DMK government in Tamil Nadu appointed a special committee headed by P.V. Rajamannar, a former Chief Justice of the Madras High Court, to examine the working of the Centre-state relations (with special reference to Tamil Nadu) and recommended changes in the allocation of powers between the Union government and the states. The committee submitted its report in May 1971.

Some of the observations made by the committee are, "There are unitary trends, and in the allocation of powers there is a strong bias and tilting of the scales in favour of the Centre". It attributed the presence of the Congress as the ruling party, both at the Centre and in most states, as responsible for the development of the unitary trends.

Some of the important recommendations made by the Rajamannar Committee are as follows:

- The committee recommended for the abolition of the Planning Commission repeal of the Industries (Development and Regulation) Act of 1951. It suggested that in place of the Planning Commission a statutory body consisting of scientific, technical, agricultural and economic experts should be constituted.
- Regarding Finance Commission, the committee suggested that it should be a permanent body with its own Secretariat. It also suggested that they should be given equal representation in the Rajya Sabha.
- To ensure real autonomy for the states, the committee also suggested the transfer of a number of items, not only from the Concurrent to the State List in the Seventh Schedule of the Constitution, but also from the Central to the State List. It recommended the abolition of Articles 356 and 357 of the Constitution. The commission called for the vesting of the residuary power of legislation and taxation solely with the State Legislatures.
- On the financial relations between the Union and the states, the committee emphasized for 'the greater devolution of taxes, so that in actual practice, the need for grants-in-aid under Article 275 is either eliminated or is minimized.' Further the committee sought to widen the tax base devolution of resources to the states by including corporation tax, customs and export duties and the tax on the capital value of assets in the divisible pool.
- Regarding the All-India Services, the committee observed, "Recruitment through the Union Public Service Commission may be discontinued". The committee recommended that recruitment to the All-India Services be made by holding an examination confined to each State.
- The committee also suggested immediate formation of an inter-state council as provided under Article 263 of the Constitution.

Sarkaria Commission

The demand for greater autonomy to the states gathered further momentum. In 1983, the Council of Chief Ministers of the Southern states was set-up to "promote the cause of co-operative federalism between the states and the Centre", calling for equitable distribution of resources between the Centre and the states. On 24 March, 1983, in response to vociferous demand by several opposition leaders, the then Prime Minister Indira Gandhi appointed a commission under the chairmanship of R. S. Sarkaria, a retired judge of the Supreme Court, to study the Centre-State relations.

After five years of deliberations, the Sarkaria Commission submitted its report on Centre-State relations in 1988. The commission suggested a series of concrete steps to strengthen federalism and prevent the misuse of Article 356 for restructuring Union-State relations. The Sarkaria Commission advocated co-operative federalism and recommended greater financial autonomy for the states

Some of the main recommendations of Sarkaria Commission:

- Article 356 which empowers the Union government to impose upon President's rule and the deployment of armed forces for law and order should be made use of sparingly and only at the request of the state.
- Article 258, the Centre's right to confer additional authority on the states, should be used liberally by the Centre.
- The role of the states in expanding the Concurrent List should be enhanced. The Centre should consult states on the Concurrent List. And the residuary field, other than the taxation, should be placed in the Concurrent List.
- The Commission also recommended the need to amend the Constitution in order to give the states greater power and responsibilities.
- The Governors of the states appointed by the Centre should be non-political, non-controversial persons. They should be appointed in consultation with the Chief Ministers.
- The bills reserved for the President's assent should be disposed off within four months.
- Governors, after relinquishing there office should not be eligible for any other appointment or office of profit under the Union or state government.
- The states' shares in revenues generated by them should be increased.
- The Commission recommended for the constitution of the Inter-State Council (ISC) and the revival of the regional councils to enable both Centre and states to work out consensus on federal issues.
- It also recommended that the five Zonal Councils to be re-constituted afresh under Article 263.
- It also recommended the streamlining of the National Development Council and the Planning Commission. Further, it said that the National Development Council should be renamed and reconstituted as the National Economic Development Council (NEDU).
- The commission also recommended for appointment of an expert committee by Union government to recommend reforms in taxation.
- Regarding All India Services, the commission suggested that it should be further strengthened, and every All India Service Officer, whether he is a direct recruit or a promoted officer should be required to put in a minimum service under the Union government. It also suggested for a regular consultation on the management of All India Services between the Centre and the State governments.

The major recommendations of the Sarkaria Committee have been ignored. Further, these recommendations were not given any statutory form.

Post 1990s - Emerging trends in Union-State relations

One of the major trends in federalism in the post-1990s is the resurgence of state governments as vibrant players in India's political system. The states are making themselves heard and felt politically and economically more than ever before since Independence. Prominent role of the states, in the post 1990's Indian political system, can be attributed to following reasons: The decline of the one-party dominance, both at the Centre and in states; the rise of the regional parties; formation of coalition governments at the federal level; and the efforts to deregulate several sectors of the economy (liberalization) made such a change possible. According to Ian Copland in the 1990's, "one feature of political transformation is the diffusion of power downward and greater autonomy and power for the states".

According to Lawrence Dsaez, "The shift from one-party dominance to coalition politics and multi-party governance, coupled with the process of economic liberalization initiated by India in the 1990s altered the federal calculus. As an outcome of these developments, a transformation in the federal relations from inter-governmental competition between the Central government and the states to inter-jurisdictional co-operation between the states can be seen. As a consequence, the states no longer need to rely exclusively on the central government for their economic and industrial development. The transformation from co-operative federalism to inter-jurisdictional competition has prompted states to compete with each other for further foreign investments inflows."

Rise of Federal Market Economy

Rudolph and Rudolph attributes the changing phase of Union-State relations to India's move from a command economy to a federal market economy in the post-1990's. Under conditions of a federal market economy, the states command a larger share of economic sovereignty than under the centrally planned economy. Rudolphs identify the following factors for the emergence of the 'federal market economy': Economic liberalization launched in 1991 by the Narasimha Rao Congress Government led to the dismantling of the permit-license raj and an increasing reliance on market. The decline of Central public investment and the growth of private investment have given the federal states a larger role in the economic liberalization and in promoting investment and economic growth.

Economic reforms assigned greater powers to the State governments and infused greater competition for control over them. As a consequence of these reforms, the states have become the principle arena for private investment. States are directly negotiating with the global agencies like World Bank for aid and assistance for the developmental projects. For instance, Andhra Pradesh has secured support from the World Bank; DFID is also working to support state-level reforms in Andhra Pradesh, West Bengal, Madhya Pradesh and Orissa.

Moreover, by the end of the 1990's the State Chief Minister became the key player in the federal market economy. In the post-Economic liberalization era, the Chief Ministers of various states have been playing a prominent role. For instance, the Andhra Pradesh and Karnataka Chief Ministers travelled all over the world to meet the business leaders, and were also able to attract and woo investors and persuade the likes of Bill Gates to endorse the idea of investing in these states.

Some of the other trends visible in the context of Centre-region relations in the post-1990's era are as follows:

- The unprecedented participation of the regional parties in the federal government in the post-1990's era is due to the shift from dominant-party to multi-party politics and the rise of state parties.
- The Supreme Court's ruling in the *Bommai vs Union of India,* delivered in March 1994, curtailed the constitutional power vested in the Central Government to dismiss a State government under article 356 of the Constitution.
- Another emerging feature that can be seen in the Union-State relations in the 1990's is the greater acceptance of decentralization and the greater devolution of political and economic power to the states by the Union. Not only Central governments but also States themselves are undertaking modest degree of devolution. For instance, the devolution of powers to Panchayat (village) level institutions is being taken more seriously.
- Many new States have been formed. The central government's ability to create new states recently led to the further consolidation of the Indian federation. The three newly created States are: Uttaranchal, Jharkhand and Chhattisgarh.

Therefore in the 1990's, the State governments were playing a key role in the national politics with the emergence of a federal market economy. According to Sumit Ganguly, the logic of economic liberalization is working in favour of a deeper and full federalism. The states in India's federal system command more economic and political sovereignty than they did under a planned economy. As a result, the real power and decision-making had moved away from the Centre to the states. In the 1990s, province-states were no longer preoccupied with the question of autonomy from the Centre but were exerting power within and over the Centre. Politically, the shift from one-party dominance to fragile coalition governments has changed the balance among institutions at the Centre.

SUMMARY

- Article 1 of the Indian constitution describes India as a Union of States. The framers of the Indian constitution intended to make the Union government strong enough to tide over the difficulties created by the fissiparous tendencies at the time of Independence.

- The Constitution of India clearly demarcates the division of powers between the Union and the Sstates. Basically, there are three broad areas of Centre-state relations. These are: legal, administrative and financial relations.
- The legislative powers between the Union and the states are enumerated into three lists, i.e. the Union List, the State List and the Concurrent List. Residual powers are vested in the Union.
- The Finance Commission oversees the division of financial resources between the Centre and the states. Its function is to ensure orderly and judicious devolution of resources from the Union to the States.
- The Planning Commission advises the Union government regarding the desirable formula for the transfer of resources to the states as recommended by the Finance Commission
- The National Development Council is one of the key organizations of the planning system in India. The main responsibility of NDC is the approval of Five Year Plans and look into the issues related to economic development in the country. It is entrusted with the responsibility of laying down guidelines for the formulation of a national plan.
- The Inter-State Council is a forum for effective co-ordination and co-operation between the units in the federal system. It was established to provide a platform for both the Union and the states to discuss and deliberate on the matters of common interest.
- Some of the unitary trends in the working of India's federal polity, which led to the major source of confrontations are as follows: the one-party dominance both at the national and state politics, centralization of institutions like Planning Commission, and All India Civil Services. The arbitrary dismissal of the State governments and imposition of President's Rule (misuse of Article 356), and the partisan role of the Governor.
- To address the concerns on growing centralizing tendencies in the political process, various commissions and committees were appointed since Independence to look into the controversial issues of Union-State relations. Some of them are the Administrative reforms committee, the Rajamannar Committee (1971) and the Sarkaria Commission (1983).
- One of the major emerging trends in the Indian federalism, in the post 1990s, is the resurgence of State governments as vibrant players in India's political system with the emergence of a federal market economy. Prominent role of the states in the post 1990's Indian Political System can be attributed to following reasons: the decline of the one-party dominance, both at the centre and the states, the

rise of the regional parties, formation of coalition governments at the federal level and the efforts to deregulate several sectors of the economy (liberalization). Today, the states in India's federal system command more economic and political sovereignty than what they did under planned economy. As a result the real power and decision-making moved away from the Centre to the states. Politically, the shift from one-party dominance to fragile coalition governments has changed the balance among institutions at the Centre.

QUESTIONS

1. "Indian Constitution is federal in form but unitary in spint". Comment.
2. Bring out the main characteristics of the Indian Federal system.
3. What are the problem areas in the relationship between the centre and the states in India?
4. What are the recommendations of the Sarkaria Commission?
5. Examine the role, organization and functions of the planning commission and its apex body NDC (National Development Council).
6. Analyse the major issues creating tension between the centre and the state.

9

Local Government Institution in India

After reading this chapter, you will be conversant with:

- Urban Local Government
- Rural Local Government

INTRODUCTION

The process of urbanization which began with the onset of Industrial Revolution had remarkably altered the socio-economic and political systems all over the world. The age old customs, traditions, feudalism, were replaced by new ones. The feudal economy based on agricultural system was replaced by the industrial and commercial economy. The royal absolutism and monarchical form of government declined and gave rise to democratic institutions where the citizen played a crucial role in deciding the governing body of the nation. All these changes shifted the emphasis from rural areas to urban towns with the role of cities being emphasized in the process of developmental activities. The cities were considered to be the engines of growth, resulting in a massive inflow of people into urban areas leading to socio-economic and political problems. The national government was concentrating more on nation building activities and taking care of national interests and was unable to cater services to the urbanites. It was felt that administration of urban affairs would be better looked after if it were entrusted to people residing in the area itself as they would be in a better position to understand their local problems rather than the national government placed miles away. Thus, the process of entrusting local services to local people began which heralded urban local government in modern period.

Although, urban local government was not new to India as one finds detailed references in Kautilya's Arthashastra and Megasthene's Indica regarding the administration of Patalitputra, the capital city of Mauryans which occupied a place of significance during ancient times in India. Although urban areas flourished during medieval period, the rulers did not take much interest in the development of self-governing bodies. Unsanitary conditions prevailed in the city of Madras where the British army was stationed. The soldiers suffered from malaria and other diseases on account of such unsanitary conditions. Therefore, the British regime in India decided to establish an urban government on the lines of its experience back home. In 1688, the first Municipal Corporation was established in Madras followed by Calcutta and Bombay in 1772 and 1793, respectively. After independence, the process of entrusting civic affairs to local people continued and depending on the size of the area and number of people residing in it, various types of urban local bodies have been established. After detecting some flaws in the functioning of urban local bodies, the government passed the 74th amendment to the Constitution providing constitutional status to urban local bodies heralding a new phase of their ascendancy.

Elements of Local Government

There are certain important elements of urban local bodies found in almost all parts of the world irrespective of the country and the prevailing political system.

- It is observed all over the world that the governments at the national level and provincial level are more concerned about policies having wider ramifications. They primarily deal with the issues of larger interests of the nation and people showing little concern about the civic affairs. It is assumed that civic affairs are looked after by the governments at the local level by popular representation assisted by civil servants. In majority of the cases, popular elements in the form of elected representatives are inducted into the administrative process to look after the local issues as the government is involved in policies and issues of wider interest and policy decisions. The day-to-day services which can be provided at the local level like sanitation, water supply, roads, and street lights, etc. are entrusted to the local bodies. This is particularly true in the unitary form of government where the central government handles the issues and policies pertaining to national and international developments and the local bodies primarily deal with the above stated functions of providing direct services to the people.
- It is found that certain local problems are peculiar and unique to some areas and can be understood by local residents only. The officials or any other individuals empowered to solve such problems cannot solve them unless they are aware of the pros and cons in detail. Under such conditions, local inhabitants are in a better and appropriate position to handle such issues.
- Since a local self-government is also the representative government of the area, local problems are bound to receive prompt and timely attention reducing delay in the decision making process and offering quick solutions. One finds that officials are not needed to involve themselves in the local issues.
- Certain local functions like sanitation, cleaning of roads, sewerage, maintenance of public health, and water supply, etc. are performed better by the local government as they have better knowledge of local affairs rather than any other higher agency located outside the local area.

- Some functions necessitate the co-operation and participation of the local people and such functions could be discharged by the local bodies having local representation more easily and efficiently.
- The aspiration and the interests of the people are exhibited in the form of a request for the creation of a local government body headed by responsible and accountable elected representatives guiding and controlling the administrative staff and resources in the accomplishment of goals of the local government institutions;
- The popular representatives get an opportunity at the local government level to understand the dynamics of a working democracy. Thus, it provides administrative training ground for the political executives. In other words, local bodies become the base to provide recruits to the state and central governments.
- The local bodies, providing services to the people at local level, enable the state and central governments to address the issues which are of greater importance and international in character. This is true in the case of natural calamities like famine, where the local government institutions play a significant role.
- The impact of the local government on the citizens is more compared to the functioning of central and state governments. The influence of a local government is easily visible to the citizens.

The local government system in India is described below under two separate heads as 'A' and 'B'. Part A deals with urban local government and Part B with rural local self government.

URBAN LOCAL GOVERNMENT

The 74th Amendment

The dismal conditions of the local government institutions in India, persisting even after forty three years of independence made the government headed by Rajiv Gandhi, the then prime minister, to constitutionalize the local self-government institutions to function with dignity and autonomy. In the year 1992, amendments were made to the Indian Constitution to strengthen the rural and urban bodies to ensure effective delivery of goods and services to the people. The 74th amendment was a step in the direction of according legal and constitutional status to urban local bodies. The amendment heralded a new era in the Indian political and administrative system. Although detailed provisions were enumerated in the constitution regarding the functions of the state and central governments it was not done in case of urban local bodies which were despised by both central and state governments. They did not like the emergence of urban local bodies, since they were considered as contenders for power. Although many committees and reports recommended strengthening of these urban bodies, they were conveniently put aside by all governments irrespective of political affiliations. The pathetic condition of these local bodies was described in the said amendment act in the following manner.

"In many states local bodies have become weak and ineffective on account of variety of reasons, including the failure to hold regular elections, prolonged suppressions and inadequate devolution of powers and functions. As a result, urban local bodies are not able to perform effectively as vibrant democratic units of self-government."

According constitutional status to urban bodies is a welcome step to empower people at the local level to manage their own affairs. They would be able to provide solutions to grievances more swiftly as elected representatives would be controlling administration. The 74th amendment strives to bring drastic changes in the functioning of urban local bodies by eradicating ills of the prevalent system. The provisions of the amendment are designed to ensure popular and active participation of the people in the local government affairs. The following are, inter-alia, some important provisions of the said amendment.

- **Constitutional status:** The state government, irrespective of their political affiliations, decried the dominating attitude and role of central government regarding administrative directives and financial grants. The dominating role irked many a state governments, some of whom adopted confrontational approach towards central government to get their work done. However, these very state governments treated their local bodies with the same indifference, by not granting enough autonomy and finances. The weakened urban local bodies bore the brunt of being inefficient and were consistently strangulated by state governments. As controlling authorities, the state governments had dissolution powers regarding urban local bodies. Such conditions, to a large extent, were rectified by the 74th amendment which accorded constitutional status to urban local bodies, thereby strengthening them vis-a-vis state governments. The jurisdiction of legislative affairs and the finances for the local bodies were clearly demarcated by the amendment and the state governments were barred from entering the jurisdiction demarcated for the local bodies.
- **Regular elections:** It was observed in the past that state governments consistently and intentionally did not conduct elections to urban local bodies on a regular basis since it would strengthen popular representatives. The state governments did not want people to use elections to urban local bodies as a referendum to their policies and activities. Even elected members of the legislative assembly did not like regular elections to urban local bodies as popular representatives at the local level would diminish their hegemony over welfare activities and provision for civic facilities. The 74th amendment rectified the flaw by making it obligatory on the part of the state government to conduct elections regularly. The regular elections would facilitate people to be at the helm of affairs regarding civic facilities and also development. The elected representatives would be accountable to the citizen for non performance of their duties towards citizens.

- **Reservation for women:** Women played a negligible role throughout the period of development of democratic institutions in India. They were not allowed to enter several fields including politics. This state of affairs did not continue for long as they began to conquer male bastions. But politics still eluded them as only few privileged women could enter it, although they constituted almost half of the Indian population. They failed to enter the political field because of social and economic hurdles. Even though women could not get the reservation bill passed pertaining to reservation of one-third seats in the parliament, the 74th amendment provided the same as a positive sign of women's development. The amendment paved the way for the development of women and their active participation in politics, and highlighted the problems of women in particular and citizens' grievances in general.

Constitution of Urban Bodies

In the past, urban local bodies were constituted without any scientific and rational basis. The priority was given to political and social considerations which made urban local bodies unviable regarding generation of financial resources. This directly impinged on efforts of urban local bodies to generate additional resources which compelled them to depend on the state government for finances, and thus, urban local bodies became the limbs or extensions of the state governments. To remedy such flaws, the amendment provided for certain norms to be considered for the establishment of urban local bodies as follows:

- Number of people residing in the area.
- The density of population of the area.
- Sources of income generation.
- Number of people engaged in agricultural and non-agricultural activities.
- Other economic factors.

The 74th amendment to the Indian constitution provided for three types of urban local bodies as shown below:

Three types of Municipalities:

- Nagar Panchayats for areas in transition from a rural area to urban area;
- Municipal Councils for smaller urban areas;
- Municipal Corporations for larger urban areas.

Thus, it is found that the constitutional amendment provided for these three categories to take care of civic affairs at the local level on the basis of the level of urbanization, population and economic activities. A small developing urban area or a transitional area could be called 'Nagar Panchayat' with its population heading towards diversification in economic activities and gradual increase in employment opportunities. Municipal Council could be constituted in case of such urban area which is developed, and at the same time having ample economic activities and employment opportunities for the people. A Municipal Corporation could be constituted in case of areas which can be termed as completely urban and economy is completely dependent on economic activities like industries, commerce, and service sectors.

According to the amended constitution, urban local bodies shall be filled by elected members from the territorial constituencies based on the recent census. The delimitation should be such that each representative of an urban local body would represent almost equal number of citizens. This uniformity enables popular representatives to offer better services to people. Added to this, individuals having specialized knowledge and experience in the affairs of municipal administration should be included to enhance its efficiency. The urban local body should consist of members of the Lok Sabha and the members of the legislative assembly of the state whose constituencies are a part of the urban local body. The association of the national and state level political representatives serves two purposes. Firstly, they would be able to know the functioning of urban local bodies; and secondly, the members of urban local body would be able to present their views and grievances pertaining to finances, staff and development.

One finds that the amendment gave sufficient scope and flexibility to state governments regarding the inclusion and constitution of members of urban local bodies. It is observed that almost all states have preferred a council or corporation representing the local body. The council corporation consists of members who are directly elected by the people, and each member representing a ward. The council is headed by the Chairman and the corporation is headed by a Mayor. In addition to the members and the head of local body, some states have preferred standing committees which are empowered to take some important decisions. There is a permanent body of officials to assist the council headed by the municipal commissioner. Thus, one finds the existence of a body of members elected directly by the people as the head of the local body and permanent staff headed by the commissioner constituting the main elements of an urban local body.

The municipalities are given tenure of five years and in case of dissolution, a new body should be constituted within six months of the dissolution. The constitution empowered the state governments to resort to dissolution of municipalities under the following circumstances:

- If the urban bodies do not perform well according to the provisions of the act.
- If they fail to comply with the orders of the state government.
- If they exceed their conferred powers.
- If finances and credit-worthiness of municipal bodies is at stake.

Finances

A Finance Commission is constituted to review the financial relations between the state government and urban local bodies. The commission would review financial position of the urban local bodies and make such recommendations to the Governor of the state, which would strengthen local bodies. The recommendations would include the principles according to which grants should be made to the local bodies, the distribution of finances, net proceeds of the taxes, tolls, fines, and allocation of finances to the municipalities according to their shares. The commission would ensure that the financial relations between the state governments and municipalities would be based on sound fiscal principles rather than political exigencies. Besides, the commission is expected to ensure financial viability and independence of municipalities, so that they are not dissolved on the ground of financial unavailability.

The amendment empowered the state governments to authorize municipalities to collect certain taxes, fees, duties and tolls with certain procedures subject to legal norms. The state government, in the interest of the municipalities could completely assign certain taxes, tolls, fees and duties collected by it to the municipalities. Besides, the government can provide certain grants from the consolidated fund of the state to ensure certain important functions by the municipalities. Added to the above sources of finances, other revenue sources include local taxes imposed by the municipalities, certain user charges, profits from commercial ventures, and shared taxes with the state government.

Urban local bodies should resort to appropriate blending of internal and external financial resources to sustain their positive and fruitful existence. Since there is so much scope to increase finance from the external sources, the urban local bodies should tap potential tax sources in its area of functioning. During the process of taxation and tapping of additional resources, the urban bodies should be within the purview of legislative and constitutional limits. Added to this, socio-economic and political conditions should be studied in such a way that generation of additional resources in no way scuttles the source of revenue.

Functions Assigned to Urban Bodies

The twelfth schedule added to the Indian constitution under article 243 allotted certain functions to the local bodies which are as follows:

- Urban planning, including town planning.
- Regulation of land-use and construction of buildings.
- Planning for economic and social development.
- Roads and bridges.
- Water supply for domestic, industrial and commercial purposes.
- Public health, sanitation conservancy and solid waste management.
- Fire services.
- Urban forestry, protection of the environment and promotion of ecological aspects.
- Safeguarding the interests of weaker sections of society, including the handicapped and mentally retarded.

- Slum improvement and up gradation.
- Urban poverty alleviation.
- Provision of urban amenities and facilities, such as parks, gardens and playgrounds.
- Promotion of cultural, educational and aesthetic aspects.
- Burials and burial grounds, cremation grounds and electric crematoriums.
- Cattle pounds, prevention of cruelty to animals.
- Vital statistics including registration of births and deaths.
- Public amenities, including street lighting, parking lots, bus stops and public conveniences.
- Regulation of slaughter houses and tanneries.

Impact of Decentralization Process

Although the process of decentralization is not new to the Indian system of governance, it had been rejuvenated by the 74th amendment. The amendment brought drastic changes, although not in structural form, in some areas which go a long way in the process of social development as it provided reservation to the most neglected or deprived sections of Indian society, i.e. the women. It is they who have been really empowered through the 74th amendment to energize urban local bodies. The functioning of urban local bodies in the last decade clearly shows that women had really come out to participate actively in civic affairs. Added to it many other positive results have been observed which symbolize the emergence of a truly urban government in which the citizens would actively participate. The other results of urban local government energized in the form of 74th amendment are as follows:

- Women benefited the most.
- People have taken keen interest in civic affairs as they directly impinge upon their day-to-day life.
- The state governments have constituted State Finance Commissions to suggest ways of improve the local finances and also distribution of revenue between the state government and the local bodies.
- Regular elections are taking place in many states.

CRITICAL APPRAISAL

Urban local government is considered to be more concerned with the day-to-day services like sanitation, supply of drinking water, sewerage cleaning, street lighting, etc. The expectations of the people were belied in many areas of urban affairs. The urban local governments failed to deliver services to the people. Every urban area is besieged by innumerable problems like lack of interest of people in civic affairs except politicians, growing urban poverty, inadequate housing facilities, failure to supply adequate drinking water, lack of sanitation facilities particularly to the urban poor, inadequate public transportation, growing traffic congestion, lack of planning for development of the urban areas, lack of sufficient health services to urban poor, insufficient civil society participation, inadequate education services, increasing air pollution, lack of care for environment, insufficient facilities for the disposal of solid waste, and lot more. Citizens should not depend on urban local bodies for all the services. It is their bounded duty to adhere to laws of the urban local bodies to facilitate it in providing better services. They should pay local taxes, cess and dues, so that urban local bodies are financially strengthened and need not depend on state governments for finances. Once the local bodies and people co-operate in the generation of financial and other resources, true democratic centralization begins at the local level.

PANCHAYATI RAJ INSTITUTIONS (PRIs)

To deal with the socio-economic and political problems at the rural and urban level, the framers of the constitution desired to entrust the responsibility to urban and rural local bodies under the Directive Principles of State Policy which created Village Panchayats enjoying commensurate authority. To this end, community development projects were taken up in 1952 without peoples participation resulting adversely. Therefore, the Government of India appointed a committee called 'Committee on Plan Projects' headed by Dr. Balwant Rai Mehta. The committee after extensive tour and discussions with officials and non-officials recommended, inter alia the following aspects:

- Three tiered structure of Panchayati Raj bodies from village to district, hierarchically linked.
- Bestowing genuine transfer of power and adequate resources for effective functioning.
- Devolution of power to these bodies in addition to channeling all the development functions through these bodies.

The three-tiered system entails Village Panchayat at the village level, Panchayat Samithi at the block level and Zilla Parishad at the district level. Among the three tiers, Panchayat Samithi or block was visualized as most effective and strong body. The organically linked Panchayati Raj structure as given by B.R.Mehta committee is described below:

Village Panchayat: The Village Panchayat will be at the grass root level. It is an elected body with co-option of two women members, one from Scheduled Caste and one from Scheduled Tribes. The Sarpanch or the president will be elected by the elected representatives of the Village Panchayats.

Functions

The Village Panchayat has to discharge the following obligatory functions and also act as an agent of the Panchayat Samithi.

- Provision of water supply for domestic use.
- Sanitation.
- Maintenance of streets, drains and tanks.
- Lighting of the village streets.
- Land management.
- Maintenance of records relating to cattle.
- Relief of distressed.
- Maintenance of village records.
- Supervision of primary schools.
- Welfare of backward classes.
- Collection and maintenance of statistics.
- An agency to collect land revenue desirability.

Finances

The Village Panchayat should be entrusted with the following main sources for their finances:

- Property or house tax.
- Taxes on markets, bazaars.
- Taxes on vehicles like cars, bicycles, boats and pack animals.
- Octroi or terminal tax.
- Conservancy tax.
- Electricity tax.
- Water tax.
- Income from cattle ponds.
- Fees charged on sale and registration of animals within local area.
- Fees from slaughter houses.
- Grants from Panchayat Samithi.

The budget of the Village Panchayat should be approved by the Panchayat Samithi.

PANCHAYAT SAMITHI

Panchayat Samithi is an intermediary level elected statutory body endowed with comprehensive functions, bestowed with requisite authority and resources. It should be free from governmental interference and control. The state government shall have to give guidance. The following are the details of the covering areas, functions and sources of finances of the Panchayat Samithi.

Area

The area of Panchayat Samithi shall neither be too large and unmanageable, nor too small negating the principles of economy and efficiency. It should be financially viable and within the reach of the common people. The committee, inter alia recommended that the existing block be constituted as a Panchayat Samithi.

- It is a unit of rural local government.
- It is the sole authority for the development of the following:
  - agriculture.
  - animal husbandry.
  - co-operation.
  - minor irrigation.
  - village industry.
  - primary education.
  - local communications.
  - sanitation.
  - health.
  - medical relief.
  - local amenities.

The committee recommended the following sources of finance for the governance of Panchayat Samithi:

- A fixed percentage of land revenue collected within the block area.
- Cess on land revenue, water rate.
- Tax on professions and trade.
- Surcharge on duty on the transfer of immovable property.
- Rents and profits accruing from property, e.g., ferries, fisheries.
- Tolls and leases of roads.
- Pilgrim tax.
- Tax on entertainment.
- Primary education cess.
- Proceeds from periodical fares and markets.
- A share of the motor tax.
- Voluntary public corporations.
- Grants from government.

Composition

The Panchayat Samithi shall have an elected chairman with twenty members. All the Sarpanches are the members of the Panchayati Samiti. The elected representatives are authorized to co-opt two women members interested in matters relating to women and children. At least one woman from the Scheduled Castes and Scheduled Tribes, constituting five percent of the total population of the Panchayat Samithi area, should be co-opted. Apart from these, two members must also be co-opted from the local area, who have rich experience in administration, public life or rural development. Cooperatives within the jurisdiction of Panchayat Samithi should also be represented. The elected body of Panchayat Samithi along with co-opted members shall remain in the office for five years.

ZILLA PARISHAD

Composition

Revenue district shall be the jurisdiction of the Zilla Parishad. It was considered to be a coordinating unit unlike Panchayat Samithi, in addition to performing supervisiory functions. All the presidents of the Panchayat Samithi are members of Zilla Parishad. The members of the legislative assembly representing the district are also the members of the Parishad including medical and health, agriculture, veterinary, engineering, education, backward classes, welfare, public works, and other development departments. The chairperson is to be elected by the members of Zilla Parishad. One of the district officers will have to act as the secretary of Zilla Parishad. Among other things, **B.R. Mehta committee** recommended the following:

Functions

The committee desired that the Zilla Parishad shall be, at the risk of repetition, a coordinating and supervisory body and never discharge executive functions. The functions of the Zilla Parishad are enumerated below:

- It has to approve the budgets of Samithis in the district.
- It must distribute funds given by the government to the Panchayat Samithi.
- It has to co-ordinate and consolidate the block plans in the district.
- It has to process the request for grants to the state government.
- It has to supervise the functions of the Panchayat Samithi in the district.

However, the state governments must be given discretionary powers to organize Panchayati Raj bodies to suit their conditions. While some consider that Zilla Parishad is an effective and strong body, some vote for the Panchayat Samithi. Some states have adopted the two-tier system while others followed three-tiered structure.

Ashok Mehta Committee

Main Recommendations: During the period of the Janata Party rule, a committee headed by Ashok Mehta recommended, inter-alia, the creation of a Mandal Panchayat instead of the Panchayat Samithi. This Mandal Panchayat was to be smaller than the latter so as to take the administration to the door steps of the people. Thus, Panchayat Raj was to be two tiered structure. Few states like Andhra Pradesh have adopted this system. The concept of reaching people appears to be laudable though in practice it proves otherwise. The Mandal Panchayat does not have the requisite finances to take up development functions as the resources mobilized in the area are not sufficient to meet the demands of the salaries of the personnel working at the *mandal*. Whatever the development takes place, it is on account of the grants given by the state government only. It amounts to state that the local self government units are reduced to local government units and made subservient to the state government.

73rd Constitutional Amendment: A Mile Stone In the Local Self-Government in India

The intent of having local self-governments found place in Directive Principles of State Policy (Article 40) and since then, appeared in different forms in different states from time to time. Two committees chaired by Mehtas laid down the foundation for working of PRIs in the country, but many other committees recommended for constitution at status to PRIs. The following are some of the chief provisions of the 73rd constitutional amendment, which came into being on 24 April 1992:

- Empowerment to weaker sections by means of reservations in the local self-government bodies to the tune of one-third seats for women members.
- Devolution of powers and commensurate finances to Panchayati Raj bodies to uphold their dignity and autonomy.
- The Panchayati Raj officials must be trained to provide effective assistance in the field of administration, and also finances.
- Conducting elections every five years by the State Election Commission.

GRAMSABHA

Another notable development in the Panchayat Raj system was the creation of 'Gram Sabha', quite in the spirit of democratic functioning of the system at the grass root level. Article 243(b) of the Indian constitution provided the creation of Gram Sabha.

Gram Sabha meetings are convened at least twice a year. The first meeting discusses the developmental plans and approves the budget and the second meeting is concerned with approving the activities and also the accounts. The meetings have to be convened by the president of the Village Panchayat and presided over by him. The decisions are reached by a simple majority vote. But in practice, it is observed that the system has been surviving more on paper, since only the entry of such meetings are found in the book or register without any meeting being actually held.

State Finance Commission

Yet another remarkable development in the light of long experience of working of Panchayati Raj system that took place was the 73rd amendment of the Indian Constitution. The said amendment recognized the Panchayati Raj bodies as constitutional bodies, empowered with requisite finances apart from conducting elections to the Panchayati Raj bodies as a constitutional obligation as in the case of State Legislatures, and Parliament. State Finance Commission was created to grant and disburse the funds to Panchayati Raj bodies. The State Finance Commission is also a constitutional body, the composition of which is also being determined by the state governments since they have the discretion to appoint the chairperson and the members. Those who do not possess any experience in the field of local government and rural development are drafted for the purpose, which should be forbidden.

CRITICAL APPRAISAL

Empowering the rural local bodies with requisite authority and finances to enable them to be autonomous and continue to operate with dignity and independence was long overdue. Despite the required amendments in the constitution, the attitude of state governments did not change much. Though the powers are given through their respective acts, in practice they are all usurped by the state governments. The state governments resort to appointing their officials to discharge certain functions which fall under the purview of the Panchayati Raj bodies. Further, the finances, i.e. grants are not released in time. Sometimes, the elected representatives have to come out to the streets to demand the release of finances. It may be appropriate to state that the entire arena of Panchayati Raj functioning vis-a-vis state government centres around the psychological dictum 'Love-hate relationship'. The state leadership needs the rural leadership's support in the general elections, but it is afraid that the same leadership would likely to be a contender for power in the future.

Rajiv Gandhi government brought two constitutional amendment Act (64th & 65th) for this purpose, but could not sucessed in passing them through Rajya Sabha even though Lok Sabha passed them. The critics of these bills thought that they were encroaching upon the states' jurisdiction. After Narsimha Rao government came into power in 1991; these bills were passed with modifications.

SUMMARY

- The history of local self governments in India dates back to Mauryan Empire and even the British government recognised its utility and tried to give it a modern outlook.
- As a compromise between strong advocacy of Gandhians for Village Swaraj and Ambedkar's strong criticism of ills inflicting the rural society, the local self-governments found the place in Directive Principles of State Policy (Article 40).
- The Seventy-fourth Constitutional Amendment Act accorded Constitutional status to local self-governments in urban areas, providing for a Nagar Panchayat for a transitional area, a Municipal Council for a smaller urban area and a Municipal Corporation for a larger urban area.
- The 74th Amendment Act also provides for Ward Committees, State Finance Commission, District Planning Committee and Metropolitan Planning Committee.
- Schedule Twelfth contains the list of subjects for the municipalities.
- The 73rd Constitutional Amendment Act deals with Panchayati Raj Institutions, which provided for an optional three tier system. Gram Panchyat, Panchayat Samiti and Zila Parishad. The list of objects for PRIs has been given under Eleventh Schedule.
- Both these Constitutional amendment sets provide for regular elections of local bodies by State Election Commission, one third seats to be reserved for women, reservation of seats for SCs, STs, and backward class of citizens.

QUESTIONS

1. Discuss the major features of 74th Constitutional Amendment Act.
2. What are the major recommendations of Balwant Rai Metha Committee report? Compare the report of BR Metha Committee with Ashok Metha Committee.
3. Critically analyse the features of 73rd Constitutional Amendment Act and challenges to its effective implementation.

10

Indian Party System

After reading this chapter, you will be conversant with:

- Meaning and Definition of Political Parties
- Role and Function of Political Parties
- Evolution and Features of Party System in India
- Party System in India
- National and Regional Parties
- Coalition Government

Introduction

Political parties are widely regarded as indispensable to the proper functioning of a democratic society. They act as a link between the people and Government. Political parties nominate candidates for office. Parties are a means by which people of broadly similar interests can meet, organize and campaign. They are the vehicles through which individuals and groups work to secure political power. Political parties serve as a forum in crystallizing public opinion. The party, which secures the majority in the legislature, forms the government and the other parties form the opposition. The opposition parties scrutinize the use of power and force by the ruling party. Further, they also expose the shortcomings of the Government. Political parties promote a specific ideology or a specific interest group and act as a channel of communication between the Government and the masses. Political parties provide due representation to different sections of population. They enlighten the masses about the political situation and the various problems faced by the country. In the words of Huntington, "Parties provide the institutional means of initiating, sustaining and accelerating change, and of absorbing the impact of that change" .

DEFINITIONS

According to Leacock, "By a political party we mean, more or less organized groups of citizens who act together as a political unit. They share or profess to share the same opinions on public questions, and by exercising their voting power towards a common end, seek to obtain control of the government".

According to Gettell, "A political party consists of a group of citizens more or less organized, who act as political unit and who, by the use of their voting power, aim to control the government and carry out their general policies."

Maclver says, "A political party is an association organized in support of some principle or policy which, by constitutional means, endeavour to make the determinant of government".

According to Edmund Burk, "A political party is a body of men united for promoting their joint endeavours of the national interest upon some political principles in which they believed".

From the above definitions, the conclusion drawn is that four things are essential for the formation of a party. First, people should be organized. Second, there should be similarity of principles. Third, the aim of a political party should be to attain political power. And fourth, a political party should use constitutional means for attaining political power.

ROLE AND FUNCTIONS OF POLITICAL PARTIES

In modern political systems, political parties play a significant role. Some of the important functions performed by the political parties are as follows:

- Parties play a pivotal role in educating masses about the political situation and help them to form an opinion. Political parties, during the time of elections, hold discussions on various social, economic and political issues. They also mobilize the masses to actively participate in the political process. An important trait of a well-structured political party is to clearly tell the electorate about the various problems faced by the country.
- Political parties play a crucial role in running the government. They also influence the decision-making process. The party that gains maximum number of votes during elections forms the government. Since the party in power represents the entire population and their aspirations, it is called as the representative form of government. The wishes of the people are articulated through government.
- Political parties are central to an understanding of how politics works. They provide a link between citizens and the government, and between the electorate and the representative institutions. They act as the transmitter of ideas, opinion and approaches to social needs and national goals.
- Apart from the ruling party, the opposition parties also have a pivotal role in a Parliamentary form of government. They check on the party in power and curtail any despotic tendencies. An opposition party exposes various loopholes in the administration and brings them to the notice of the people. The criticism by the opposition party makes the ruling party to be careful in its activities.

- Political parties provide due representation to different sections of the population. They unite different segments of the society on common goals and attain political power to form the government. They use mass media, public forum and local organizations to disseminate their views and build public opinion. Without political parties, it is impossible to implement any programme aimed at the benefit of the people.
- Apart from the above mentioned functions, some of the other functions of the political parties include the nomination of the candidates for the offices of the government, and the presentation of alternative sets of policies. Further, parties also serve the purpose of creating leadership by recruiting and training activists.

PARTY SYSTEM

The party system essentially means the way the political parties interact with one another within the politically competitive nature and beyond. G. Sartori describes a party system as, "The system of interactions resulting from inter-party competition". There are three types of party systems in various governments in the world today: (a) The single party systems, (b) The two-party systems, and (c) The multi-party systems.

Party System in India

India has witnessed evolution of a multi-party system. In 1952, seventy four parties contested elections, while this number has been consistently increasing since 1989. According to one estimate, there are over two hundred political parties in India. The mention of a political party is not found anywhere in the Constitution of India. However, the Tenth Schedule of the Constitution, added by the Constitution (Fifty-second Amendment) Act, 1985, deals with the disqualification of a person for being a member of either House of Parliament [Article 102(2)] or the Legislative Assembly or Legislative Council of a State [Article 191(2)], on the ground of defection from a political party. Electoral system of India is largely based on the British pattern. The Constitution did not provide any details about the electoral system and left it to the Parliament to determine. Accordingly, the Parliament passed a number of laws to regulate the electoral system. Some prominent laws enacted for this purpose include the Representation of People's act, 1950 and 1951; Presidential and Vice-Presidential Election act, 1952 and Delimitation act, 1952.

The two major categories of political parties are: national and state parties. As of today, there are six national parties (seven after the split in the Janata Dal in August 1999) and thirty eight regional parties recognized by the Election Commission of India. If a political party is recognized in four or more states, it is considered as a national party. The national parties are Indian National Congress, Bharatiya Janata Party, Communist Party of India, Communist Party of India (Marxist), Bahujan Samaj Party, and Janata Dal. Telugu Desam in Andhra Pradesh, Assam Gana Parishad in Assam, National Conference in Jammu and Kashmir, Muslim League in Kerala, Shiv Sena in Maharashtra,

Akali Dal in Punjab, All-India Anna Dravida Munnetra Kazhagam and Dravida Munnetra Kazhagam in Tamil Nadu, Bahujan Samaj Party and Samajwadi Party in Uttar Pradesh, and All-India Forward Block in West Bengal are the prominent state parties.

Features of Party System

India has a multi-party system with the presence of a large number of political parties at the national and regional level both. In spite of the presence of a large number of parties, the Congress party dominated the political scene for several decades since Independence (except from 1977-1980 and 1994 onwards). For the first two decades after Independence, the main arena of political competition at both national and state levels was within the Congress party, but with increasing frequency since the mid-1960's, regional parties have successfully challenged Congress hold on various states. The membership of political parties is small and party discipline not rigid. The parties are characterized by fragmentation, splits, polarization, mergers and defections. Political parties are yet to mature in terms of policies, ideologies and programmes. There is no clear-cut ideological difference in the policies and programmes of parties. All parties subscribe to democracy, socialism and secularism. Party system has been greatly influenced by cultural diversity, social, ethnical, caste, religious pluralism, traditions of the nationalist movement, contrasting style of party leadership, and clashing ideological perspectives. Leadership occupies an important place in the party system and a number of parties are formed around distinguished personalities. Factionalism, internal dissensions, and splits are some of the other major features of Indian Party system. It can thus be said that party system has not yet reached that stage of development where ideologies are strong and parties are able to structure meaningful electoral issues.

Evolution of Party System in India

The evolution of the party system can be traced to the days of India's struggle for independence. The Indian National Congress was the first political party that came into existence in 1885. According to A. S. Narang, the party system did not develop from within because "unlike the West, social and economic change did not precede political development. The growth of science and technology was slow and the development of the country's economy poor and uneven. Society as a whole remained traditional. The commitment to modernity, invoking a radical change in the traditional value system and social relationships, therefore was weak and ambivalent. Thus, the situation provided hardly any ground for the development of the party system. Like capitalism, the development of party system also proceeded from an application of external stimuli. The British provided it as a part of historical process". The British political ideas and system, the prevailing situation in India, differences of religions, sects, linguistics blocks, ethnic groups, castes, sub-castes, and underdeveloped economy and tribes have played a prominent role in shaping the system before and after independence. Since independence we can identify three phases in the functioning of the Indian party system:

- Single-party dominance.
- Decline of the single party dominance.
- Multi-party and coalition era.

1. Single-Party Dominance - Congress Party

The Indian National Congress is considered to be the oldest and the largest political outfit. It was formed in 1885 and was the most powerful force behind the country's struggle for independence. The Congress primarily has been a centrist party. Congress, under the leadership of Nehru followed the approach of planned development in democratic framework. It remained as the most important political organization in India after independence. During the initial decade it was also in favour of agrarian reform, enlargement of public sector and economic planning. Congress believed in non-alignment and peace amongst all nations. The non-alignment strategy of Nehru provided newly independent nations with an alternative to domination by the superpowers. The Congress, right from the beginning, supported secularism and opposed the use of religion for political ends.

Coming to the social base, it draws support widely from across the country from all classes and groups. It has mass support in every district, town, city, and the state. The party was able to appeal to a wide segment of the poor (including lower castes and Muslims) through its ideology of social equality and welfare programmes, while appealing to the more prosperous voters usually from upper castes by preserving private property and supporting village community leadership.

After Independence, the Congress party remained in power till 1977. The Congress Party won the elections in 1952, 1957, 1962, 1967 and 1971. The Congress retained the character of the nationalist movement in seeking to balance and accommodate social and ideological diversity. The Congress sought to resolve or avoid internal conflict, balance interest, and blur ideological distinctions in its search of consensus. The Congress emerged as a party of consensus, with factions representing various ideologies. For the first two decades after Independence, the main arena of political competition at both national and state levels was within the Congress party. According to Rajni Kothari, "Congress was able to maintain its position as a party occupying most of the space in the political system because there was plurality within the dominant party which made it more representative, provided flexibility, and sustained internal competition. At the same time, it was prepared to absorb groups and movements from outside the party and thus prevent other parties from gaining strength." Moreover, the Congress occupied not only the broad centre of the political spectrum, but also most of the left and right as well. Even though there were many opposition parties, dissidents and other interest groups, these groups outside the margin did not constitute alternative to the ruling party. Further, the Congress also forged patronage links with regional and local forces, thus creating chain of authority that stretched from the capital city to villages (Anil Kohli). The main reason for dominance of Congress was lack of viable alternative to the Congress, not a clear-cut polarization of political forces. Hence, the Congress, which functioned as a broad based national movement before Independence, successfully transformed itself into the dominant political party of the nation. Moreover, the opposition parties were highly fragmented. The 1967 election, which the Congress lost, marked the beginning of the decline of the one-party dominance, both in terms of percentage of votes and seats. During the same year, Indira Gandhi, by splitting the Congress, established her supremacy both in the party and the government and decided to go directly to the people thereby receiving a fresh mandate in 1971 mid-term polls. The split resulted in the centralization of power. It also led to the end of the 'consensus' approach in decision-making and heralded in plebiscitary politics. Therefore, it weakened the Congress party organizationally.

2. Decline of the Single Party Dominance

The 1977 elections acquired prominence as they were held in the backdrop of emergency. The opposition parties for the first time defeated Congress at the Centre. The success of the Janata Party in 1977 elections gave hope for the possible emergence of a two-party system, however, this was short-lived. The internal bickering and factionalism in the party had tarnished its overall reputation. The Congress had split into groups again in 1978. The results of the 1980 elections showed the continuing ability of the Congress to play the central role in maintaining and restructuring political consensus in India. The second phase was still characterized by one-party, though Congress was no longer dominant. Beginning of the plebiscitary mode of electoral politics saw the emergence of genuine competition to the congress, both at the state and at the national level. By late 1980's, non-congress parties started dominating state legislature. Increased competitiveness and coalition politics have brought the Congress-dominat system at the Centre to an end. In all the states, regional parties have successfully challenged the Congress hold on various states. This narrowing of the Congress base has had a dramatic effect on the nature of the opposition. The actual and potential opposition to the Congress was thus reduced to regional and ethnic pockets. State assembly elections further consolidated the position of regional parties. To sum up, the 1980's dominance of the Congress was not the dominance of one party all over India. In the words of Myron Weiner, "The Congress party that won in 1980 was not the Congress party that had governed India in the 1950s and 1960s, or even the early 1970s. The party was organizationally weak and the electoral victory was primarily Gandhi's rather than the party's".

3. Multi-Party and Coalition Era

The end of Congress party dominance and the lack of a clear single-party majority since late 1980's ushered in an era of coalition politics. Further, by late 1980's opposition parties started dominating state legislatures leading to narrowing of the Congress base. Congress lost the1989 parliamentary elections. The elections clearly inaugurated a multi-party system at the national level. Here a shift from a predominant party system to a coalition party system can be seen. In the 1989 elections, although the Congress (I) remained the largest party in the Parliament with 197 seats, it was unable to form a Government. Even though the Congress (I) regained power in 1991, it was no longer the pivot around which the party system revolved. The Congress (I) won 227 seats, up from 197 in 1989, but its share of the vote dropped from 39.5 percent in 1989 to 37.6 percent.

The 1996 mid-term polls further strengthened this situation and showed a clear trend of decline of Congress hegemony and emergence of multi-party system and a coalition phase. In the 1998 general elections, the Congress party managed to get only 141 seats and its vote-share further declined. At the regional level, half of the states were ruled by the non-Congress parties.

Yogendra Yadav identifies the reconfiguration in the political system after 1995 elections and identified the emerging trends. He calls this the 'second democratic upsurge'. The consolidation of the party system at the state level cannot be aggregated at the national level. There is a clear picture of emergence of bipolar consolidation in various states without yielding bipolarity at the national level and more over the two-party system at the national level seems to be improbable. The Congress definitely shows signs of a long-term decline at a time when the task of occupying the middle ground has become difficult. This phase also signaled a move towards a competitive multi-party system, which can no longer be defined with reference to Congress. Another emerging trend is the rise of the caste-based parties especially in the North, the rise of the OBC's in Uttar Pradesh and Maharashtra, and tribal in Gujarat and Rajasthan. Increasingly, caste is not a local consideration which works in favour of a candidate of one's own caste. Now, caste identities and affiliations are imagined at the level of the state. Finally, with no party in a position to get absolute majority at the national level, there is a clear evidence of the emergence of the rainbow coalition of parties at the centre. Thus, one can say that the emergence of multi-polarity is a clear indication that the politics has entered a coalition phase. This was amply demonstrated in the 1999 general elections with the National Democratic Alliance (NDA) coalition forming the government under the leadership of A. B. Vajpayee.

BHARATIYA JANATA PARTY (BJP)

The Bharatiya Janata party is distinct due to its non-association with the Congress. Instead, it grew out of an alternative nationalist organization, the Rashtriya Swayamsevak Sangh (RSS). The Bharatiya Jana Sangh, was renamed the Bharatiya Janata party (BJP) in 1980.

The main political ideology of the BJP is that it opposed the separate code of civil laws, and supported nuclear defense capability. The BJP believes that all Indians constitute one nation despite various differences. The party wishes to promote a feeling of oneness and national unity amongst the people. It is determined to preserve democratic institutions and values. The BJP gives importance to restoration of moral and human values. It stresses vocational and technical education as well as the setting up of agro-industrial institutions in each district. It declares that economic factors should be considered for reservations. Residential schools for all children of poor families of all castes should be set up. The BJP encourages cottage industries, especially for women. It wants to end corruption and promote value-based politics. It opposed secular democracy advocated by the Congress party, and favoured restrictions on the foreign investment.

In 1984, the Bharatiya Janata party won only two seats in the Lok Sabha. In 1989 it improved its position and sent eighty eight members to the Lok Sabha. It became the main opposition in the Lok Sabha. The BJP attained national prominence by raising the Hindu nationalism in the early 1990's. It secured power in four of the northern states in the 1991-1992 election. It expanded its support base in the northern Hindi-speaking areas, especially among urban middle-class traders. The decline of Congress (I) in the1990s led to the emergence of BJP as the largest national party. In the general elections of 1991, the Bharatiya Janata Party expanded its support more than any other party. Its number of seats in the Lok Sabha increased from eighty-five to one hundred nineteen and its vote share grew from 11.4 percent to 21 percent. It became the main opposition in the Lok Sabha. It secured power in four of the northern states in the 1991-1992 elections. In the aftermath of the Hindu activists' dismantling of the Babri Masjid in December 1992, the evocative symbolism of the Ram Janmabhumi controversy had apparently lost its capacity to mobilize popular support. Nevertheless, the BJP, by giving more emphasis to anti-corruption and social issues, achieved unprecedented success in south India, where it won twenty eight percent of the vote and came second in elections in Karnataka in November. In 1996 the BJP-led coalition, headed by Atal Bihari Vajpayee remained in power only for thirteen days. Again, it came to power in 1998, but exactly after thirteen months, was voted out by the slender margin on record—just one vote. In 1998 elections, nearly eighty five percent of the BJP's parliamentary presence came from the seats it won in Uttar Pradesh, Bihar and Madhya Pradesh, plus the three western states of Gujarat, Maharashtra and Rajasthan. In the 1998 Lok Sabha elections, the BJP increased its seats tally from 161 to 179 seats. It's vote share rose by an impressive five percent.

BJP emerged as the single largest party in the 1999 general election and formed the Government. However, bowing to the pressures of coalition politics, it had to compromise on a few issues like construction of Ram Temple, abolition of Article 370, and establishment of Uniform Civil Code and has temporarily put its ideology in the shelf to be able to function smoothly as the dominant partner in the 24-ruling party coalition.

The rise of BJP has been phenomenal, not because of its growing strength, but because of the declining popularity of the Congress. Though its strength is mostly concentrated in the north, the BJP has made inroads especially among the urban middle classes into other parts of India. Today, its strength has gone up to 182 with a vote share of 24 percent. The reason for the phenomenal growth of the BJP, according to Atul Kohli is due to following reasons, "The BJP's ideology and organization have given it advantages. Unlike most Indian parties, it is tightly disciplined and can count on a significant organizational base. Second, its commitment to India as a 'Hindu nation' has enabled it to redefine Indian nationalism and to provide substitute of sorts for declining nationalist legacy of Congress." Further, most of its growth in the early 1990's came from the social appeal of its redefined religious nationalism. It's support base is especially among the elite and educated middle class. By the late 1980s, the Congress decline was creating a growing political vacuum. The rapid rise of BJP since 1990 must be seen in this light.

The social base of BJP has been widening too CSDS post-poll survey of the 1998 elections indicate that the BJP is no longer an exclusivist party, but one that now reaches out to a much wider range of the electorate in terms of class, caste and religion. As a right-wing political party, the BJP had initially obtained more votes from the higher castes, upper classes and educated people. According to the 1998 general election results, the BJP has become a more broad based party. The key to the BJP's gain in the 1998 is its inroads into other backward classes (OBC) votes. The BJP has increased its base among the Scheduled Castes and Scheduled Tribes at the cost of both the Congress and the United Front.

COMMUNIST PARTIES

The Communist Party of India (CPI) was formed on 26 December, 1925. Communists participated in the Independence struggle and as members of the Congress Socialist Party, became a formidable presence on the socialist wing of the Indian National Congress. Starting in 1951, the CPI shifted to a more moderate strategy of seeking to bring communism to India within the constraints of the democracy. In 1957, the CPI was elected to run the state government of Kerala but the government did not last long due to the imposition of President's rule in 1959. The CPI relies mainly on mass organizations for its activities, fronts and movements. The CPI, traditionally has significant base of electoral support in West Bengal, Kerala, and Bihar.

The CPI differs from the CPM in its policy matters. The Communist Party of India was ideologically close to the Soviet Union, while the CPI (M) was a follower of the China camp. Support for the CPI is more evenly spread nationwide. The CPI share of the parliamentary vote has more than halved from 5.2 percent in 1967 to 2.5 percent in 1991. In the llth Lok Sabha elections, it won twelve seats while in the 12th Lok Sabha it occupied only nine seats. In it won three seats in West Bengal, two in Tamil Nadu, two in Kerala and three in Bihar.

In 1964, a large leftist faction of the CPI leadership, based predominantly in Kerala and West Bengal, split from the party to form the Communist Party of India (Marxist) or CPI (M). The CPI (M) is a well-organized party, with a fairly stable electoral base among the lower-middle and lower classes especially of rural West Bengal. It also established its stronghold in Kerala, Tripura, Andhra Pradesh and Assam, though its influence has been declining over the years. In West Bengal, the CPM-led Left Front government has been in power since 1977. The CPI (M) has ruled the state with a coalition of other leftist parties. The party has also dominated West Bengal's parliamentary delegation and in Kerala the Front led by CPM was in power.

In the 1990's, CPI (M) share of the vote has gradually increased from 4.2 percent in 1967 to 6.7 percent in 1991. It has largely remained confined to Kerala, Tripura, and West Bengal. From 1977 to 1989, the CPI (M) dominated Tripura's state government. It won two parliamentary seats in 1971, 1980 and 1984, but it lost all of it's seats in 1977, 1989, and 1991. In 1996 and 1998, it won 32 seats. The United Left Front has also been contesting elections on a single platform. In 1996, CPI (M) played a key role in the formation of United Front Government with the help of like-minded parties.

REGIONAL PARTIES IN INDIA

Regional parties are those parties which represent the interests of particular linguistic, religious, regional or cultural groups. They exclusively operate within a limited geographical area of a state and mostly participate in elections only within that state. Regional parties play a significant role in the political life, given social, cultural, and historical diversity of the country. The federal system also enabled the regional parties to obtain power by taking up issues of regional concern. The regional parties come into power because of some popular stand that they take up on some local issues. Their political programmes are usually restricted to the specific Issues of the concerned region. These parties are powerful in their own regions. The important regional parties include DMK, AIADMK, Telugu Desam, Akali Dal and National Conference.

Regional parties with strong social bases in their communities and/or regions have been a feature of Indian politics since Independence. Due to the presence of wide range of socio-cultural and ethnic diversities, many regional parties came into existence. The growth of regional parties can be attributed to the following reasons. Firstly, the emergence of regional parties can be seen in the light of protection and promotion of their respective cultural, linguistic, regional and ethnic identity. Regional parties like Shiv Sena emerged on the appeal of the 'sons of the soil'. It perceived that the interests of the locals are supposedly being endangered by migrants from the other parts of India. Secondly, they emerged as opposition parties to the Congress, which was the dominant party ruling at the Centre. Over the years, the national parties have neglected to give adequate importance to their regional and state units. Further, due to the Centre's frequent interference in the affairs of the state and imposition of the President's rule in the non-Congress ruled states, they perceived Central government to be working against their interests. Therefore, the regional parties demanded more autonomy and less intervention by the Centre in the affairs of the state. Apart from these, some other reasons for the growth of the regional parties is due to the failure of the developmental plans over centralization.

The importance of regional parties has been growing in the past three elections. They have come to play an effective role in the formation of Governments. With the decline of Congress (I) in the 1990's, party system became more fragmented and the regional parties gained more prominence at the national level. The most striking feature of the 1996 elections was the spectacular rise of regional parties. Regional parties played a vital role in the formation of the National Front (1989-1990) Government at the Centre. Moreover, regional parties played a key role in the formation of the present NDA government.

Further, with no single party in a position to get a clear majority, coalition governments have come to stay. Hence the single largest party forms a coalition of regional parties to form a Government at the Centre. These coalition partners have assumed an equal footing with the national parties and they cannot afford to antagonize them, as various ministers are chosen from these regional parties. Hence, in the era of coalition governments, the national parties cannot afford to push the regional parties under the carpet.

In Tamil Nadu, the two main regional parties are All India Anna Dravida Munnetra Kazagham (AIADMK) and Dravida Munnetra Kazagham (DMK). Regional political parties have dominated Tamil Nadu state politics since Independence. In 1949, charismatic film scriptwriter C. N. Annadurai founded the DMK in an attempt to achieve the goals of Tamil nationalism through the electoral process. The DMK played a prominent role in the agitations that successfully defeated attempts to impose Hindi as the Official National Language in the mid-1960s. Although the DMK has failed to gain a foothold outside Tamil Nadu, the party has expanded its social base within the state, by raising the Tamil Nationalist sentiment, demand for greater state autonomy and an end to northern domination. One of the main planks on which the DMK came to power was by successfully raising the issue of imposition of Hindi as an Official Language in the Southern States. The DMK defeated the Congress in 1967 elections in Tamil Nadu and took control of the state Government. After Annadurai's death in 1969, M. Karunanidhi took the leadership of the party and government. In 1972, M. Ramachandran, popular Tamil actor, known as M.G.R., splitted from the DMK to form the All-India Anna Dravida Munnetra Kazhagam (AIADMK). Under his leadership, the AIADMK dominated Tamil politics at the state level from 1977 through 1989. After his death, the DMK gained control over the state government. The AIADMK, under the leadership of Jayalalitha recaptured the state government in 1991. However, in 1996, the DMK once again regained the power. AIADMK won eighteen Lok Sabha seats in the 12th Lok Sabha. In the 2001-2002 assembly elections, AIADMK won a majority of seats under the leadership of Jayalalitha.

Andhra Pradesh was considered to be the citadel of Congress party as it continuously ruled the state for three decades. However, Telugu Desam Party broke this trend in the 1980's. In 1982, N. T. Rama Rao (popularly known as N.T.R. in Telugu-language films) formed the Telugu Desam party and within nine months the party came into power with a thumping majority. The party ruled the state from 1983 to 1989. It also won thirty of Andhra Pradesh's 42 parliamentary seats in 1984. With the objective of enhancing regional autonomy, N.T.R. played a key role in the formation of the National Front Coalition Government in 1989. However, in the elections, the Telugu Desam lost control over the state Government to the Congress (I). It was able to win only thirteen seats in Parliament in the 1991 elections. The Telugu Desam returned to power in Andhra Pradesh after winning the state legislative assembly elections in November 1994. In the 1999 assembly elections, the Telugu Desam party once again retained power under the leadership of N. Chandrababu Naidu.

The Akali Dal was first formed in the early 1920s as a reform group to bring the gurdwaras (the Sikh shrines) under the control of the orthodox Sikh community. Initially, the party was open only to members of the Sikh community of which it claimed to be the sole representative. It was confined primarily to the Punjab only. At the time of partition, the Akalis had sought an independent Sikhistan, but through agitation of the 1950's for linguistic states, the Akali demand was translated to that of a Punjabi-speaking state of Punjabi Suba.

During the 1960s, the Akali Dal played an important role in the struggle for the creation of Punjab as a separate state with a Sikh majority. Even with the majority Sikh population, the Akali Dai's political success has been limited by the Congress ability to win votes from the Sikh community. The Akali Dal won nine of Punjab's thirteen parliamentary seats in the general elections of 1977 and seven in 1984 but only one in. the 1971 and 1980 elections. The Akali Dal headed coalition governments in 1967 and 1977 and formed the state government in 1985, but it lost state government elections to the Congress (R) in 1972, and to Congress (I) in 1980 and in 1992. As the 1980's progressed, the Akali Dal became increasingly factionalized. In 1989 three Akali Dal factions ran in the elections, winning a total of seven seats. The Akali Dal factions boycotted parliamentary and state legislative elections that were held in February 1992. As a result, voter turnout dropped to 21.6 percent and the Congress (I) won twelve seats in Parliament and a majority of seats in the legislative assembly. Akali Dal again came to power in 1997. It lost the recent assembly elections to Congress.

The National Conference, based in Jammu and Kashmir, is a regional party, which, despite its overwhelmingly Muslim following, refused to support the All India Muslim League during the Independence movement; instead it allied itself with the Indian National Congress. The National Conference was closely identified with its leader, Sheikh Mohammed Abdullah. After the death of Sheikh Abdullah, his son Farooq Abdullah became chief minister of Jammu and Kashmir. The National Conference remained Jammu and Kashmir's dominant party through the 1980s and maintained control over the state government for most of the period. In parliamentary elections, it won one of Kashmir's six parliamentary seats in 1967, none in 1971, two in 1977, three each in 1980, 1984 and 1989. However, popular support for the National Conference was badly eroded by allegations of electoral fraud in the 1987 state elections which were won by the National Conference in alliance with the Congress (I) and the widespread corruption of the subsequent state government under the leadership of Farooq Abdullah. There was a little popular sympathy for Farooq Abdullah and the National Conference even after the government was dissolved and President's rule declared in 1990. Jammu and Kashmir remained under President's Rule through 1995. The National Conference came to power after the President's rule. But in the 2002 assembly election, it lost power to the Congress and Mufti Mohammed Syeeed coalition combine. During the late 1980's, the Assam Gana Parshid (AGP) rose to power in Assam on the crest of Assamese nationalism. Immigration to Assam primarily by Bengali Muslim from neighboring Bangladesh had aroused concern that the Assamese would become a minority in their own state. The

Assam Accord was signed between Rajiv Gandhi and Assamese nationalists on 15 August, 1985. The Assam Accord also included a compromise on the voter eligibility issue, settled the issue of the citizenship status of immigrants, and stipulated that new elections were to be held in December. Assamese student leaders formed the AGP after signing the accord, and the new party won the December 1985 elections. The victory of AGP did not end the controversy over Assamese nationalism. The AGP was unable to implement the accord's provisions for disenfranchising and expelling illegal aliens, in part because Parliament passed legislation making it more difficult to prove illegal alien status. The AGP's failure to implement the accord along with the general ineffectiveness with which it operated the state government undercut its popular support, and in November 1990 it was dismissed and President's Rule declared. As the AGP floundered, other nationalist groups of agitators flourished. The United Liberation Front of Assam (ULFA) became the primary militant organization raising Assamese nationalism. While the All Bodo Students' Union (ABSU) and Bodo People's Action Committee (BPAC) led agitations for a separate homeland for the central plain tribal people of Assam (often called Bodos). By 1990, ULFA militants ran virtually a parallel government in the state, extorting huge sums from businesses in Assam, especially the tea industry. The ULFA was ultimately subdued through a shrewd combination of ruthless military repression and generous terms of surrender for many of its leaders. The ABSU/BPAC-led mass agitation lasted from March 1987 until February 1993 when the ABSU signed an accord with the state government that had been under the Congress (I) control since 1991. The accord provided for the creation of a Bodoland Autonomous Council with jurisdiction over an area of 5,186 square kilometers and 2.1 million people within Assam. Nevertheless, Bodo agitation continued in the mid-1990s as a result of the demands of many Bodo leaders who insisted that more territory be included under the Bodoland Autonomous Council.

COALITION GOVERNMENTS

One of the recent developments in the study of parliamentary democracies is the coalition party system. Coalition parties, to a large extent, exist only in parliamentary form of countries with multi party system. Coalition governments are formed when no party gains absolute majority in the elections. A coalition government is one in which the cabinet is composed of members of more than one party. It is an alliance between more than two political parties. It is a working relationship between parties with similar interests. Coalition is the result of bargaining between parties who have their own political interests. Once in power, the partisan concerns of coalition members become visible. The NDA alliance led by BJP was one such coalition government.

A coalition government lacks necessary mandate to put forward bills pertaining to national issues. Sometimes, a coalition government may encourage splits within the ruling parties. This is because the party with a majority seats may encourage 'horse trading' keeping aside the conventions of political parties. In fact, coalition governments pose a major threat to the Parliamentary system because the survival of the government depends on the confidence of the house. In recent years, Italy, France and India are the countries which are prone to a more fractured mandate and encourage coalition governments. This is because of lack of focus among political parties 'in power'. Secondly, the much-needed electoral reforms are not implemented so far.

Indian Party System: Challenges

The party system in India faces a number of challenges. Not only they have declined in terms of their ideological orientation and commitment to the welfare of the masses, but also in the recent past they have shown tendencies of fragmentation, factionalism and regionalism. Formation of alliances for seeking power irrespective of any strong ideological or programmatic commitments is another major trend emerging in Indian Party system. Politics in India is centered on casteism, communalism and personalities which led to the fragmentation of political parties and has resulted in more caste-based political violence in the society.

Strong trends of changing of party or group loyalty are endemic in party organizations in India. Criminalization of politics and politicization of criminals and the maintenance of public ethics is another area of concern. Parties enter into opportunistic alliances to maintain their influence within the party and government to remain in power. The instability at the Union level or in the states can be attributed solely to the growing number of parties. Alliances and coalitions are made, broken and changed at whim. In recent years, fragile coalitions are leading to unstable governments at the Centre.

SUMMARY

- Political parties are essential for the successful working of the parliamentary system of government. Political parties are indispensable to any democratic system. They play a crucial role in the electoral process in setting up the candidates and conducting election campaigns. Political parties act as a link between the people and the government.
- Some of the important functions performed by the political parties are as follows: educating and mobilizing the masses, holding discussions on various social, economic and political issues, influence the decision-making process, provide due representation to different sections of population, etc.
- India has a multi-party system with the presence of a large number of political parties both at the national and regional level. Since Independence, Indian National Congress has governed at the Centre for most part of the time. The end of the Congress dominance ushered in an era of coalition politics. the prominence of the regional parties further increased in the era of coalition governments.

- Since independence we can identify three phases in the functioning of the Indian Party System: a) Single-party dominance, b) Decline of the single-party dominance, and c) Multi-party and coalition era.
- Some of the major drawbacks of the Indian party system are,strong trends of fragmentation, factionalism, and formation of alliances, which is being increasingly witnessed. As a result of these fragile and unstable coalitions, the new economic reforms, initiated in the early 1990's, could not be carried with vigour.

QUESTIONS

1. Write an essay on the nature of the party system India.
2. What are main features and emerging trends of the party system in India? Discuss.
3. Examine the role played by the regional parties in the Indian Political System.
4. "India has parties, but no sound party system." Comment.
5. What do you mean by political party and party system? Analyse the role and functions of political parties.
6. Critically analyse the growth of the BJP in India polity.
7. Write short notes on the following:
   a. Communist Parties.
   b. Coalition Governments in India.

11

Pressure Groups

After reading this chapter, you will be conversant with:

- Meaning and Definition of Pressure Groups
- Significance of the Pressure Groups
- Similarities and Differences between Pressure Groups and Political Parties
- Relationship between Pressure Groups, Interest groups and Lobbies
- Functions, Techniques and Drawbacks of Pressure Groups
- Pressure Groups in Indian Context

Introduction

In a modern political system, pressure groups occupy an important place and they exist in almost all-political systems. In recent times, they are not only considered as essential for democracy but also regarded as the champion of individual interests. Due to increasing intricacy of economic and social life, and better communications, Governments worldwide today recognize the right of pressure groups to represent distinct interests in the society. As a consequence, pressure groups are playing an important role in politics. In democracies apart from the political parties, pressure groups play an important role in transmitting the views of different sections of society to Government and politicians, and thereby, act as a link between the people and the government.

DEFINITIONS

Pressure group may be defined as follows:

- A body, organized or unorganized, that actively seeks to promote its particular interests within a society by exerting pressure on public officials and agencies. Pressure groups direct their efforts towards influencing legislative, and executive branches of Government, political parties, and sometimes-general public opinion. (The Columbia Encyclopedia)

- An organized body of individuals who share some goals and who try to influence public policy.
- Any interest group that is not part of the Government and does not itself seek to govern the country in its own name, but seek to influence that government for its own purposes. (Encyclopedia Britannica)

Pressure groupss vary enormously in their motivation, size, organization and degree of activity. For examples, group of trade union's (autoworkers, mineworkers), business organizations, environmental groups, All India Manufacturer's Organization (AIMO), Associated Chambers of Commerce (India), Federation of Indian Chambers of Commerce, and Forum of Free Enterprise.

SIGNIFICANCE

The aim of all pressure groups is to uphold their interests by trying to influence government. They do not intend to capture the political power or nominate candidates, but do seek to influence government policies and activities. In a sense, we can say a pressure group is a collective whose members want to influence laws. They try to realize their aims by propaganda using newspapers, pamphlets, books and radio, lobbying, and personal contacts with men in power. In most of the modern democracies, political parties are not in a position to provide an adequate representation for diverse interests and opinions. Moreover, due to the increasing government control, people are not in a position to exercise their influence over decision-making process made during intermediary period of elections. As a result, the prominence of pressure groups increases farther. Pressure groups increase participation and access to the political system. They provide an important mechanism by which citizens can influence government. Pressure groups provide a means by which ordinary citizens can participate in the decision-making process, as well as maintain a check on government activity. Similarly, governments can be better informed of the electorate's sensitivities to policies, because of the pressure articulated by these groups.

Pressure groups, apart from promotion of sectional interests also have a beneficial impact on political system. As Trueman succinctly states, "Pressure groups improve the quality of the government. It makes government more efficient by enhancing the quality of the decision-making process. Information and advice provided by the groups helps to improve the quality of government policy and legislation. Pressure groups enable new concerns and issues to reach the political agenda, thereby facilitating social progress and preventing social stagnation, for example, women and environmentalist movements. Pressure groups increase social cohesion and political stability by providing a 'safety-valve' outlet for individual and collective grievances and demands. Pressure groups assist the surveillance of the government by exposing information it would rather keep secret, thereby reinforcing and complementing work of opposition through political parties. Pressure groups, thereby, improve the accountability of decision makers to electorates".

PRESSURE GROUP AND POLITICAL PARTIES

Political parties and pressure groups are the main organizations, which allow for participation in the political system. Political parties and pressure groups must not, however, be confused. They resemble each other so far, as they both seek to realize their objective by influencing the decision-making process. Pressure groups are different from political parties. Political parties seek representation and power, whereas pressure groups seek political influence. Political parties put up candidates for election to public office and carry out activities to secure their election, but a pressure group seeks to influence both the government and the parties. Parties often focus on the national interest, whereas pressure groups may be concerned with sectional issues/single issues. A sectional interest represents common interests of a particular section of society. Political party is generally a much larger organization than the pressure group. Generally in a democracy, political parties' primary function is to nominate candidates for the elective office and seek to win active support of millions of voters and has policies on a wide range of issues. Pressure groups try to influence legislation by mobilizing public opinion. They seek to influence government policy through indirect means, such as lobbying, public protests and media campaigns. Political parties are active both within and outside the legislature, but pressure groups are active only outside the legislature. In a democracy, most members of the Parliament represent political parties, and parties closely influence policy development and operations of both the Parliament and the executive. Pressure groups provide a means of popular participation in national politics between elections. They are sometimes able to gather sufficient support to force government to amend or even scrap legislation.

PRESSURE GROUPS AND INTEREST GROUPS

Interest groups are defined as, "A group of people who share common traits, attitudes, beliefs, and/or objectives who have formed a formal organization to serve specific common interests of the membership". For example, interest groups would include book clubs, bowling leagues, swimming clubs, church organizations, and homeowner's associations. They do not normally try to influence legislators, political parties, or candidates. Interest groups commonly have formal access to membership, dues, elected officers, regular meetings, and they often provide information and regular opportunities for communication through newsletters or magazines, sponsor recreational or educational activities, organize volunteer public service projects, make deals for group discounts or group insurance, or so on. Larger interest group organizations may have full-time paid officers or professional staff to manage and to supplement the efforts of member-volunteers in furthering the work of the organization. However, sometimes an interest group is also a pressure group. When any interest group tries to influence the government in the pursuit of its aims, it becomes a 'pressure group'. Not all interest groups try to exert influence on government; many such businesses and trade unions do so only as part of their more general activities of promoting their interests. Sometimes a group begins as only an interest group, and then becomes a pressure group. According to Harry Eckstein, "Interest groups become pressure groups because they seek to obtain favourable policy decisions or administrative dispositions". For example, interest groups exercise pressure upon government in order to obtain laws and administrative decisions that are convenient to them.

Of late, the distinction in usage between the term's interest group and pressure group has accordingly become less significant in ordinary language. Sometimes, it is also possible that a pressure group will form first and it will later become an interest group. For example, the doctors of a community may join together in order to prevent competition from newcomers by pressurizing politicians to allow them to set professional licensing standards. After succeeding in this, they may recognize that they have a common interest in education, providing training facilities for assistants, or in buying resources collectively. The group may continue as a pressure group but also provide other services that have nothing to do with laws. Thus, interest groups, acting as pressure groups, have become increasingly important as a means by which individuals can attempt to influence governments regarding their particular requirements.

PRESSURE GROUPS AND LOBBIES

The major distinction between pressure groups and lobbies are as follows: The former, is interested in influencing both the legislature and public opinion. The latter concentrates mainly on legislature while is in session and is concerned with the passage or defeat of particular bills. Lobbyists, often deal directly with governmental decision-makers, supplying technical information, making political threats or promises, and supplying friendship, entertainment, and other favours. Their indirect methods include the use of the mass media, mailing and telephone campaigns. According to Gabriel Almond, "Standard lobbying techniques include, appearances before legislative committees, mailing or otherwise providing information to individual legislators, and similar activities."

In some cases, pressure groups and lobbies carry effective and widespread publicity and propaganda in favour of certain causes and try to pressurize the government in passing the necessary legislation. Of late, lobbyists no longer confine their activities to the buildings where legislators meet. They visit legislator's offices, invite them to dinner and vacation retreats, and offer to pay them for lectures. According to Rogan Kersh, "In 1960, there were 360 registered lobbying groups in Washington. In 2001, there are more than 45,000. This shows how much power do lobbying groups wield in politics".

FUNCTIONS

Pressure groups and lobbies discharge the following functions:

- Pressure groups and lobbies carry on effective and widespread publicity and propaganda. They try to pressurize government for passing the necessary legislation and prevent the passing of certain types of bills, which are against their interest.

- Pressure groups take up electioneering in favour of candidates, who they think, will uphold their causes. At the same time, they also function in tandem with some of the political parties.
- Pressure groups establish necessary contacts with the ruling establishment from time-to-time and try to achieve their objectives. However, they may also arrange for violent movements and strikes if their interests are in danger.
- Pressure groups and lobbies play a significant role in creating and moulding public opinion. They promote discussion and debate and muster public opinion on key issues. They make use of mass media, newspapers and billboards in order to influence the public opinion.
- Pressure groups and lobbies represent and uphold various types of interests and causes. For instance groups, such as the trade associations, labour unions, professional associations, ethnic and religious organizations represent and fight for varied causes.
- Pressure groups and lobbies do many public relations work. According to V. O. Key, "Public relation efforts are essentially of two types. An intensive short-term campaign may be designed to whip up public opposition to or in support of a particular legislative measure. And the long-term effort is to manage basic public attitudes towards support of a broad point of view or to create a favourable sentiment towards a particular corporation or industry."
- Pressure groups play an important role in implementing changes to public policy. They act as a check to the power of executive. Many groups are actively involved in implementing political decisions and evaluating their relative success or failure.
- Pressure groups also perform citizen-centric activities as they provide ordinary citizens with an important means of participating in politics and communicating their demands to decision-makers. They provide expertise and assistance to ordinary electorate. They provide a useful channel of communication between the governments and the people.
- Apart from the above mentioned functions, the pressure groups perform a role in educating citizens about specific issues, enhance democratic participation, pluralism, and diversity. They also provide an important access point for those seeking redressal of grievances. They also represent minorities.

TECHNIQUES

Some of the techniques of the pressure groups are as follows:

- Exerting grassroots pressure on the various branches of government. Some are successful at influencing even local government.

- Consulting with ministers or contacting public officials in person, by telephone, fax, e-mail, postcard and letter.
- Contributing funds, loans, equipment, publicity and volunteers.
- Making use of legislative committees, influencing parliamentary committees.
- Electting friendly candidates (for example a political candidate can be elected on a single platform), influencing the elections.
- Initiating legal action through injections or appealing higher courts, and seeking the intervention of the courts, if possible.
- Promoting social movements, joining with groups and individuals sharing goals to engage mass mobilization, protest demonstration and other forms of direct action.
- Publicizing interest group views by influencing party platforms and moulding public opinion.
- Campaigning for, or opposing certain candidates at elections.
- Demonstrating outside the Parliament and government offices or marching on the streets.
- Pressure groups indirectly influence government opinion through media or directly by lobbying state members and the parliament via petitions, letters and deputation's.

Drawbacks of Pressure Groups

Some of the major drawbacks of the pressure groups are as follows:

- Many organized pressure groups undermine the policy-making process since people with vested interests dominate them.
- Many groups are not democratically organized and have no legitimate power because they are unelected.
- Pressure groups encourage unrealistic expectations among the electorate of what government can actually do, leading to growing disillusionment with modern politics in the long run.
- There is unequal distribution of resources and influence between the groups. Cumulative inequalities between groups are widening as some groups are more effective than others in securing funding.
- Pressure groups improve participation, but in an unequal way, benefiting the wealthy sections of society and disadvantaging the weakly organized.
- Pressure groups themselves may not be representative of their members. Their officers are not usually elected. Few groups have procedures for consulting their

members. As a result, the group members may not share the views expressed by the group officials.

- Pressure groups, sometimes adopt undesirable tactics like bribing the legislators.

PRESSURE GROUPS IN INDIA

Organized groups working in India may be classified as business groups and industry groups, trade union groups, peasant groups, student groups, and the like.

Business and Industry Groups

In India the business and industry groups are independent of the control of the political parties. These groups are extremely powerful. Prior to Independence, the business associations existed in India. For instance, in 1887 the Indian Chamber of Commerce was established in Calcutta for the purpose of acting as pressure group. After Independence, various business and industry groups developed in India to protect and promote their particular interests. For example, many business groups are a part of industry and commerce, such as Federation of Indian Chambers of Commerce and Industry (FICCI), Confederation of Indian Industries (CII), All India Manufacturer's Organization (AIMO), Associated Chambers of Commerce and Forum of Free Enterprise. These groups are considered to be powerful as they control over the larger part of the society's economic capital resources and ownership. As a result, it becomes difficult even for a socialist minded government to impose upon the capital policies to which it is firmly opposed. The business groups influence the decision-making process of the government in their favour through lobbies. Most of the business groups support the party in power and try to maintain good relations with the important ministers and bureaucrats. In order to protect their interests the business groups use press as an instrument.

Trade Unions

The Trade Union movement occupies a prominent place in the social process. Since Independence, the trade unions are exerting considerable pressure on the government in the policy formulation and to influence decisions in their favour. The strength of the trade unions is well recognized by the political parties and the Government. Most of the trade unions are associated with one or the other political parties. Different political parties have their own trade unions. For instance, the Indian National Trade Union Congress (INTUC) established in 1948 is the trade union wing of the Congress Party. Similarly, Bharatiya Mazdoor Sangh (BMS) and All India Trade Union Congress (AITUC) are the trade union wings of the Bharatiya Janata Party (BJP) and Communist Party of India (CPI), respectively. Trade unions are extremely vocal in their demand and militant in their methods. They adopt strike, gherao, bandh, demonstrations and marches. Some of the major demands of the trade unions are an overall increase in their wage structure, the right to bonus, regulation of working hours and overtime payment, and better working conditions, higher wages, employee's insurance, medical and housing facilities. The trade unions were successful in achieving their demands.

Some of the major drawbacks of the trade unions are that they are poorly organized and financed. And most of the trade unions are under the control of outside leadership and the membership turnover is great. Further, in India the trade unions are not in a position to work as independent pressure groups due to their close affiliations with their respective political parties. Moreover, the political parties utilize trade unions as their political weapons.

They work more as an agent of a particular party. As a consequence, they are not in a position to articulate their interests effectively. According to Mynor Weiner, "Rival unionism is rampant, unions are led by outsiders, and control of unions is often in the hands of political parties seeking to use them at their own ends."

Student Groups

The origin of the student groups can be traced back to the nationalist movement. During the pre-Independence period, the student groups took active role in non-cooperation (1920) movement and Quit India Movement in 1942. "After Independence", according to Philip G. Altbach, "the student movement had lost its sense of unity and ideological purpose the nationalist fervor of the pre-Independence period has been replaced by generally unorganized and sporadic agitation usually aimed at specific grievances." Many student unions are affiliated to political parties, for example, the Akhil Bhartiya Vidyarthi Parishad is the student wing of RSS, All India Student's Federation is controlled by the Communist Party of India, and National Student Union of India is the student wing of the Indian National Congress.

One of the reasons for increasing student activism is due to unresponsive nature of the university authorities and an uncertain future. Some of the major activities with which the student groups are associated with include, demand by students on university authorities for facilities, reforms in education system, opposition to fee hike, and job opportunities. Student unions exerts pressure on the university authorities by means of strikes, damage of property, and physical attacks on university personnel. Students also involve in local political conflicts, social issues and agitation. Student unions have become the extension counters and recruitment ground for political parties, as most of them are associated with one or the other political parties. Of late, student unions have become means to pressurize government. For instance, implementation of Mandal Commission Report over reservations for OBC's in 1989, led to agitations by different student groups all over India. Bowing to students' pressure, it led to the withdrawal of the report. With Political parties and politicians taking active role in students' union activities, they are further exploited to serve their narrow ends.

Peasant Groups or Farmers Organizations

Prior to Independence, All India Kisan Sabha was founded in 1936 as federation of state movement to look after the interests of the peasants. Initially it began as a Congress front but quickly came under Communist control. Similarly, the Socialists set up their Hind Kisan Panchayat and the Communists' United Kisan Sabha. After Independence, different political parties have started their own peasants organizations which are being used as political instruments. Recently, some more organizations have come up, such as Shetkari Sanghathan (SS) led by Sharad Joshi, and Bharatiya Kisan Union (BKU) led by Mahendra Singh Tikait. Both these organizations are effective in influencing national policies on prices, and taxation structure. Bharatiya Kisan Union in west Uttar Pradesh, Punjab, and Haryana, and the Rajya Ryota Sangha in Karnataka are the other farmers unions which are active. The major activities of the peasant groups is to exert pressure on the government, for instance, availability of seeds and fertilizer at a cheap rate, higher prices for agricultural products, development of irrigation facilities, rural credit scheme, insurance of crops, lowering of electricity rates, easier term loans for agricultural investments, representation of farmers in all decision-making bodies of the government, waiver of loans given to small and marginal farmers, implementation of land reforms, etc. Some of the major drawbacks of the peasant groups are that they are inarticulate and uncoordinated. Caste rivalries, inadequate financial resources, and factionalism are some of the reasons for non-effective functioning of the peasant groups in India.

Apart from the above-mentioned pressure groups in Indian political system, there are a large number of professional and anomic groups like the lawyers, who have their bar associations. The medical practitioners have their Indian Medical Association, Similarly, the teachers, engineers, technicians and artists have their own groups. Numerous religious organizations like the Vishwa Hindu Parishad, Bajrang Dal and Rashtriya Swayamsevak Sangh; various separatist groups seeking greater regional autonomy, like the All-Party Hurriyat Conference (Kashmir) are examples of different types of pressure groups which are active in politics.

SUMMARY

- Pressure groups are an essential dimension of any modern political system. Pressure groups are formed by people to protect or promote a specific interest. In democracies, apart from the political parties, pressure groups play a significant role in carrying across to government, views of different sections of society. In a sense, they act as a link between the people and the government.
- Unlike political parties they do not intend to capture the political power and form a government. Their main aim is to influence legislative and executive branches of government, political parties, and public opinion and try to influence public policy. The role of pressure groups became paramount due to their

increasing influence on decision-making process. The information and advice provided by the pressure groups help to improve the quality of a government policy and legislation.

- They provide a means by which ordinary citizens can participate in the decision-making process as well as maintain a check on the governmental activity. Apart from these functions, they also perform a role in educating citizens, articulate issues and act as an important access point for those seeking redressal of grievances.
- Pressure groups adopt various techniques to influence the laws, such as lobbying, publicizing interest group views, and moulding public opinion.
- In spite of the various advantages of the pressure groups, some of the major drawbacks of the pressure groups are that they can endanger democracy, if adopt corrupt practices. Despite these drawbacks, pressure groups have become essential part of modern politics. Pressure groups gave people more power over their lives what social scientists call "agency", in a way that work, politics and education never did.

QUESTIONS

1. Examine the significance and role of pressure groups.
2. What are the different techniques adopted by the pressure groups to achieve their objectives?
3. What are different kinds of pressure groups working in India? Also describe their salient features.
4. Write an essay on trade incomes and farmer organisations in India.
5. Highlight the difference between political parties and pressure groups, and interest groups and pressure groups. Illustrate with some examples.

12

Mass Movements

After reading this chapter, you will be conversant with:

- Meaning of the word Mass Movements
- Theories of Social Movement
- Types of Social Movements
- Emergence of Mass Movements in India
- Peasant Movements
- Dalit Movements
- Tribal Movements
- Trade Union Movements and
- Women Movements.

A democratic country provides for the participation of people in political activities. It is the people who make or unmake the leaders through periodic elections. The people are provided with the freedom to take part in the decision-making process to improve the social, political and economic conditions. The institutional arrangements in a democratic country provide scope for people to express their demands as well as grievances. But due to lack of adequate arrangements, there is an increasing trend towards discontent which is making people resort to non-parliamentary activities like protests, strikes, *dharnas*, *gheraos* and *bandhs*. Masses are involving themselves in direct action, particularly the oppressed sections of the society. They are attempting to bring about a change in the power structure that is in favour of the majority.

In the past few decades, there is an increasing tendency to organize different types of mass or social movements all over the world. This development urges anyone to have an understanding as to what exactly are social movements, what builds up these movements and the like. The following is a description of the above queries.

MEANING

A social movement or a mass movement is a collective attempt to bring about a change or resist any change. The central concept of a social movement is that, the people intervene in the process of social change. Rather than responding passively to the flow of life or to its troubling aspect, people seek to alter the course of history. In achieving that, they undertake a collective action. Individuals consciously act together with a sense of engaging in a common enterprise. Moreover the social movements possess a considerable measure of internal order and purposeful orientation. It is in fact this organization that strengthens the movement to challenge the established institutions. Thus, a social movement can be described as a more or less persistent and organized effort on the part of relatively a large group of people to bring about or resist change. However, the number of persons participating is not the criteria to describe any movement as a collective action. The movement must have a leader to guide and plan the actions and the power to sustain the movement. Social movements, however, are different from pressure groups or institutional movements. Institutional movements are highly organized, permanent and primarily occupation based. Social movements are spontaneous and not issue specific.

THEORIES OF SOCIAL MOVEMENTS

There are basically four theories that describe the rationale of the people that makes them undertake a joint action. Various opinions have been expressed with regard to the cause of social movements. One set of observers are of the view that the roots for any movement are found in social misery, social and economic deprivation. Another set of observers are of the opinion that the widespread discontentment and oppression are the causes for social movements. It is also stated that conditions for living in a society are becoming intolerable which prompts people to take part in social movements. The following is a brief explanation of each of the approach.

Mass Society Theory

This approach was suggested by William Kornhauser in 1959 wherein he argued that mass society is impersonal, industrialized and highly bureaucratized that makes people feel isolated. This emptiness is filled by the social movements as they bring about a sense of belongingness. He also observed that in a society where social ties are weaker, there are more chances of social movements.

Sociologist like Dough McAdam, explained that the main reason for people to risk their lives in social movements is because of their strong desire to set right the wrongs and to overcome the injustices and not to isolate themselves as they are firmly rooted in families and communities.

Deprivation Theory

According to this theory, people deprived of things deemed valuable in society whether money, justice, status or privileges, join social movements with the hope of redressing their grievances. This theory was well explained by Karl Marx. He claimed that the excessive capitalistic exploitation was leading to impoverishment of the working classes that compelled them to overthrow their oppressors. However, Karl Marx recognized that abject misery and exploitation do not necessarily result in revolutionary fervour. He pointed out that the suffering of under classes whom Marx labelled as *Lumpenproletariat* can be so intense and their resulting alienation so massive that all social and revolutionary consciousness is dead end. Karl Marx also gave an explanation to another type of deprivation called relative deprivation where the people believed that they must join movements on the basis of their evaluation of what they think they should have compared to what others have. However, this theory which has excellent insights into revolutions also holds a surprise. Because of improving conditions, human desires for even better conditions, which at times spark revolutions. Theory of relative deprivation is further elaborated under another condition is characterized as 'rise and drop' or 'J Curve' hypothesis as explained by James Davies. He contends that revolutions are likely to take place when a prolonged period of social and economic betterment is followed by a period of sharp reversal. People fear that the gains they achieved with great effort will be lost and their mood becomes revolutionary.

Moral issues and Ideological Commitment

According to sociologists like James Jasper and Dorothy Nelkin, people join social movements even out of moral shock a sense of outrage at finding out what is 'really' going on. They feel they must choose sides and do what they can to bring about a difference. For example animal activists say organization like People for Ethical Treatment towards Animals (PETA) try to convince people based on the justification that animals suffer in order to make products for human consumption. Environment is another issue that attracts people on moral grounds.

Resource Mobilization Theory

This approach takes a different path altogether. The proponents of this theory claim that it is always necessary to know the forces that energize and activate a social movement. They emphasized on the factors like availability of resources for pursuing particular goals and the system of interpersonal relationships. People are seen to participate in social movement not as a result of deprivation, but as a response to a rational decision-making process whereby they weigh the costs and benefits of participation. In many cases resources and organizations outside the protest group are crucial in determining the scope and outcomes of collective action. External support is essential for movements of the poor. Most of the time the success or failure of the social movements is determined by the political factors in which it becomes entangled.

Thus, the above-mentioned theories, give us an understanding as to what are the reasons that instigate people to join various social movements. These movements help people to relate the individual to the larger society and make them aware of social concerns. It is through these movements that governments get to know the needs and demands of the people both in general and specific terms.

TYPES OF SOCIAL MOVEMENTS

Social movements may be classified on the basis of the purpose and interest like linguistic, religious, sectarian, caste, peasant, workers, tribal, ethnic, women's environmental, civil rights and human rights. With regards to the organization or strategies adopted they can be classified into moderate and militant, peaceful or violent and constitutional and unconstitutional movements. With respect to the demands or goals, movements can be reform movements, revolutionary movements, resistance movements, revivalist movements and expressive movements.

A reform movement can be described as a mass movement that seeks to change only one specific aspect of a society. A revolutionary movement pursues objectives that aim to change the society through challenging fundamental values or seek changes within the existing value framework. A resistance movement can be described as a movement that arises not only for the purpose of instituting change, but also to block change or to eliminate a previously instituted change. A revivalist movement seeks to take the system back to its original pristine purity. Finally expressive movements usually arise among under privileged sects, who do not seek comprehensive social change. Their aim is not to save the world, but save the individuals from a world that is progressively degenerating. Most of the movements try to involve people in the political process and bring about political awareness among the people. Some movements aim at bringing about a change in the lives of the downtrodden as well as women.

EMERGENCE OF MASS MOVEMENTS IN INDIA

India is not new to social movements. With its vast size, diversities, inequalities and finally in the process of development, India experienced a number of movements. The Indian National Movement is an explicit example of movements during, pre-independence period. Even after attaining Independence, in spite of adopting a democratic system of governance, there was dissatisfaction and frustration among people with regard to nature, role and behaviour of the state functionaries.

Once India became an independent country, the leaders adopted a Constitution based on Westminster model that fulfilled the aspirations of the people. The framers of the Constitution envisaged a model of mobilizing the masses through Parliamentary

Democracy, curb the influence of the dominant classes and evolve a professional middle-class as the new governing elite. Further it provided social and economic justice to the poor in the entire democratic process. Though liberal democracy was inaugurated, it was mostly the upper and middle classes that were participating in the affairs of the state. A large number of illiterate, poverty stricken, ignorant citizens, hardly had any change in their lives and were alienated from the entire political process. At this juncture, it became imperative for the political leaders to set up favourable conditions and establish a rapport between the people and the institutions. Though the task was hard but to achieve it was not impossible. In actual practice the Indian leadership ignored the need to do equal service to all sections of the society. They failed to realize that the social base of society is completely different where in each section of the society has to be taken care of independently. With no substantial effort on the part of the leaders, there was no improvement in the economic conditions of the landless, depressed sections, tribes, peasants and the like. Regional imbalances became widespread. Numerous ethnic groups based on language, race, religion or culture felt alienated from the political process and failed to acquire the benefits of economic developments. Thus from early 1970's there was a tendency of centralization of power, while the secular values were on a decline which prompted popular movements or mass movements. The following is a brief description of some of the movements that had an impact on the social, political and economic realm of the nation.

PEASANT MOVEMENTS

Indian economy is primarily an agrarian economy. The majority of the populations' main occupation is agriculture. Before independence, India was a poor country and its agriculture was primitive in nature. Further there was complete domination of the feudal lords over the lands and there was an unequal distribution. So, after independence, the government agriculture policy had to evolve a two-pronged strategy. On the one hand there was a need to modernize agriculture and increase production and on the other bring about a uniform ownership system. In the early 1960s new agricultural policies were introduced popularly under the banner of Green Revolution primarily to increase production. The policies were designed to provide financial support to the landowners and in turn increase their output by assuring access to all irrigational facilities. It was however only the rich and middle-class farmers, who could secure loans, invest in fertilizers and procure high-yield variety seeds. As the agriculture policies did not mention about redistribution of the agriculture product, the condition of small and marginal farmers deteriorated drastically. Further, the constant oppression and exploitation by the rich farmers became rampant.

In rural areas, the land reforms and agricultural policies were not properly implemented. Land reforms benefited the small and marginal farmers but not the landless. Further the mechanization and commercialization and state-sponsored rural development programmes benefited the rich and middle-class peasants. Consequently, the number of landless agricultural labourers, mostly unemployed, increased. At this juncture, the rural poor realized the need for a collective action in order to fight injustice and also against the state that does not protect their rights. Most of the time, the peasants demand higher wages and better working conditions. These movements were organized by the *kisan sabhas* and the agriculture units of Communist parties. The main purpose of all these movements is to strive to improve the economic conditions of all those who earn their livelihood by toiling in agricultural fields and related work.

The support extended by the political parties is crucial as most of these movements lack resources as well as organization. Further the rural poor are heterogeneous wherein they differ in their perceptions and attitudes. Therefore it is not possible for any organization to take a stand on economic and political issues that cut across various areas and cultural divisions. In a state where the peasant movement is strong it obviously suggests that there was complete oppression of landlords. One result is lack of faith in democratic process. When we consider the Naxalite movements they are popular among peasants in various states. However, these Naxalite movements failed to provide a common and unified programme and organization that led to rank and division of the peasants ideologically and regionally. Political parties like CPI, CPI (M), have organized various agitations all over India to highlight the concentration of land in the hands of landlords, former princes, zamindars and monopolists in order to make the public alert about the need for new agrarian reforms.

Peasant Movements before Independence: Some of the popular peasant movements that inspired the peasants at a later stage prior to independence were the Tebhaga movement or uprising in the north of Bengal in 1946 and the other was the Telangana in former Hyderabad state in 1946–48.

Box 12.1

The Telangana struggle began in 1946 demanding the abolition of illegal extractions by the nawabs and also the cancellation of peasant debts as the condition of the peasants was deplorable. The tenants were compelled to do forced labour. With pent-up emotions sporadic strikes were organized against forced labour and also for securing better wages. The landlords with the support of police retaliated by firing at workers. These incidents culminated in Telangana insurrection in which the village communities grabbed the land of rich landlords in 300 villages and distributed among peasants and the labourers.

The Tebhaga Movement of 1946–47, was launched by the share-croppers to retain two-thirds of agricultural produce for themselves and also demanded a reduction in the rent paid to the landlords. The movement was led by Bengal Provincial Kisan Sabha in Dinajpur from where it later spread to eleven other districts. In this movement the share-croppers refused to pay any share of the crop to the landlords.

DALIT MOVEMENTS

The main cause for the rise of Dalit movements or Dalit consciousness was the failure of government in framing policies that brought about social transformation and the process of democratization. A dalit refers to hitherto untouchables who were called Harijans or Children of God. The Constitution of India refers to them as Scheduled Castes.

In the Varna system or caste system of Hinduism, the society was first categorized into privileged and under-privileged. This downtrodden were considered as untouchables or even un-seeable. This feeling of untouchability was so well ingrained in the psyche of the upper castes that they had a great amount of control over the lives of the downtrodden from life to death. During the British rule, radical changes were made to serve the imperial needs be it in political, social or economic system of India. Principles like competition and individualism replaced the caste, colour and creed prejudices. Further the rise of socio-religious movements, demand for representative institutions augmented the rise of dalit consciousness. The period from 1920s to 1940s witnessed a steady rise of political consciousness that created a need for a separate, distinct and independent dalit identity. This urge for separate identity also gave rise to a consciousness of special judicial, political and constitutional safeguards and privileges as well. Further the literature of the times built about the perception of separate dalit identity. At this juncture the role played by Dr B. R. Ambedkar needs to be highlighted. He took a bold stand and became a leading Dalit figure of the depressed classes before and after Independence. During the Second Round table Conference held in London, 1930–1931, Ambedkar made one of his most brilliant presentation in front of the world leaders regarding the status of Dalits. He stated "The Depressed Classes cannot consent to subject themselves to majority rule in their present state of hereditary bondsmen. Before majority rule is established their emancipation from the system of untouchability must be an accomplished fact. It must not be left to the will of the majority. The Depressed Classes must be made free citizens entitled to all the rights of citizenship in common with other citizens of the State". Ambedkar was of the opinion that the deep-rooted caste prejudice and religious orthodoxy confined the nationalist movement to largely representing the aspirations of the dominant castes for political and economic power. It was in fact the result of Ambedkar's interventions at the Round Table Conference that the Indian Constitution guaranteed Fundamental Rights, established universal suffrage, abolished untouchability and guaranteed reservation in legislature and government services for dalits, *adivasis* and minorities. Dr B. R. Ambedkar is considered as the 'pariah of social outcastes' as he pioneered the cause of the upliftment of the dalits.

After independence, the government made conscious attempt to uplift the conditions of dalits, tribals and backward classes. The Constitution of India not only guaranteed equality in all the spheres but also abolished untouchability (Article 17) and made special provisions for the upliftment of the SCs, STs and ECs. The Constitution provided for reservations for SCs, ST's and BC's in legislative bodies, governmental jobs and educational institutions. Further the universal adult franchise facilitated the dalits to participate in political affairs and exercise their right to vote and also contest in elections. In fact some constituencies have high concentration of dalit population who have the power to decide the future of the candidates. So in most cases political parties fight among themselves in securing the support of dalits.

The constitutional provisions brought about a change in the policies and programmes adopted by the state, a change in the caste-ridden society and improvement in the dalit conditions of work. Reservations provided new occupational opportunities to the dalits. However it is not true that the entire section of dalits has witnessed a change, in spite of adopting a democratic, secular and socialist Constitution, poverty, illiteracy, bonded labour and oppression are still dominant. Majority of population of dalits live below poverty line. Moreover even though dalits have so-called social attributes like political and economic power, rank and esteem, there are occasions where in they are looked down upon.

With reference to the resurgence of dalits, though there were anti-upper castes movements prior to independence, for long period of time dalits never considered them as a collective block. The Congress Party out of its own interest began to reform them as they are a major source of vote bank. Congress in fact was the ultimate beneficiary as well as the final arbiter of their destiny. However with the failure of government in alleviating the living conditions of dalits, by late 60's these deprived sections took matters into their own hands and believed that it is only activism that will do justice to them. They completely rejected the Gandhian model which, emphasized on tackling the problems peacefully and through non-violent means. Instead they believed in the Ambedkarite model that represented 'self-respect' which appealed to most especially younger generations of dalits. According to dalit leaders, the main reason for injustice is the upper castes holding political power. This prompted them to lead movements to contest in elections. Bahujan Samaj Party is the best example that challenged the traditional Congress vote banks.

So in simple terms, the empowerment of dalits is threatening the mainstream political parties. Their appointments are not limited to the post of ministers but expanded much more though their empowerment differs from state to state yet the strategies followed by them are identical. On the whole dalit movements today are anti-caste movements. They are neither apolitical nor support one single party. They have emerged as a new cult that has the power to mobilize and influence political process.

TRIBAL MOVEMENTS

India is one of the few nations in the world noted for its tribal population. Most of the tribal population lives in remote forests without any access to socio-economic inputs. Their long years of isolation created an all-together a different social system. In order to integrate the tribals into mainstream population there was a need for adopting certain policies. But unfortunately, lack of necessary perception both at formulation and implementation created the emergence of movements.

Having adopted a democratic system of governance after Independence, the tribal population also became a part of the democratic order. The new state was committed to bring about welfare of the people in general and tribes in particular Accordingly, Constitution of India under Articles 15(4), 146, 244(1) and 339 provided special provisions for the administration and control of tribal areas for the welfare of the people therein. Seats were reserved in legislatures and administrative services for SCs and STs. The Constitution also guaranteed the protection of their culture and language even after becoming a part of mainstream. However, the emancipation of tribals is not an easy task because the powerful feudal lords with their vested interests have to be removed first. Moreover the government did not specify a development policy exclusively for tribals but in the general interest of the country. The main reason for the failure of programmes initiated for the welfare of the tribals is elitist bias and lopsided priorities. The bureaucracy decides what is good for the tribes without concerning them or involving the tribal populace. Further there was no concept of project formulation and appraisal.

The impact of industrialization was in mineral rich areas and that have done no good to the tribes. Establishment of large-scale industries in some states led to large-scale displacement as well. They were dislodged from their traditional habitations. Consequently, they joined the ranks of landless labourers without any training, aptitude or for any semi-skilled job. The landlords turned them into bonded labourers. Furthermore, it was realized that the administrative staff entrusted with the job of welfare of tribes turned apathetic to the needs of the tribes and never carried out programmes on the pretext of inadequate funds. There was also rampant corruption and gross abuse of power. The personnel are unaware of the needs of the tribes, their social, cultural traditional and linguistic values. Instead of improving the conditions the personnel became the exploiters of the tribes. The administrative staff could easily get away because of the illiteracy of the tribal populace.

The lack of scientific and objective information among the power structures, lack of interest among the protectors and lack of enthusiasm among the administrators resulted in the deterioration of the living conditions of the tribals. There was hunger and malnutrition pervading in most of the tribal areas. At this juncture, there was an emerging trend of tribal consciousness and mobilization. The tribals realized the need to act collectively and carve out an identity for themselves. These sentiments often lead to the beginning of a sub-nationalist movement of awakening. The political crisis in the north-east particularly Nagaland, Mizoram, Manipur and Meghalaya have been demanding autonomy or independence for the past many years. The main reason for the display of these secessionist tendencies is firstly, the distinctiveness of the region and the people, internal structural contradictions within the society of north-east, thirdly, conflict of interests between the local and national bourgeoisie and finally the location of region on the national frontiers especially Burma, Bangladesh and China. Another important point that has to be borne in mind is that some movements are violent while others are non-violent. Religious differences also intensify the movements.

Finally, if tribal aspirations are continuously ignored, their movements are likely to reach enormous proportions which later becomes difficult to manage. Most of the time these movements are banned by the government as they have the tendency to create law and order crisis rather than understanding the genuine political and democratic aspirations of the people. The solution is not suppression but to understand a holistic perspective of the real trouble and make efforts to integrate the tribes in to the mainstream, assuring their identity.

TRADE UNION MOVEMENTS

India though primarily, is an agriculture economy; it constitutes a sizable working class as well. Establishment of new industries after Independence resulted in an increase in the industrial workforce. People working in large and small factories, permanent and temporary, casual and contract, skilled and unskilled, educated and uneducated workers form the industrial workforce.

In usual parlance, the terms 'trade union movements' and 'labour movements' are used interchangeably. However, one important point to be noted is that the trade unions constitute the institutionalized core of labour movements. The main reason for referring to a trade union as a movement is because of its formal structure, membership, organizational hierarchy which are absent in other forms of movements. The main purpose of any trade union movement is to improve the conditions of the workers.

The history of trade union movement is closely related to the Indian National Movement. Prior to Independence, all movements whether political or economic, aimed at the overthrow of colonial system. During the Gandhian phase, most of the movements were economic in nature than political. Workers movements confronted both British imperialism and Indian capitalists. By the end of World War II, the Communist and Congress supporters greatly reduced because each party began to question the tactics or methods followed by the other party as against the colonial rulers.

After Independence there was growing discontent and dissatisfaction among the workers as there was more emphasis on establishing capitalism which to a great extent led to suffering and exploitation of large sections of the country. Inflation and price rise resulted in a fall in the real wages of the workers. These deplorable conditions of the workers instigated a resistance movement among the working class all over the country. In the initial years after Independence, most of these movements were led by All India Trade Union Congress or AITUC. By the end of World War II two leading workers organizations came into existence, namely, AITUC and Indian Federation of Labour. With a split in AITUC in 1948, a new organization called Hind Mazdoor Sangh was formed under the leadership of M. N. Roy while the other half in AITUC had become the Indian National Trade Union Congress (INTUC) in 1949. The main aim of INTUC is to place the industry under national ownership and control. However, nothing exclusive could be done as the members within INTUC were divided and had reservations about nationalization of industries. Being affiliated to the Congress Party, it always co-opted with government directives that derived gains because of its proximity to the government. During the fifties and sixties, these worker unions attained ideological views that industrial relations must reflect the interests of the working class and that the organized labour is at the forefront of the progressive forces. The Communist Party of India (CPI) and Communist Party of India, Marxist (CPI [M]) began to have an influence over these unions. Each party had a separate trade union organization called AITUC, which is renowned for its military outlook though confined to the heavy industries and public sector undertakings. Most of the time the movements led by these unions were centered around a revision in pay structure and pleaded for better conditions of work and minimum wages. In July 1960, a major strike was called out by the representatives of All India Railway Men's Federation, National Federation of Post and Telegraph Employees, All India Defence Employees Federation and The Confederation of Central Government Employees. The representatives demanded payment of dearness allowance as per the provisions of First Pay Commission, distinction between different types of workers namely, skilled, semi-skilled and unskilled employees. This movement however was declared as illegal under Essential Services Maintenance Ordinance, which led to firing, injuring and killing the activists. The same year, there were other struggles led by white collar employees, teachers of schools and colleges. In fact most of the movements were led by the central and state government employees under the leadership of All India State Government employees Federation. During 1965–1975, there was an increasing number of strikes as the unorganized sector as well, became more active and vocal. The country witnessed various agitations in different parts mainly because of rise in prices, shortage of commodities and mounting unemployment. Central and state government employees also joined in protests against the growing economic difficulties affecting almost all sections of the people.

WOMEN'S MOVEMENTS

Women activism usually cuts across different socio-economic strata and other interests. Though a great unifying force, women movements lack correct means to organize themselves. These movements are not to create community feelings but create community awareness. Women's movements are always not gender-specific, but they aim at societal transformation where in power is used to suppress women. Feminism is an attempt to reorganize the differences in sexes and division of labour. It cannot be stated that it is in the last few decade that there is a rise in women's movements. Even prior to Independence women have played an active role in the freedom struggle movement.

Gandhi once declared "I would boycott that legislature which will not have a proper share of women members". In fact Gandhi was the only Indian leader who thought of the power of massive vote bank to get rid of corruption and caste ridden murky politics. Apart from his great service to the society in the form of abolishing untouchability, he also tried to bring about a change in the lives of women. He stressed that the main cause of evil is not legal inequalities but the greed for power and fame and deeper still in mutual lust. Gandhi encouraged women in fighting for their rights. He wanted women not to imitate the west but apply methods suited to the Indian genius and environment. Commenting on women workers in 1947, Gandhi stated, India can proclaim that she can make progress not through the atom bomb but through non-violence alone and that women alone can take the lead in this, for God has endowed them with great power. If women resolve to bring glory to the nation, within few months they can totally change the face of the spiritual background of the women.

Role of Women in Politics

Prior to Independence most of the movements were led against the imperialistic rule and it was then women began to participate. Be it the movement led by Gandhi or the Communist party, there was a large participation of women. Their presence was also felt in various peasant and working class movements as well. In the post-Independence era, however, women movements became more global and there was an increase in militancy among women. Most of the movements centered on issues like peace, human rights, imperialism, racism, pollution and development models of growth.

There are three women organizations, though each organization is affiliated to a political party. They are All India Women's Conference (AIWC) affiliated to Congress Party, National Federation of Indian Women (NFIW) allied with Communist Party of India and finally All India Democratic Women's Association (AIDWA) associated with Communist Party of India, (Marxists). Each group has a different outlook with regard to the role of women in the society and responds differently to the issues. AIWC was formed in 1927 and actively participated in the freedom struggle movement. After independence it pressurized the government to improve the living conditions of women. It was responsible to make government enact the Special Marriage Act (1954), the Hindu Marriage Act and Divorce Act (1955), Inter-state Succession Act (1956) and Dowry Act (1961). With reference to NFIW, it was formed in 1954 mainly to restrain the oppression of women supported by unequal property rights. It aims at transformation of social relations of power which oppress not only women but also other social groups. This organization committed itself to alleviate the conditions of women in factories and other oppressed groups like peasants and tribals. It also strives to provide justice to rape victims and victims of police tyranny. With respect to AIDWA, it came in to existence in 1981. The organization has taken up the issue of equal rights for women. It draws support mainly from agricultural labourers, peasants, working class and professional groups. AIDWA concentrates more on dowry problems and pressurize the government to formulate and implement policies on anti-dowry.

In the recent years, these organizations have concentrated more on mobilizing people to highlight gender identity. Special attention today is given to the role of women in the society and certain evils that are still practiced like Sati. Though women's groups were successful in getting the bill passed against Sati, they were unsuccessful in incorporating suggestion into the Women's reservations in the Parliament. This suggests that on the one hand these organizations have to pursue their goals and expose women's oppression and on the other struggle against the entire general oppressive structures.

Women and Trade Unions

In the last few decades there has been an increase in protest movements organized by women in companies and factories. The main reason for the emergence of these movements is that it was realized that certain issues cannot be solved by the hierarchical party organizations. Further the women work force is often a low paid job and lacks authority. There are basically two main organizations that support women in the informal sector. They are Self Employed Women's Association (SEWA) based in Ahmedabad and Working Women's Forum in Madras. These organizations are run by middle-class women and are less hierarchical and flexible. They respond quickly to the needs of women in society. Most of the women organizations are interested in providing legal aid, health care and counseling to women than involving themselves in violent movements, public demonstrations and campaigns.

SUMMARY

- It becomes very clear that unless and until there is subjugation and prejudices involved, mass movements do not arise. In fact the Indian struggle for Independence itself was a mass movement. Before Independence, the movements focussed on the overthrow of British imperialism which included all categories. of people.
- After Independence, the gross absence of a powerful enemy and different perceptions to get rid of evils created differences which finally gave birth to a variety of movements. Much of the peasant and workers movements demand for land reforms, distribution of land, minimum wages and allowances while tribal movements insist on preservation of forests and right over forest products.
- Women movements are directed against injustice and oppression. In most cases these movements are sporadic while some are organized. Similarly some movements are local and regional like tribal or peasant movements. Some movements shake up the entire country like the workers movements.
- Over a period of time there has been a slight shift in the ways adopted to achieve the purpose. Earlier movements were more involved in settling ideological issues like anti-capitalism, class revolution and class struggle. Movements today are not in leading revolutions or revolutionary overthrow of governance of the state. In reality these movements bring about change without a change in the government. Movements today are more global in nature which affects not only one specific section but entire human population.

- Some of the contemporary issues that attract world attention are anti-racism, anti-nuclearism, disarmament, environmentalism, regionalism and ethnicity and civil liberties.

QUESTIONS

1. Explain the deprivation theory of social movement
2. What are the different kinds of social movements and discuss at least one of the social movements at large?
3. Analyze some of the important issues involved in the contemporary women movements in India.
4. Briefly analyze the worker's movements since independence. Suggest some measures for strengthening the Trade Union Movement in India.
5. Briefly analyze the evolution of the Peasant Movements in India.
6. Explain the different reasons for social movement.

13

Electoral Politics in India

After reading this chapter, you will be conversant with:

- Election Commission
- Election Process
- Electoral Reforms
- Anti-Defection Law
- Voting Behaviour
- Election Funding and
- Criminal and Political Nexus in Elections

INTRODUCTION

Elections are an instrument through which modern states create amongst its citizens a sense of the political awareness, involvement and participation in public affairs. For a genuine representative government, there has to be a good electoral system. The architects of the Indian Constitution attached the highest significance to independent electoral machinery for the conduct of elections hence the need for an independent Election Commission was felt which would ensure fair and free elections at all levels. Consequently, the Election Commission of India under Article 324 states:

'The superintendence, direction and control of the electoral rolls for and the conduct of all elections to Parliament and to the legislature of every state and of elections to the offices of President and Vice President held under this constitution, including the appointment of election tribunals for the decision of the doubts and disputes arising out of or in connection with election to Parliament and to the legislatures of the states, shall be vested in a omission.'

The constitution provides for universal adult franchise. Every citizen who is eighteen years or above has voting rights irrespective of religion, race, caste, sex or place of birth and elections are to be conducted under the supervision and direction of an independent authority called the Election Commission. In addition to the elections to the two Houses of Parliament and the state legislatures, the Election Commission is also responsible for the conduct of elections to the offices of the President and Vice President of India.

The Legal Framework

Under the constitution, provision is made for an Election Commission which is entrusted to deal with the following matters that are listed here.

- Election of the President of India.
- Election of the Vice President of India.
- The Union Parliament and the composition of its two chambers.
- Qualification of members of Parliament.
- Composition of State Legislatures.
- Qualifications of members of State Legislatures.
- Duration of Parliament and the State Legislatures.
- Elections to Parliament and State Legislatures.
- Reservation of seats in the House of the People and the State Assemblies for the Scheduled Castes and Tribes.
- The determination of population for purposes of election.

Under Article 327, Parliament is vested with the supreme power to legislate on all matters relating to elections, including elections to State Legislatures. Under Article 328, the states have also been vested with certain limited powers of legislation with respect to elections.

THE ELECTION COMMISSION

To ensure free, fair and impartial elections, the constitution establishes the Election Commission, an autonomous body. In other words, electoral machinery is centralized in an independent statutory body called the Election Commission and the commission is responsible for direction and control of the elections to Parliament and State Legislatures (Article 324).

The superintendence, direction and control of the preparation of the electoral rolls and the conduct of all elections to Parliament and to the Legislature of every state and of elections of the office of President and Vice President held under this constitution shall be vested in a commission mentioned to in constitution as the Election Commission.

The Election Commission shall consist of Chief Election Commissioner and such number of other Election Commissioners, as the President may from time-to-time fix and the appointment of the Chief Election Commissioner and other Election Commissioners, subject to the provisions of law made by Parliament.

Before each general election to the House of People and to the Legislative Assembly of each state and before the first general election and thereafter before each biennial election to the legislative council of each state having such council, the President may also appoint after consultation with the Election Commission, such regional commissioners as he may consider necessary to assist the Election Commission in the performance of the functions conferred on the commission by clause (1).

Subject to the provisions of any law made by President, the conditions of service and tenure of office of the Election Commissioner and the Regional Commissioners shall be such as the President may by rule determine. Provided that the chief election commissioner shall not be removed from his office except in the manner and on similar grounds as a judge of the Supreme Court and the service conditions of the Chief Election Commissioner shall not be varied to his disadvantage after his appointment. Any other Election Commissioner or a Regional Commissioner shall not be removed from office except on the recommendation of the Chief Election Commissioner.

The President or the Governor of a state shall, when so requested by the Election Commission, make available to the Election Commission or to a Regional Commissioner such staff as may be necessary for the discharge of the functions conferred on the Election Commission by clause (1).

Thus the Election Commission may be a multi member body under the headship or leadership of the Chief Election Commissioner.

Removal of Chief Election Commissioner

He may be removed by the process of impeachment on charges as applicable for the removal of the judge of the Supreme Court. A resolution to this effect must be passed after issuing at least fourteen days notice to him by both the Houses of Parliament by absolute majority of the whole House with two-thirds majority of the members present and voting.

Regional and Deputy Commissioner

To assist the Chief Election Commissioner in the performance of his duties, there exists large paraphernalia of the officers and the subordinate to him. Among them are the Regional Commissioners, Deputy Election Commissioner, Secretary, Under Secretary and Research Officers.

Functions of Election Commission

The main functions of the Election Commission may be enumerated as discussed in the following subsection.

- To prepare electoral rolls for the elections and suitably revise them after every decennial census and before every general election to the Union and State legislatures.
- To supervise the machinery of elections throughout the country to enable free and fair elections.

Election Commissioners of India

Sukumar Sen	1950 to 1958
K. V. K. Sundaram	195 8 to 1967
S. P. Sen Verma	1967 to 1972
Dr Nagendra Sing	1972 to 1973
T. Swaminathan	1973 to 1977
S. L. Shakdhar	.1977 to 1982
R. K. Trivedi	1982 to 1985
R. V. S. Peri Sastri	1986 to 1990
V. S. Ramadevi	1990 to 1990
T. N. Seshan	1990 to 1996
M. S. Gill	1996 to 2000
J. M. Lyngdoh	2000 till date

- To notify dates and schedules of elections so that nomination papers are filed and properly scrutinized before elections take place (The Returning officer notifies to all the contesting candidates the date, time and place for the formal scrutiny of nomination papers).
- To appoint officers inquiring into disputes relating to electoral arrangements
- To empower the President of India or the Governor of the state for requisitioning of staff necessary for conducting elections.
- It can cancel polls in the event of mass-scale rigging or other irregularities.
- To act like a court for settling matters as giving recognition to a political party or allotting a symbol for electoral purposes including de-recognition of a party or withdrawal of its symbol.
- The commissioner advises the President on a matter relating to the disqualification of a Member of Parliament and to the Governor about the disqualification of a member of the State Legislature.
- To advise the government whether elections can be held in a state under President's rule in order to extend the duration of emergency there after a year.

ELECTORAL PROCESS

Registration of Voters and Revision of Lists

Considering the vastness of the country, the size of its population, prevailing illiteracy, inadequacy of the means of communication and indifference of political parties the enrolment of voters is a difficult task. Moreover, the revision of rolls is a time consuming process which impedes the holding of elections quickly. Some procedure should therefore be evolved under which the electoral rolls are subjected to constant revision so that they are always kept up-to-date and the commission may hold state or countrywide elections within a short time. The objective can easily be attained if political parties cooperate in the venture.

Fixing the Election Date

The Election Commission in consultation with the union or state government fixes the date of election as the case may be.

The Nominating Process

The electoral process is formally set in motion by the Presidential announcement calling upon electors in all parliamentary constituencies to elect their representatives to the Lok Sabha. Similarly the Governors of the state issue notifications calling upon electors to elect their representatives for the legislative assemblies.

At the same time election commission issues notifications specifying the timetable for nominations, scrutiny, withdrawals of nomination and polling. Candidates must meet the requirements laid down in the constitutions. They may also contest as independents. Shortly after the dead-line of filing of nomination papers passes, the papers are scrutinized by the returning officers who reject those which are invalid and come out with a list of the validly nominated candidates in each constituency, arranged alphabetically. The list of candidates is finalized only after the last date for withdrawals.

Grounds for Rejecting a Nomination Paper

The Election Commission set out the conditions which would justify a returning officer to reject the nomination paper of any candidate. The grounds for rejection of nomination papers are;

- If a candidate is clearly not qualified to be a member of the House of the people or of a state legislative assembly.
- If he was disqualified according to law to be such a member.
- If he has not taken the oath or affirmation as required by the constitution.
- If his nomination paper has not been delivered on time.
- If his nomination paper had been delivered to the returning officer or to an authorized assistant returning officer by a person other than himself or his proposer.
- If his nomination paper has not been delivered at the place specified in the public notice issued by the returning officer.
- If his nomination paper has been delivered to a person other than the returning officer or any of his authorized assistant returning officer.

- If his nomination paper was not substantially in a prescribed form.
- If his nomination paper has not been signed either by him or by his proposer or by both in the places meant for such signatures in the nomination paper.
- If the proper deposit has not been made by him in accordance with the law already explained.
- If his signature or the signature of his proposer on the nomination paper is not genuine.
- If he does not belong to schedule caste and he files nomination paper to contest a seat reserved for the schedule castes.
- If the proposer is not an elector of that constituency or is ineligible to be a proposer.

Recognition of Parties

The election commission determines which political parties will be recognized, on both national and state levels and what symbols will be assigned to each party. The political parties, not meeting the criteria of a national party or a state party, is known as registered party.

Selection of the Candidate

The selection process has a considerable bearing on the quality of leaders to be chosen for political parties as well as of individuals on the nature of the electoral process and on the character of leadership and the orientation of the political system. The procedure varies from party to party.

Election Campaign

A political campaign is always an interesting happening in the political life of a nation. It attracts a great deal of attention inside a country. The campaign is the period when the political parties put forward their candidates and arguments with which they hope to persuade people to vote for their candidates and parties. Candidates are given a week to put forward their nominations. The returning officers scrutinize these nominations and if not found to be in order can be rejected after a summary hearing. Validly nominated candidates can withdraw within two days after nominations have been scrutinized. The official campaign lasts at least two weeks from the drawing up of the list of nominated candidates and officially ends forty-eight hours before polling closes.

During the election campaign the political parties and contesting candidates are expected to abide by a Model Code of Conduct evolved by the Election Commission on the basis of a consensus among political parties. The model code lays down broad guidelines as to how the political parties and candidates should conduct themselves during the election campaign. It is intended to maintain the election campaign on healthy lines, avoid clashes and conflicts between political parties or their supporters and to ensure peace and order during the campaign period and thereafter, until the results are declared. The model code also prescribes guidelines for the ruling party at the centre or in the state to ensure that a level field is maintained and the ruling party does not misuse the official machinery during election campaign.

Once an election has been declared, parties issue manifestos outlining the programmes they wish to implement if elected to form a government. It also includes strengths of their leaders and the failures of opposing parties and their leaders. Slogans are used to popularize and identify parties and issues and pamphlets and posters distributed to the electorate. Through rallies and meetings candidates try to persuade, cajole and encourage supporters and denigrate opponents in their constituencies. Personal appeals and promises of reform are made, with candidates in a constituency and try to influence as many potential supporters as possible. Party symbols abound, printed on posters and placards.

ELECTORAL REFORMS

Need for an electoral reform has been debated right from the time of the first general elections in 1951–1952. Successive Election Commissions, various other Commissions and committees have made suggestions in this direction. The government itself has from time-to-time formulated some proposals. The Election Commission of India, after every General Election has been making proposals for electoral reforms. A committee with representatives of all leading political parties under the chairmanship of Dinesh Goswami, a leading member at Parliament, made a thorough study of electoral problems and proposed a number of recommendations. The report of the committee was unanimously adopted by the Parliament. The Lok Sabha has also unanimously passed a resolution on electoral reforms. Successive governments at the centre have been making promises about electoral reforms. From booth capturing, snatching of ballot papers and stuffing them in ballot boxes, intimidation of voters, in fact, every form of electoral malpractice has been on the increase in every election. Muscle power and money power has been very much on the increase. It is in this context that an urgent need for electoral reforms has become necessary and yet nothing tangible has happened so far. Unless electoral reforms are brought about and strictly implemented, democratic elections will become an ornamental euphemism than a reality.

Electoral reforms should address the following issues:

- Criminalization of politics.
- Misuse of unaccounted money.
- Electoral irregularities such as rigging, booth capturing and proxy voting.

- Autocratic and unaccountable political parties.
- The problems of defection for personal gains.

To make elections more free and fair, certain electoral reforms were initiated and introduced from time-to-time by election commissions. Some of the suggested reforms are as follows:

Code of Conduct for Political Parties

Parties have often become a collection of greedy and corrupt persons who are willing to use any means to have their hold on state power. Therefore, a code of conduct dealing with aspects of electioneering such as meetings, processions, speeches and slogans have been accepted by political parties. A party must obtain prior permission of the administration for holding a public meeting, for using the loud speaker or any other facility in connection with the meeting. A party organizing a procession should in advance determine the time and place of starting the procession, the route thereof and the time and name of its disbanding.

Pictorial representation should be decent and moderate and should focus on the objects of party instead of highlighting the misdeeds of rival parties. On the eve of the Third General Elections, the election commission circulated a code to all the political parties in India and to the state governments, exhorting the latter to secure acceptance of the code by all parties contesting general elections in their states.

Electronic Voting Machine

Electronic Voting Machine (EVM) retains all the characteristics of voting by ballot papers, while making polling a lot more expedient. Being fast and absolutely reliable, the EVM saves considerable time, money and manpower. It helps to maintain total voting secrecy without the use of ballot papers and enables early announcement of results. The EVM is 100 per cent tamper proof. And, at the end of the polling, press a button and you have the results.

Computerization of Rolls

The Election Commission has taken the computerization of the electoral rolls throughout India which might lead to improvements in accuracy and speed with which the electoral roll can be updated.

Issue of Photo Identity Cards

In order to improve the accuracy of the electoral roll and prevent electoral fraud, the Election Commission initiated for the introduction of photo identity cards for voters. The Commission is providing ways and methods to deal with the problems with the issue of cards and difficulties in keeping track of voters, especially the mobile urban electorate.

Curbing Illegal Election expenditure

Excessive illegal and illegitimate expenditure in elections is the root cause of corruptions. Most election expenditure is illegal and is incurred in buying votes, hiring hoodlums and bribing officials. This is the major cause of corruption siphoning off money at all levels. Cleansing elections is the important way through which corruption and misadministration can be curbed.

Booth Capturing and Rigging

On the question of booth capturing, rigging and intimidation of voters, the proposals of the Goswami Committee to the effect that EC should be empowered to take more stringent action should be accepted and implemented in full.

The Commission recommends: (a) Under section 58A of the Representation of the People Act, 1951, the Election Commission should be authorized to take a decision regarding booth capturing on the report of the returning officers, observers or citizen groups. Also, the Commission should be empowered to countermand the election and order a fresh election or to declare the earlier poll to be void and order a re-poll in the entire constituency and (b) EC should consider the use of tamper-proof video and other electronic surveillance at sensitive polling stations constituencies.

ANTI-DEFECTION LAW

Definition of Political Defection

If any person who had been allotted the symbol of any political party and who has got elected as a member of either House of Parliament or of a Legislative Assembly or Legislative Council of a state or of a Union Territory willingly renounced allegiance to such political party, he is said to have defection.

Causes of Defection

The causes of defection are several. Firstly, the ambition for capturing power the politicians fight for power and government offices.

Secondly, there was big difference between the emoluments, status and benefits attached to the office of a Minister and that of an ordinary MLA. If an MLA was offered or promised ministership, he/she did not hesitate to leave the party on whose ticket and symbol he was elected. There are also instances wherein legislators lost faith in the policies and programmes of the party to which they originally belonged and developed genuine liking for the ideology of some other party and therefore they crossed the floor. But most of the defectors were motivated by their selfish motives and lust for power. Thirdly, the lack of competent and dynamic leadership within parties leads to factionalism within those parties. This was also responsible for defection.

Fourthly, the difference or ignorance of the illiterate and narrow-minded electorate to acts of defection by their representatives.

Committee on Defection

The practice of defection was becoming a menace hence a senior member of the Congress party in the Lok Sabha, Venkatasubbaiah introduced a resolution which demanded that a high level committee consisting of representative of political parties and constitutional experts be formed by the government 'to consider the problem of legislators changing their allegiance from one party to another and check their frequent crossing of the floor in all its aspects and make recommendations in this regard'. The Lok Sabha adopted the resolution on December 1967 and the committee was constituted three months later.

Recommendations of Committee of Defection

The committee on defections made its own recommendations in January 1969.The recommendations are discussed below.

- Political defectors should be debarred form occupying any office such as Prime Minister, Speaker, Deputy Speaker or Chairman of any statutory corporation for a period of one year from the date of defection.
- The size of Ministry in a state should be ten per cent.
- The defectors should be barred from becoming ministers up to one year from the date of defection, unless they get elected after resigning.

Due to various reasons the Home Ministry abandoned the idea of introducing the Bill in Parliament. Prime Minister Indira Gandhi directed the Law Ministry to examine the suggestions and to recommend whether or not those could be incorporated in the proposed bill. The Ministry after examining pointed out the difficulties involved in the suggestions. About the suggestions that a defector should be disqualified from the membership of the legislature the difficulty found was that the reason for disqualification laid down in the constitution were personal and did not cover political beliefs or associations.

With regard to the suggestion of limiting size of the council of Ministers, the difficulty seen was that the constitution did not contemplate any such limitations and any restrictive legislation to declare by the Supreme Court as unconstitutional.

In the suggestions that the elector should be given the right to recall a defecting legislator the difficulty presumed was that the term of office of the legislator had been laid down in the constitution and a legislator should be made to resign and seek a fresh mandate from the voters for which each newly elected legislator should deposit with the leader of his party an undated letter of resignation that could be used in the event of his defection. The difficulty pointed out was that the member concerned could at any time write to the speaker of the Assembly or Chairman of the Legislative Council to cancel his letter of resignation.

It was also suggested that all political parties should be compulsorily registered on the basis of their aims and objective or only such parties whose membership reached a specific percentage of the electorate should be recognized for the purpose of election and all the candidates should belong to one such party. This suggestion led to the violation of all Fundamental Rights of freedom of speech and association and it was also pointed out that Parliament could not pass a law providing for compulsory registration of parties.

Support to the Bill on defections evoked unfavourable responses from the opposition parties hence the idea of introducing the Bill in the Parliament was abandoned.

Citizens realized that their votes have no sanctity after the elections are over. Even if a candidate is elected to form a government, there is no guarantee that the candidate will not defect to a party with a different agenda and ideology, thereby betraying peoples' verdict for their selfish gains. Hence the tenth schedule of the constitution incorporated by 52nd Amendment was popularly known as the Anti-Defection Act. It was meant to ensure that people's mandate is respected.

Anti-Defection Law, as enacted in 1985 when Rajiv Gandhi was Prime Minister, empowers the Speaker or Chairman of the House concerned to decide on the question of disqualification of a member who defects. It provided for the disqualification from Parliament of any member who voted against the dictate of the party leadership (called party whip) on any motion but permitted a third of members of any party to oppose party whip and still retain their seats, recognized as having split from the original party. The new amendment will take away the one-third-member provision and disqualify anyone that votes against party whip and invalidates the dissenting vote of any member who votes against a party whip to topple a government.

The law also recognizes splits in and mergers of parties. A split is recognized if at least one-third of the total membership of the legislature party defects. If more than two-thirds of the member of legislators of a party decides to join another party, it is recognized as a merger. In that case, the remaining legislators of the parent party will not be disqualified. As a result splits are engineered and constitutional coups are planned with precision and careful conspiracy. In effect, anti-defection provisions have completely failed in achieving the intended results.

VOTING BEHAVIOUR

Elections are indispensable for the democracy and franchise is the most important means to participate in a political system through elections. Hence a study of voting behaviour therefore helps in the understanding of democratic system. Periodic elections enable almost every political party to come to power and form the government. No definite judgments therefore can be given about voting. Here is an attempt to investigate the factors influencing voting in view of the social and political conditions.

Voting—A Negative Question

Most of the citizens do not exercise their vote. Their attitude is negative about voting. They have the right to vote but they neither believe in the electoral system nor do they confide in the political system. Hence they abstain from vote.

To some voters, voting is a futile exercise. Further, more voters in rural areas do not vote. The reasons for this are the lack of political information and consciousness and long distances between the polling booths. Rural voters are politically less aware man others.

The socially and economically downtrodden also do not show interest for voting. Thus voting behaviour is related to an individual's socio-economic status, confidence in political system, communalism and several other factors. But once a voter takes active participation in voting he usually retains it and becomes more concerned about political affairs. People who vote are politically aware when compared to those who do not vote. The nature of elections and its usefulness also determine voting behaviour. For instance, some voters are interested in national elections while others are interested in state and local polls.

In voting for a candidate a voter takes into account several factors such as:

- The family set up.
- Social conditions.
- The political environment.

Family: Each individual associates himself or herself with family, locality, caste and other related associations and organizations to which he relates. For instance, family gives an individual his or her identity. Voting decisions are taken by consulting family. The mature opinion of family still prevails.

Caste: Caste is an important social institution which gives the citizen a sense of belongingness. The selection of candidates is often made based on caste. Hence the influence of caste on voting behaviour is undoubtable.

Caste has been politicized and politics uses caste as its base to attain power. Thus caste associations have a major role to play in voting.

Class: The class consciousness is equally important while dealing with the voting behaviour. The class is an economic institution which reflects the income level of a voter. In the urban areas, the class based organization and associations influence the voting behaviour of individuals. Political parties invariably take advantage of this consciousness.

Socio-Economic Factors: Age, education, income, sex, religion, ownership of land, past financial status and future expectancy are the socio-economic determinants of voting and are equally important. For instance, the older citizens are more conservative in voting while the young are more radical. The majority of people who are educated do not attach much importance to the head of the family in giving their vote. The intellectually elite is more inclined towards the opposition. The propertied section does not support the revolutionary but support, the establishment.

In India the role of money cannot be denied when it comes to voting behaviour. Constitutionally, limitations have been imposed on election finances yet votes are sold for money. In rural areas voters are lured by money. The political situations and problems play a fundamental role in influencing voting. In a democratic set up, the citizens regard voting as a means to fulfill a political purpose like the establishment of a government. Therefore the economic, cultural and linguistic problems assume a political colour and during voting all problems are subordinated to political preference or non-preference. The Political conditions that effect voting can be local, national as well as international.

Political Parties

One of the most important institutions affecting voting is the political parties and its leader. In India, importance is given to candidate's individual capacity and personal merit such as his or her straightforwardness, experience and service but party organization is more important than the candidate. The organizational capacity, resources and collective thinking of a party surpass those of any candidates. In India votes are claimed in the name of the party leader, such as Gandhiji, Pandit Nehru and Indira Gandhi. These leaders have become the symbol of stability, democracy and progress. Therefore, the voters change their preference about parties through associating them with a leader.

Political parties organize campaigns and communicate the issues through discussions and propaganda. This dissemination of information leads to a higher political consciousness which influences voting. The ruling party influences franchise through tempting announcements and concessions made. With few exceptions voting behaviour in India has been peaceful. Though gradually, people have realized the importance of their votes and despite problems voting behaviour has been responsible and cooperative in the democratic system. Voting has influenced the political system through mass participation.

ELECTION FUNDING

The exercise of raising funds for political parties has become a vicious circle. Business houses are the main source for funds to political parties. But they also demand their pound of flesh while shelling out the funds. They are often obliged by the ruling dispensations at the centre and in the states in form of contracts, licenses or permits and numerous other ways.

It is evident that pressures from big industrialists, for the donations, reached notorious levels, often embarrassing the ruling dispensations. Big Houses appointed their liaison men in state capitals. They are described as touts or middleman and entrusted with the task of clinching a deal. They are the agents through whom money is paid to political parties and their leaders. Industrialists consider these payments investments because they yield rich results.

However, donations by business and trade establishments have become overt and often exposed and discredited politicians and their parties. New ways to collect funds are devised and defence was considered the safest means, as there was much risk-free money to be made. Huge commissions are paid on defence deals. These are supposed to be highly guarded secrets. The payment of commissions on arms purchases is considered by political parties as the best means of funding themselves. Until the Bofors deal was exposed, it was not known how much money changed hands. Though the Bofors transactions are still covered in mystery, it took its toll on a government with the largest-ever majority in the Parliament. Another example of this is the recent Tehelka sting operation that exposed the multi-level corruption in the defence ministry.

The problem of political funding is a complex one. Political parties need hefty contributions from companies and from other desirable sources. The greater the contribution, the greater is the risk of dependence, corruption and lack of probity in public life. There is a need for transparency to avoid any illegal and unfair influences of money in politics. Laws with regard to transparency should be general in nature and enforced with respect to everyone and not just political parties or candidates, but also to the donors as well. In fact, it is essential to strengthen regulation and the mechanisms and capabilities of supervision and controlling entities. Quite often, funding and commitments do not reach the parties, but rather go directly to the candidate and his or her inner circle of supporters. This is a fact today in the context of the image and credibility crisis that party organizations have been undergoing and the emergence of regional leaders due to the regionalization process. This tends to make transactions between donors and beneficiaries become even more secretive. Hence, the senior leaders or party members may often not be aware of private contributions (many of them dubious in origin and in quite large sums). Consequently, any proposals for reforms concerning political funding should revolve, among other things, around the following four main objectives. These are:

- Reducing the influence of money by diminishing its impact (by shortening campaigns, establishing ceilings on expenditure and limiting individual contributions).
- Improving the utility of money by investing it on more productive activities for the sake of democracy and not just squandering it on propaganda and negative campaigns.
- Stopping or at least curtailing, as much as possible, current levels of influence peddling and political corruption.
- Strengthening public disclosure and transparency mechanisms with respect to both the origin and the use of funds.

At present, different acts regulate the flow of funds to political parties both from internal as well as external sources and consolidating such laws should enact a comprehensive legislation providing for regulation of contributions to the political parties and towards election expenses. The new law should aim at bringing transparency into political funding and should permit corporate donations within higher prescribed limits and keep them transparent. It should make all legal and transparent donations up to a specified limit tax exempt and treat this tax loss to the state as its contribution to state funding of elections. Political funding should be a separate head in the accounts and annual reports of the company. This will ensure transparency. This will be in addition to the existing conditions laid down in the Companies Act, 1956 for making donations to political parties.

The law should contain provisions for making both donors and recipients of political funds accountable. The government should encourage the corporate bodies and agencies to establish an electoral trust which should be able to finance political parties on an impartial basis at the time of elections.

Audited political party accounts like the accounts of a public limited company should be published yearly with full disclosure under predetermined account heads.

CRIMINAL AND POLITICAL NEXUS

It is generally believed that there is a nexus between political parties and anti social elements which leads to criminalization of politics. Criminals are joining politics. Thus lawbreakers have become lawmakers. This has proved detrimental to democracy of the country. Many legislators and members of parliament are having criminal record. In this background, the Supreme Court took the view that elections would be a farce if the voters were to remain unaware of the background of their candidates. Though it agreed that such candidates ought to be disqualified from contesting elections, it acted with judicial self-restraint and emphasized that 'at the outset, we would say that it is not possible for this court to give any directions for amending the Act or the statutory rules. It is for Parliament to amend the Act and the Rules'.

The Court held that the right to information and the right to know the background including the criminal past or assets of candidates was a fundamental right under Article 19(1) (a) of the Constitution and that the information was fundamental for survival and effective functioning of democracy. In its judgment of 2 May 2002, it directed the Election Commission to call for information on affidavit from each candidate seeking election to Parliament or the State Legislature as a necessary part of the nomination papers on:

- Whether the candidate has been convicted acquitted discharged of any criminal offence in the past if any.
- Whether the candidate was accused in any pending case of any offence punishable with imprisonment for two years or more and in which charge was framed or cognizance taken by the court of law. If so, the details thereof.

The assets (immovable, movable and bank balance) of a candidate and of his or her spouse and that of the dependents; liabilities, if any, particularly of any overdues of any public financial institution or government dues and educational qualifications of the candidate.

The Vohra Committee appointed by the government stated in strong terms that the nexus between crime syndicates and political personalities was deep. According to the Central Bureau of Investigation (CBI) report to the Vohra Committee: 'All over India, crime syndicates have become a law unto themselves. Even in the smaller towns and rural areas, muscle men have become the order of the day. Hired assassins have become part of these organizations. The nexus between the criminal gangs, police, bureaucracy and politicians has come out clearly in various parts of the country.' The Committee quoted other agencies to state that the mafia network is 'virtually running a parallel government, pushing the state apparatus into irrelevance.' The report also says 'in certain States like Bihar, Haryana and Uttar Pradesh, these gangs enjoy the patronage of local politicians cutting across party lines and the protection of the functionaries. Some political leaders become the leaders of these gangs or armed senas and over the years get themselves elected to local bodies, state assemblies and national Parliament.'

There were grave incongruities in the existing provisions of sub-sections (1), (2) and (3) of Section 8 of the Representation of the People Act, 1951 (RPA 1951), illustrating the case of a rapist, convicted and sentenced to ten years imprisonment, being disqualified only for six years under sub-section (1) and while not able to vote, being free to contest elections even while serving the last four years of his sentence in prison.

The Commission recommends that the Representation of the People Act be amended to provide that any person charged with any offence punishable with imprisonment for a maximum term of five years or more, should be disqualified for being chosen as or for being, a member of Parliament or Legislature of a state on the expiry of a period of one year from the date the charges were framed against him by the court in that offence and unless cleared during that one year period, he shall continue to remain so disqualified till the conclusion of the trial for that offence. In case a person is convicted of any offence by a court of law and sentenced to imprisonment for six months or more the bar should apply during the period under which the convicted person is undergoing the sentence and for a further period of six years after the completion of the period of the sentence. If any candidate violates this provision, he should be disqualified. Also, if a party puts up such a candidate with knowledge of his antecedents, it should be de-recognized and de-registered.

Any person convicted for any heinous crime like murder, rape, smuggling or dacoity should be permanently expelled from contesting elections. Criminal cases against politicians pending before courts either for trial or in appeal must be disposed off speedily, if necessary, by appointing Special Courts.

A potential candidate against whom the police have framed charges may take the matter to the Special Court. This court should be obliged to enquire into and take a decision in a strictly time bound manner. Basically, this court may decide whether there is indeed a prima facie case justifying the framing of charges.

The Special Courts should be constituted at the level of High Courts and their decisions should be appealable to the Supreme Court only. The Special Courts should decide the cases within a period of six months. For deciding the cases, these courts should take evidence through Commissioners.

As per the provisions contained in sub-section (4) of section 8 of the Representation of the People Act, 1951, the disqualification referred to in sub-sections (1) and (2) of that section shall not take effect for a period of three months from the date of conviction if the person convicted is a member of Parliament or the Legislature of a state. However, if within the said three months an appeal or application for revision is brought in respect of the conviction or sentence, the disqualification will not operate until that the court disposes of appeal or application.

The Commission feels that the benefit of this provision should be available only for the continuance in office by a sitting Member of Parliament or a State Legislature. The Commission recommends that the aforesaid provision should suitably be amended providing that this benefit shall not be available for the purpose of his contesting fresh elections.

The Commission also feels that the proposed provision laying down that a person charged with an offence punishable with imprisonment which may extend to five years or more should be disqualified from contesting elections after the expiry of a period of one year from the date the charges were framed in a court of law this should equally be applicable to members of Parliament and State Legislatures as to any other such person.

SUMMARY

- India is a constitutional democracy and has periodical elections. Elections are critical to the maintenance and development of democratic tradition.
- An independent Election Commission has been established under the Constitution in order to carry out and regulate the holding of elections in India. The Election Commission is a constitutional body entrusted with the task of holding free and fair elections throughout the country. The members constitutionally appointed by the President.
- The Election Commission's effort in weeding out non-serious candidates and candidates with criminal background proves to be a Herculean task.
- The stringent enforcement of the anti defection law does not seem to uphold with the floor-crossing of the elected representatives.
- Some argue that the voting behaviour of the citizens is highly speculative especially after the lowering of the voting age to eighteen years. Another hindrance is the populist politics that are being practiced by some of the political parties to mobilize voters on grounds of religion, region, and sex and also with short-sighted policies.

QUESTIONS

1. Discuss the role of the Election Commission and enumerate some of its major functions.
2. Why are the electoral reforms significant for Indian political system? What are the major issues for electoral reforms?
3. What do you mean by political defection? What are the factors responsible for defection? How can the defection be controlled?
4. What are the factors influencing voting behaviour? Analysis.
5. What do you mean by criminalization of politics? How can this be curbed?
6. Examine the issues involved in funding of electrons in India.

14

Challenges to Indian Democracy

After reading this chapter, you will be conversant with:

- Communalism
- Regionalism
- Caste
- Corruption and Criminalization in public life

INTRODUCTION

Critics applaud the achievement of Indian democracy in procedural matters, but its substantive dimension needs qualitative improvement. The democratic legitimacy of the State is in question because the electoral process is vitiated by money and muscle power. The attempts to develop grassroots democratic institutions and to build decentralized democratic structures at the regional levels in response to the growing demands of some ethnic groups dose not seem to have been effective. As rampant corruption in public places shakes the foundation of democracy and as the instrumentalities of the constitution and the actors in the political process seem to falter, the citizens begin to wonder about the way out. Some hope on non-government organizations as a counterpoise to the manifold infirmities eroding the faith in the system.

The diversity of India after independence was visible from Center-State tensions, communalism, regionalism and linguism that became the predominant problems.

COMMUNALISM

India is a secular country consisting of various ethnic and religious groups. The diversity of its culture, religion, language and caste is obvious. Conflicts and constant tensions among such groups are also obvious. One of the most important conflicts occurs among different religions. Such kind of rivalries among different religious groups give rise to communalism.

Definition

Communalism in India refers to loyalty to one's religious group. According to Ram Ahuja, communalism refers to an ideology, which states that society is divided into religious communities whose interests differ and are, at times, even opposed to each other. This antagonism goes to the extent of falsely accusing, harming and deliberately insulting a particular community and extends to looting, burning down the homes and shops of the helpless and the weak, dishonoring women and even killing persons.

Causes of Communalism

Some of the causes of communalism are discussed in the following subsections.

1. Religious Ethnocentrism: In this, one religious group feels superior than the other religious group. This kind of feeling gives rise first to prejudices and later takes the shape of communal tensions between various religious groups.
2. Divide and Rule Policy: The religious unity to overthrow the colonial rule proved to be a threat to the mere existence of the Britishers in India. In order to split their unity the Britishers introduced the 'divide-and-rule' policy during their colonial rule to achieve their own personal ends.
3. Extreme loyalty towards one's own religious group: This leads to a feeling that one's own religious group is the in-group as against other religious out-groups.
4. Practice of Secularism: The practice of secularism in a country like India where a number of religious communities exist together is bound to cause friction because of divergent religious beliefs. When this friction takes an extreme form it can result in a communal tension.
5. Role of Religious Leaders: A leadership that can control the inflamed sentiments of members can control an unstable situation. It has been seen that in situations where religious tensions prevail, religious leaders instigate and encourage members to force the issue and use violent methods to prevail over other religious groups. Thus, religious leadership plays a vital role in either controlling a situation of communal violence or instigating violence.
6. Role of Political Leaders: Politicians make use of religious sentiments to further their own selfish ends. For them God and religion are merely instruments to attain their political goals. Political instigation plays an important role in initiating a communal tension.
7. Community Clashes: When one religious community distrusts other communities it can result in hostility, which is a favourable condition for communal violence.

8. Role of Mass Media: Misinformation misrepresentation or misinterpretation of any communal situation by the mass media can further vitiate an already existing explosive situation.
9. Fundamentalism: Increasing fundamentalism, narrow and dogmatic religious values that can be seen across most religious communities also lead to communal tensions.

Of the several challenges such as political corruption, criminalization of politics, authoritarianism and ploys employed to curb freedom of expression, separatism, secessionism, and social justice, communalism was the major challenge. It is a political animal that had been posing a series of challenges to the survival of democracy. It existed well before the partition. Communalism is a cold-blooded political mobilization as unambiguously understood in the Indian context. It was a socio-political project underlined by hate politics directed towards minorities with an aim to win elections. It seeks to establish its dominance in every sphere of Indian life. The secular democratic republican character of India is converted into intolerant communal society. The recent communal carnage in Gujarat has, in the most terrifying manner, displayed the gruesome face of the communal monster. The earlier attacks against the Christians in Gujarat, Orissa and elsewhere, the torching to death of Graham Staines have revealed the true face of fascistic intolerance.

Communalism and its fundamentalist ideology

It is the utilization of the religious divide between the people, consciously engineered and perpetuated for a political purpose. It is an ideology based upon a religious conflict for a specific political purpose. The British used this for perpetuating their colonial rule and in the process elevated it to such an extent that they succeeded in partitioning our country and left behind a scourge that continues to claim countless lives. Communalism is, hence, far removed from religion. It generates and perpetuates hatred amongst religious communities as the basis for its existence and growth.

Communalism in India

Indian population consists of Hindus, Muslims, Christians, Sikhs, Buddhists and Jains. Each of these religious groups is again divided into various sub-groups. Hindu-Muslim antagonism was an old issue but this antagonism is taking different shapes as the time is passing, but it could not be totally curbed out of the society. This rivalry between these two religious groups is the cause of the most communal riots that are now taking place in the country. Hindu-Sikh and Hindu-Christian rivalries are also evident in India.

Hindu-Muslim Communalism

The Hindu-Muslim antagonism has its beginning in the colonial rule of the Britishers. The Britishers encouraged the religious separation for their own selfish ends. The Muslim

League was formed and gained strength under the leadership of Mohammad Ali Jinnah. The league in its Lahore session defined its goal for the creation of a separate Muslim state, which was Pakistan. The Hindu-Muslim communalism is not only because of religion alone but it also has some political and social factors for its origin. Economic interests, social and cultural mores are other factors that seems to keep the communities more apart. Right from the colonial period to the recent incidents of Ramjanma Bhoomi and Babri Masjid issue of Ayodhya and communal riots of Gujarat have been constantly disrupting the communal harmony of India.

Hindu-Sikh Communalism

According to Ram Ahuja, the Hindu-Sikh antagonism started as a reform movement against the dogma of Hindu religion. The Sikh shrines (gurudwaras) were under the control of priests, who misused their position and acquired a lot of wealth. An intense agitation was started by the Sikhs (who were called Akalis) against these priests and wanted their shrines to be maintained under a body of democratic representatives, which resulted in the existence of the Sikh Gurudwara Prabhandak Committee in 1925 and liberated the gurudwaras from the corrupt priests. Later, there was Nirankari movement, which was against the induction of Hindu religious practices in the Sikh system of worship. In 1973, under the leadership of Master Tara Singh, a large number of his followers demanded autonomous status for Punjab known as Khalistan for the Sikh community. The Hindu-Sikh antagonism burst out again in the early eighties after Mrs Indira Gandhi was assassinated in October 1984 by her Sikh bodyguards. Her assassination was the result of an army attack on the Golden Temple at Amritsar to smoke out the Sikh militants.

Hindu-Christian Communalism

The Hindu-Christian Communalism is of most recent origin. Most of the riots are a result of the conversions in the tribal areas, i.e., converting the tribals into Christians. Some of the riots were the attacks of Dangs in Gujarat against the Christian tribals with attacks on their churches. On the night of 22–23 January in Manoharpur village, Keonjhar, Orissa, an Australian Christian missionary Graham Stewart Staines was burnt alive along with his two children. Dara Singh, a Bajrang Dal activist was responsible for the horrible killing. Staines was killed on the charge that he was converting the tribals into Christianity.

Communalism in pre-independence India was used by the British as a constant instrument of state power in their notorious divide-and-rule policy for maintaining the colonial order. It is in fact following the 1857 war of independence, when the Hindu-Muslim unity was demonstrated at its highest form, that the British consciously engineered a policy of communal politics. The consequent separation of electorates on the basis of Hindu-Muslim divide, the partition of Bengal and the patronage given to the Muslim League, etc. were a part of the political agenda for continuing the colonial rule.

In post-independent India, the crisis of the system that we discussed earlier is leading to growing popular discontent and this is also sought to be overcome by the ruling classes by utilizing the deep communal divide. Instead of consciously working for the eradication of the communal poison that continued to be perpetuated following partition, the communal divide was often utilized through indecisiveness and compromise for narrow political benefits.

The spread of communalism and the sharp polarization creates the dangers not only for of the country's dismemberment and lays foundation for virtual civil war conditions, but also consciously and effectively disrupts the unity of the toiling sections on whose unity rests the advance towards people's democracy. The rise of communalism today, therefore, represents simultaneously a weakening of the unity of the classes on whose strength the struggle against the class rule can be mounted. The struggle against the communal forces today is, at the same time, the struggle for maintaining the unity of these classes and, to that extent, it is an integral part of the struggle to defend and advance India.

The unity and integrity of a country of such vast diversity—religious, linguistic, of traditions and customs can only be maintained by strengthening the bonds of commonality in this diversity. Any attempt at imposing uniformity upon this diversity will shatter the unity and integrity of India. This is precisely what the communal fascist forces seek to do.

REGIONALISM

Regionalism refers to the love of a particular region. A region, more than anything else is characterized by shared sentiments of togetherness of the people. It assumes four forms in the political field namely:

- Demands of people of certain states for succession from the Indian Union.
- Demand of people for separate statehood.
- Demand for full-fledged statehood.
- Resolving inter-state disputes.

The dimensions of the politics of regionalism are:

- India being a big country the cultural and social diversity has its impact on political and social conditions. Regional economic imbalance enables the leaders of a particular region to raise demands for the creation of a separate state.
- Imbalanced economic growth across the country is being exploited by the regional leaders to launch movements such as Maharashtra for the Maharashtrians etc.
- Social backwardness, coupled with that of economic degradation induces in the minds of the people a sense of struggle for the cause of their own area or region. For this reason, the tribals of Bihar, Chota Nagpur and Santhal Paragana demanded Jharkhand, the Gorkhas of the Darjeeling demand Gorkhaland and the Bodos of Assam demanded for Bodoland.

The politics of regionalism assumes a serious form when it is sustained by factor of secessionism. The Nagas of Assam, for instance, demanded a separate and sovereign state.

Reasons for the growth of regionalism

It grew largely due to factors that are discussed in the following subsections.

Problems of economic and social development of the Indian Society

During the days of freedom struggle people were told that the innumerous sufferings and hardships they were going through were the result of British rule and that they should unite to get themselves rid of the hardships. After independence the Constitution of India assured the citizens of measures to organize village Panchayats, providing them with employment, just and humane conditions of work and free and compulsory education for children. But all these were mere promises and people were offered nothing but disappointment, more hardships, more exploitation and more injustices. Hence, instead of caring for their country as a whole they began to stress for the progress of their own state or region.

Feeling of being neglected

There was an increasing awareness among the people belonging to the backward area that they were being neglected in the matters of education and job opportunities in the allocation of central funds and grants.

Personal and selfish ends of the politicians

The regional and state leaders in order to capture power considered the weakening of the central authority and state authority in some cases.

CASTE

The idea of caste is deep rooted among the minds of the people as it has a strong foundation in our society. The problems of casteism cannot be easily wiped off and may take years for the changes to occur. The form of caste system must be changed in order to meet the nation's development. The government and non-governmental agencies should put their efforts to achieve this kind of change in our society through which we can eliminate casteism.

Caste is a fairly well-marked, separate community, whose individual members are bound to each other through endogamy [and hypergamy] and often also by a common hereditary profession or duty, actual or supposed.

Caste was not present in the beginning of human institution. There were many migrations and conflicts among various groups. Over a long period of time a homogenous culture developed and exogamy was normal. Later, with groups enclosing themselves, caste and endogamy became the rule. Discrimination on the basis of group began during this time and religious and judicial notions were developed to justify caste.

Subsequently there started the collapse and revolt against caste, leading to a virtual ousting of this system. The radicalism of Buddhism at this time was its fundamental rejection of caste and acceptance of all persons on the basis of equality. The results included more widespread democratic practices, equality and freedom. They were accompanied by abandonment of religious and judicial norms justifying caste and emergence of new ethical and juridical norms.

After this period, India fell back again into the caste system. The re-emergence of forces favouring the caste system led to a prolonged contest for supremacy between the two sides. Finally, the caste system was re-imposed, but this time practices of discrimination were even worse than before and draconian regulations were developed to ensure caste segregation. The notion and practice of untouchability was introduced. The period of colonialism and subsequent independence weakened legal aspects of caste discrimination, but at economic and social levels discrimination remained much the same.

After independence, Indian Constitution sought to prevent the perpetuation of caste and build a casteless social system. But this has not happened over the fifty-odd years since independence and shows little sign of happening in the near future. Therefore, no understanding of politics is possible without a thorough understanding of the complexities of caste. Moreover, the basic structure of the Constitution envisages a cohesive, unified, casteless society.

In ancient India there developed a social system in which people were divided into separate close communities. These communities are known as caste in English. The origin of the caste system is in Hinduism but it affected the whole Indian society. The caste system in the religious form is basically a simple division of the society in which there are four castes arranged in a hierarchy and below them the outcast. But socially the caste system was more complicated, with much more castes and sub-castes and other divisions. Legally the Government disallows the practice of caste system but has a policy of affirmative discrimination in favour of the backward classes. The worrying aspect of democracy is that political leadership is using caste to be in power.

CORRUPTION AND CRLMINALIZATION IN PUBLIC LIFE

India is a democratic country and its politics is based upon a principle that the elected representatives are responsible and accountable to the public. The elected representatives are often unaccountable because of rampant corruption in public life. We have reached a stage where political parties demand lucrative ministries. Corruption is all pervasive. This shows that the focus of the parties is not much on a better governance and being accountable to the citizens but in the enrichment of the party or the individuals.

The most disquieting aspect of the widespread corruption is the fact that it is not anymore confined to politicians or the government machinery alone. It is prevalent amongst almost every section of the society.

Ways of combating corruption

- **Role of NGOs:** Corruption can be fought by the citizen as an individual or in groups in the form of an NGO. Just as an individual first has to maintain his own integrity before he takes on the challenge of fighting corruption, NGOs which are formed mainly to fight corruption should first ensure that they themselves are clean and do not indulge in corrupt practices. It has been noticed that there are many NGOs who indulge in corrupt practices. If such NGOs also take up the issue of fighting corruption then they are not likely to be successful.
- **Spread of awareness:** Spreading awareness on the harmful effects of corruption is essential. There is extensive corruption in our system because there is a vicious cycle starting with political corruption leading to bureaucratic corruption, business corruption and criminalization of politics.
- **Creation of Anti-Corruption Bureaus, Lok Ayuktas:** Creation of Central Bureau of Investigation and Central Vigilance Commissioners are instrumental in planning a steady campaign of rooting out corruption.
- **Judiciary:** Judicial Activism has been responsible for bringing about some changes. The empowering of the Central Vigilance Commission as a more effective agency to fight corruption and particularly ensure the autonomy of Central Bureau of Investigation and Enforcement Directorate is another example of the role of the judiciary. The Public Interest Litigation is a route that can be used to approach the courts and thereby make the administration change policies or initiate action to check corruption.
- **Shaping of Public Opinion:** In a democracy, the political leaders have to respect public opinion. Shaping of public opinion hence is essential.
- **Responsible Citizens:** It is the responsibility of every citizen to fight corruption. If the citizens want the country to become economic and military superpower and create an India in which every citizen will be able to enjoy his rights and a better quality of life, fighting corruption is important.

Corruption in India cannot be eradicated by questioning ethical standards of its citizen. Removal of corruption can only be achieved by right macro-economic policies and by reducing government control. Honest political leadership is a must as a first step. Fresh ideas and entrepreneurial spirit has to replace the bureaucratic government control for a wealthier society. Supply of basic commodities needs to be higher than the demand for general population to stop bribing of government officials. An efficient tax collection mechanism supported by computerized revenue reporting systems of individual businesses would also be a step in the right direction. Qualified political leadership is required to understand and implement such policies. Most importantly, political will of these leaders will be required to take such actions. In conclusion, corruption in India exists because of the unfulfillment of the basic needs of the general population.

Criminalization

According to Oxford Dictionary, crime is an offence punishable by law. It is an evil act of doing harm or injury to others.

Criminalization of politics may be termed as a systematic act of subversion of the usual course of politics by illegal means intended to attain private gain or end. It gives rise to a situation where there are a great deal of erosion of values, organized violations of norms, rules and principles, dearth of security of life, liberty and property, lack of transparency and accountability, dominance of muscle power and black money, plunder of resources, rampant corruption, denial of justice and rule of law, and contraction of popular sovereignty leading the underworld and unconventional forces to establish substantial control over the political process.

It is well-recognized that criminalization of our polity assumed alarming proportions. Several committees and commissions have studied this problem in great detail and made recommendations for legislative action. The suggestions of the Election Commission and the Law Commission remain unheeded. The Vohra Committee Report established the growing nexus between criminals, politicians, businessmen and bureaucracy. Parliament, in its golden jubilee special session passed a unanimous resolution expressing the pious intent of decriminalizing politics. Several judgments of the higher courts have dealt at length with the problem of criminalization. These include the Delhi High Court judgment directing the Election Commission to collect and publicize information on the criminal antecedents of candidates. However, both the political parties and successive governments have done little to stop this trend.

SUMMARY

- It is important to note that Indian society was never homogenous throughout history. It was highly diverse religiously, culturally, caste-wise and linguistically but there was hardly any tension between these groups. It all began with establishment of British rule in India and most of the scholars agree that communalism is a modern phenomenon and not a medieval one. Despite measures regionalism, communalism, corruption and criminalization emerged as potential anti-national forces. Caste today has intruded into politics and is a challenge to secularism. It has become a major obstacle in the establishment of a casteless society and cemented communal connections. As regards communalism, the fundamental cause of it is political and not religion. The Indian society will continue to experience violent caste and communal eruptions as long as it does not find political and economic equilibrium in terms of castes and communities. The rise of OBCs on one hand and impact of globalization on economy on the other will continue to cause occasional eruption of violence in society for quite some time. Caste and communal polarization will be with us as long as we are not able to create more egalitarian society.

QUESTIONS

1. What factors were responsible for the rise and growth of communalism in India? Explain.
2. "Corruption has corroborated the very dynamics of Indian democracy. It has become all pervasive and has become a new trend in the society". In the light of this statement examine how corruption is eating the very core of democracy?
3. Analysis the role of castes in India polity?
4. Examine the challenges posed by criminalisation of politics to Indian Democracy?
5. Of late regionalism or separate statehood has taken a prominent place in politics. Substantiate the statement with proper examples.
6. Discuss the ways and means of combating corruption.

Bibliography

Austin, G. 2006, *Working a Democratic Constitution: A History of the Indian Experience*, New Delhi: Oxford University Press.

Bardhan, P., 1984, *The Political Economy of Development in India*, New Delhi, Oxford University Press.

Basu, D. D., *Introduction to the Constitution of India* (Agra: Wardhwa and Company), p. 237.

Basu, D. D., 2001, *Introduction to the Constitution of India* (New Delhi: Wadhwa and Company Law Publishers).

Bhargava, Rajiv (ed.), 1999, *Secularism and its Critics*, New Delhi: Oxford University Press.

Brass, P. R., 1994, *Caste Conflict and Preferential Policies* in *The Politics of India since Independence* (New Delhi: Cambridge University Press).

Brass, P. R., 1990, *The Politics of India Since Independence* (Cambridge: Cambridge University Press).

Chatterjee, P., 1999, *State and Politics in India* (New Delhi: Oxford University Press).

Chatterjee, P., (ed.), 1997, *State Politics in India* (New Delhi: Oxford University Press).

Copland, I. and Rickard, J., (eds.), 1999, *Federalism, Comparative perspectives from India and Australia* (New Delhi: Manohar).

Das Gupta, J., 2001, *India's federal design and multicultural national construction* in Kohli, A., (ed.), *The success of India's Democracy* (New Delhi: Cambridge University Press)

Das, H. H. and Choudhury, B. C., *Political Theory: Traditional and Modern Theory* (New Delhi: Mayoor Paper backs), p 238.

Frankel, Francehe R., 2005, *India's Political Economy 1947–2004*, New Delhi, Oxford University Press.

Friedrich C. J., 1968, *Trends of Federalism in Theory and Practice* (London: Praeger).

Bibliography

Austin, G. 2006, *Working a Democratic Constitution: A History of the Indian Experience*, New Delhi: Oxford University Press.

Bardhan, P., 1984, *The Political Economy of Development in India*, New Delhi, Oxford University Press.

Basu, D. D., *Introduction to the Constitution of India* (Agra: Wardhwa and Company), p. 237.

Basu, D. D., 2001, *Introduction to the Constitution of India* (New Delhi: Wadhwa and Company Law Publishers).

Bhargava, Rajiv (ed.), 1999, *Secularism and its Critics*, New Delhi: Oxford University Press.

Brass, P. R., 1994, *Caste Conflict and Preferential Policies* in *The Politics of India since Independence* (New Delhi: Cambridge University Press).

Brass, P. R., 1990, *The Politics of India Since Independence* (Cambridge: Cambridge University Press).

Chatterjee, P., 1999, *State and Politics in India* (New Delhi: Oxford University Press).

Chatterjee, P., (ed.), 1997, *State Politics in India* (New Delhi: Oxford University Press).

Copland, I. and Rickard, J., (eds.), 1999, *Federalism, Comparative perspectives from India and Australia* (New Delhi: Manohar).

Das Gupta, J., 2001, *India's federal design and multicultural national construction* in Kohli, A., (ed.), *The success of India's Democracy* (New Delhi: Cambridge University Press)

Das, H. H. and Choudhury, B. C., *Political Theory: Traditional and Modern Theory* (New Delhi: Mayoor Paper backs), p 238.

Frankel, Francehe R., 2005, *India's Political Economy 1947–2004*, New Delhi, Oxford University Press.

Friedrich C. J., 1968, *Trends of Federalism in Theory and Practice* (London: Praeger).

Roy, R. and Wallace, P., 1999, *Indian Politics and the 1998 Election: Regionalism, Hindutva and State Politics* (New Delhi: Sage Publications).

Rudolph, L. I. and. Rudolph, S. H., 1967, *The Modernity of Tradition* (Chicago: University of Chicago Press).

Rudolph, L. I. and Rudolph, S. H., 1987, *In pursuit of Lakshmi: The Political Economy of the Indian State* (New Delhi: Orient Longman).

Singh, R., 2001, *Social Movements: Old and New - A Post-Modernistic Critique* (New Delhi: Sage Publications).

Oommen, T. K. and Venugopal, C. N., 1988, *Sociology for Law Students* (Lucknow: Eastern Book Company).

Pylee, M. V., 2001, India's Constitution (New Delhi: S. Chand and Company).

Sacz, L., 2002, *Federalism without a Centre: The Impact of Political and Economic Reform on India's Federal System* (New Delhi: Sage Publications).

Sartori, G., 1976, *Parties and Party Systems: A framework for analysis* (Cambridge: Cambridge University Press).

Shah, G., (ed.), 2002, *Social Movements and the State* (New Delhi: Sage Publications).

Singh, M.P. and R. Saxena, 2008, The *Indian Politics: Contemporary Issues and Concerns*, New Delhi: Prentice-Hall of India.

Singh, M.P. and S.R. Raj, (eds.), 2012, *The Indian Political System*, Delhi, Pearson.

Vanaik, A., 1990, *The Pawful Transition: Bourgeois Democracy in India* (London: Verso).

Vanaik, A., 1997, *Communalism Contested: Religion, Modernity and Secularization* ((New Delhi: Vistar).

Glossary

POSDCORB : The term coined by Luther Gullick encapsulates in it all the activities found in an organization. The term stands for planning, organizing, staffing directing, coordinating, reporting, and budgeting.

Act : A bill passed by the legislature and enacted into law.

Adjournment : Termination of a meeting, occurring at the close of each legislative day upon the completion of business, with the hour and day of the next meeting being set prior to adjournment.

Associational Group : Formally organized group which articulates the interests of its members over long periods of time.

Auditor General : The official of Parliament whose staff audits the expenditures of government departments and who provides an annual report on instances of funds being unlawfully or unwisely spent.

Behavioural Revolution : The introduction of more empirical analysis into the study of government and politics.

Bicameralism : A system of government in which the legislature is divided into two chambers, an upper and lower house.

Bill : A piece of legislation under consideration by a legislative body.

Bureaucracy : A type of administration characterized by specialization, professionalism and security of tenure.

Cabinet solidarity : A convention that all cabinet ministers publicly support whatever decisions the cabinet has taken, regardless of their personal views. It is also known as collective responsibility of the cabinet.

Caucus : A meeting of legislators of any one party to discuss parliamentary strategy and party policy.

Charismatic Authority : Authority based on the admiration of personal qualities of an individual.

Checks and Balances : A system of government in which power is divided between the executive, legislative and judicial branches of government and these powers check and balance each other.

Citizenship : Legal membership in a community known as a nation-state.

Coalition : An alliance between two or more political units in response to opposing forces.

Coalition government : A parliamentary government in which the cabinet is composed of members of more than one party.

Coercion : A form of power based on forced compliance through fear and intimidation.

Mass media : A general term for all modern means of conveying information.

Communism : A political ideology characterized by a belief in eliminating exploitation through public ownership and central planning of the economy.

Confederation : A federal system of government in which sovereign constituent governments create a central government but balance of power remains with constituent governments.

Constituency : An electoral district with a body of electors who vote for a representative in an elected assembly.

Constitution : The fundamental rules and principles by which a state is organized.

Coup d'etat : A forceful and unconstitutional change of government, often by a faction within the military or the ruling party.

Deputy Minister : Public servant who heads each government department, manages the department, and advises the minister.

Despotism : An individual ruling through fear without regard to law and not answerable to the people.

Diplomacy : A system of formal, regularized communication that allows states to peacefully conduct their business with each other.

Direct democracy : A system of government based on public decisions made by citizens meeting in an assembly or voting by ballot.

Election Commission : The statutory body appointed by the government with the responsibility of proper conduct of Parliamentary elections.

Electoral College : The body which formally chooses the President of India.

Electorate : An area represented by one or more members of Parliament, also, the total body of electors within such an area.

Elite : A small group of people with a disproportionate amount of public decision-making power.

Equality of opportunity : The equalization of life chances for all individuals in society, regardless of economic position.

Equality of right : Application of the law in the same way to all.

Ethnic group : A group whose common identity is based on racial, national or religious association.

Executive : A small group of elected officials who direct the policy process and oversee the vast array of departments and agencies of government.

Federalism : A system of government in which sovereignty is divided between a central government and several provincial or state governments.

First Reading : Each bill introduced must be read three times before final passage. The first reading of a bill occurs when it is introduced.

Head of Government : The person in effective charge of the executive branch of government; the prime minister in a parliamentary system.

Head of State : An individual who represents the state but does not exercise political power.

Ideology : A system of beliefs and values that explains society and prescribes the role of government.

Institutional Group : Groups which are closely associated with the government and act internally to influence public decisions.

Interest Groups : Organizations whose members act together to influence public policy group in order to promote their common interest.

Interest party : A political party with a single interest of purpose.

Interim : The period of time between the end of a legislative year and the beginning of the next legislative year.

Joint Session : A session in which both the Houses meet together as they do every year on the first legislative day to hear the President's address.

Judicial Activism : The willingness and inclination of judges to overturn legislation or executive action.

Judicial review : The power of the courts to declare legislation unconstitutional (ultra vires).

Judiciary : The branch of government with the power to resolve legal conflicts that arise between citizens, between citizens and governments or between levels of government.

Justice : The virtue of protecting individuals' possessions within the acknowledged rules of conduct.

Laissez-faire : The non-intervention of the state in the economy.

Legislature : The branch of government responsible for making laws for society.

Legitimacy : Belief in the 'rightness' of rule.

List system : A form of proportional representation in which the elector votes not for individuals but for parties who have lists of candidates running for office.

Lobbying : An activity of interest groups aimed at influencing government and the public to achieve a favourable policy decision(s).

Majority Government : A parliamentary government in which the party in power has over 50 percent of the seats in the legislature.

Measure : A bill, resolution, or constitutional amendment that is considered by the Legislature.

Ministerial Responsibility : The principle that cabinet ministers are individually responsible to the House of Commons for everything that happens in their department

Ministry : The entire group of MPs appointed by the Prime Minister to specific ministerial responsibilities.

Minority Government : A parliamentary government in which the government party or allies have less than fifty per cent of the seats in the legislature.

Monarchy : Form of government in which a single person rules under the law.

Motion : A formal proposal for action made by a legislator during a committee hearing or floor session.

Multiparty System : A party system in which there are three or more major contenders for power.

National interest : Interests specific to a nation-state, including especially survival and maintenance of power.

Nation-state : A state with a single predominant national identity.

Oligarchy : A form of government in which a minority rules outside the law.

One-party-dominant : A party system in which there are political alternatives but a single system political party dominates.

Opposition : Those members of Parliament who are not part of the government of the day.

Parliamentary Inquiry : A procedural question posed by a legislator during a committee hearing or floor session. A member must be recognized for this purpose and the question answered by the committee chair or presiding officer.

Parliamentary Sovereignty : The supreme authority of Parliament to make or repeal laws.

Party discipline : The convention that all MPs within any party vote together, as predetermined in the party caucus and enforced by the party whip.

Planning : Production and allocation of resources determined by a central authority.

Political party : An organized group that makes nominations and contests elections in the hope of influencing the personnel and policy of government.

Polity : A form of government characterized by popular sovereignty but exercised within a constitutional framework to prevent oppression of the minority by the majority rule.

Popular Sovereignty : Supreme authority residing in the consent of the people.

Portfolio : The administrative responsibility carried by a minister, usually some combinations of departments and other agencies.

Prime Minister's Office : Support staff appointed by the Prime Minister to carry out political functions.

Privatization : The sale of government-owned assets or activities to the private sector.

Proclamation : The announcement of the official date a new law will take effect.

Proportional representation (PR) : An electoral system in which the share of seats won closely matches the share of popular votes received.

Quorum : The minimum number of legislators needed to begin conducting official business. The absence of a quorum leads to immediate adjournment of a committee hearing or floor session.

Race : A group of individuals differentiated through distinct physical characteristics and common ancestry.

Report Stage : The stage in the legislative process after the second reading when the House debates the committee's report on a proposed bill.

Representative Democracy : A system of government based on the election of decision-makers by the people.

Residual powers : Those powers in a federal system of government not explicitly allocated in a constitution.

Responsible Government : A form of government in which the political executive must retain the confidence of a majority of the elected legislature or assembly, and it must resign or call an election if and when it is defeated on a vote of non-confidence.

Rule of Law : Belief that all actions, of individuals and governments, are subject to an institutionalized set of rules and regulations.

Separation of powers : The separation of powers between executive, legislative and judicial branches of government.

Single transferable vote (STV) : A form of proportional representation in which electors vote for individuals rather than party lists, but they do so by ranking the candidates in their order of choice.

Single-party system : A party system in which there exists only one party and no political alternatives are legally tolerated.

Social justice : The partial equalization of wealth and income to reach a more desirable outcome.

Special (ad hoc) committee : Legislative committees appointed for special, temporary purposes, such as to investigate a problem before the government prepares legislation on the subject.

Spoils system : The assumption that after successfully winning an election, the political executive is entitled to appoint large numbers of supporters to the bureaucracy.

Standing committee	:	Legislative committees that are set up permanently and parallel to government functions.
Standing Committee	:	Subunits formed in each of the Houses that take public testimony and vote on bills usually on related subjects.
Statute	:	A specific piece of legislation.
Traditional authority	:	Authority based on birthright and custom.
Tribe	:	A community of people tied together by a myth of common ancestry.
Two-party system	:	A party system in which there are two credible contenders for power and either is capable of winning any election.
Ultra vires	:	Term used to describe an action which exceeds the conferred constitutional powers of the actor. It literally means 'beyond the power'.
Unicameral	:	A legislature consisting of one house.